BASICS

MICROSOFT®

Visual Basic

Todd Knowlton

Computer Education Consultant

Knowlton & Associates, Inc. Lubbock, TX

Stephen Collings

Knowlton & Associates, Inc. Lubbock, TX

JOIN US ON THE INTERNET

WWW: http://www.thomson.com   A service of I(T)P®

South-Western Educational Publishing

an International Thomson Publishing company I(T)P®

Cincinnati • Albany, NY • Belmont, CA • Bonn • Boston • Detroit • Johannesburg • London • Madrid
Melbourne • Mexico City • New York • Paris • Singapore • Tokyo • Toronto • Washington

I(T)P ®

International Thomson Publishing

South-Western Educational Publishing is a division of International Thomson Publishing, Inc. The ITP logo is a registered trademark used herein under license by South-Western Educational Publishing.

The names of all commercially available software mentioned herein are used for identification purposes only and may be trademarks or registered trademarks of their respective owners. South-Western Educational Publishing disclaims any affiliation, association, connection with, sponsorship, or endorsement by such owners.

Microsoft is a registered trademark of Microsoft Corporation.

Team Leader:	Karen Schmohe
Managing Editor:	Carol Volz
Editor:	Shannon O'Connor
Marketing Manager:	Larry Qualls
Art/Design Coordinator:	Mike Broussard
Cover Design:	Lou Ann Thesing
Consulting Editor:	Brenda K. Lewis
Electronic Pre-Press and Production:	Electro-Publishing

B A S I C S

BEGIN AND SUCCEED IN COMPUTER SCIENCE™

with the BASICS from South-Western Educational Publishing

Microsoft® Visual Basic BASICS introduces the Visual Basic programming language in a user-friendly, easy-to-understand format. As an initial overview, Visual Basic BASICS lays the groundwork for immediate understanding of the theory and practice of Visual Basic.

Visual Basic BASICS Text-workbook/data disk	0-538-69086-0
Visual Basic BASICS Activities Workbook	0-538-69084-4
Visual Basic BASICS Testing CD	0-538-69243-X
Electronic Instructor CD-ROM package	0-538-69085-2

Networking BASICS Text-workbook	0-538-69042-9
Networking BASICS Study Guide	0-538-69043-7
Networking BASICS Testing CD	0-538-69242-1
Electronic Instructor CD-ROM package	0-538-69044-5

Watch for additional titles in South-Western's BASICS series!

OTHER SOUTH-WESTERN TITLES

Visual Basic Programming Projects	0-538-68894-7
Electronic Instructor CD-ROM package	0-538-68895-5
JAVA: Programming Basics for the Internet (Barksdale, Turner, et. al.)	0-538-68012-1
with Visual J++ Compiler CD-ROM	0-538-68564-6
Instructor's materials available on-line	
Internet Concepts and Activities (Barksdale & Rutter)	0-538-72088-3
Electronic Instructor CD-ROM package	0-538-72131-6

Electronic Instructor CD-ROM package includes: Instructor's Manual (printed), CD-ROM which includes Lesson plans, Solutions files, and much more!

South-Western
Educational Publishing

JOIN US ON THE INTERNET
WWW.SWEP.COM

How to Use this Book

What makes a good programming text? Sound instruction and hands-on skill-building and reinforcement projects. That is what you will find in *Microsoft Visual Basic BASICS*. Not only will you find a colorful, inviting layout, but also many features to enhance learning.

Notes– These boxes provide necessary information to assist you in completing the exercises.

Objectives– Objectives are listed at the beginning of each lesson, along with a suggested time for completion of the lesson. This allows you to look ahead to what you will be learning and to pace your work.

Enhanced Screen Shots– Screen shots now come to life on each page with color and depth.

Tips– These boxes provide enrichment information about Visual Basic.

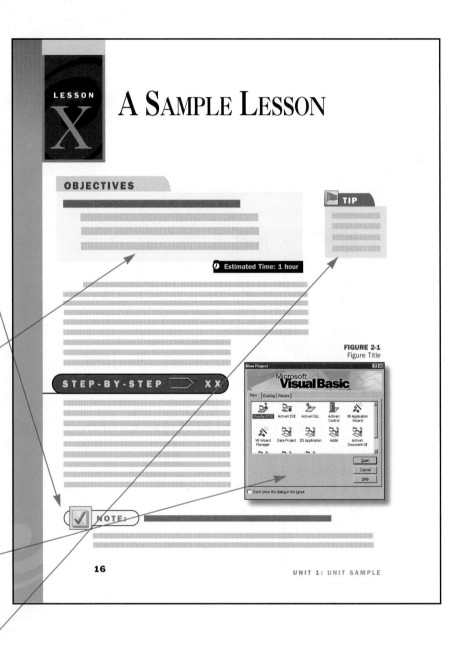

How to Use this Book

Important– These boxes provide important information about Visual Basic.

Summary– At the end of each lesson you will find a summary to prepare you to complete the end-of-lesson activities.

Review Questions– Review material at the end of each lesson and each unit enables you to prepare for assessment of the content presented.

Lesson Projects– End-of-lesson hands-on application of what has been learned in the lesson allows you to actually apply the techniques covered.

Critical Thinking Activity– Each lesson gives you an opportunity to apply creative analysis to situations presented.

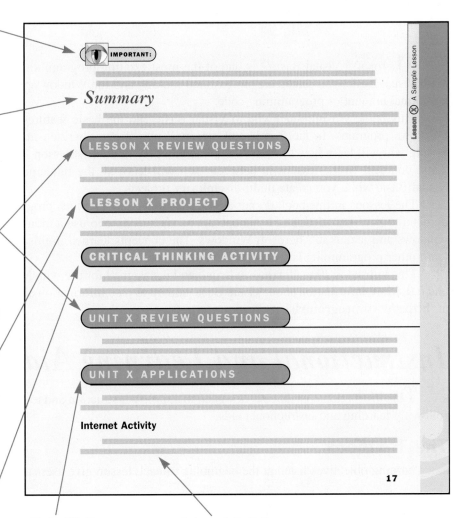

End-of-Unit Applications– End-of-unit hands-on application of concepts learned in the unit provides opportunity for a comprehensive review.

Internet Activity– Hands-on project that incorporates Internet resources for research and completion.

PREFACE

Microsoft® Visual Basic™ is one of the most exciting programming languages in use today. With Visual Basic, you can create professional-looking and fun Windows programs in minutes using a minimal amount of programming code.

This book will introduce you to Visual Basic and the basic features required to write useful Windows programs. In the first lesson, you will play a game written in Visual Basic. In the last lesson, you will learn how to create the game you play in the first lesson. You will also enhance the game yourself. In the lessons in between, you will learn all the fundamentals of programming in Visual Basic while you create multi-disciplinary projects.

The lessons in this book do not assume you have any previous programming experience. You do need to have knowledge of basic operations such as how to use a mouse and how to manipulate windows and menus in Microsoft Windows. The concepts learned in this book will prepare you to learn other programming languages, such as C++ and Java.

This tutorial is 30 to 40 hours in length and is designed for use with Microsoft Visual Basic 5.0 and 6.0. More information about Visual Basic and up to date information about this book is available at: **http://www.programvb.com/basics**

Instructional and Learning Aids

This instructional package is designed to simplify instruction and to enhance learning with the following learning and instructional aids:

The Textbook

- Learning objectives listed at the beginning of each lesson give users an overview of the lesson.

- Step-by-Step exercises immediately follow the presentation of new concepts for hands-on reinforcement.

- Illustrations, including numerous screen captures, explain complex concepts and serve as reference points.

- The case study in Lesson 14 allows students to learn from a completed Visual Basic game and then enhance the program.

END OF LESSON

- Lesson summaries provide quick reviews reinforcing the main points in each lesson.

- True/false and written questions gauge learners' understanding of lesson concepts and software operations.

- Projects offer minimal instruction so learners must apply concepts previously introduced.

- Critical thinking activities stimulate the user to apply analytical and reasoning skills.

END-OF-UNIT REVIEW

▓ Review questions provide a comprehensive overview of unit content and help in preparing for tests.

▓ Unit applications for reinforcement ask the user to employ all the skills and concepts presented in the unit.

▓ Internet activities require the user to obtain information from the Internet to complete the activity, reinforcing Internet skills.

END OF BOOK

▓ The Glossary is a collection of the key terms from each lesson.

▓ A comprehensive Index supplies quick and easy accessibility to specific parts of the tutorial.

▓ The Quick Reference lists important naming conventions and shortcuts.

Other Components

▓ The Activities Workbook provides additional exercises and activities to reinforce each lesson.

▓ The data files necessary to complete the exercises, activities, and applications in the book are packaged with the textbook.

▓ The instructor's manual provides teaching suggestions, solutions, and other resources.

▓ The Electronic Instructor package is a CD-ROM that includes features such as guidelines for scheduling users with varying abilities, lesson plans specific to each chapter, reproducible tests with answers, and solutions for exercises, projects, and activities.

Acknowledgements

We (the authors) thank Jason Duby and Trey Stoffregen of Knowlton & Associates for their work on the manuscript and the workbook. We also thank the reviewers, Kathleen Weaver of Dallas, TX and Jeff Aronsky of Pembroke Pines, FL for their insight and feedback.

We offer a special thanks to our consulting editor Brenda Lewis. Brenda worked tirelessly on this book, going beyond the call of duty. We value her suggestions and attention to detail.

Todd Knowlton & Stephen Collings

TABLE OF CONTENTS

iv   How to Use This Book
vi   Preface
xi   List of Tables
xii   Start-Up Checklist

UNIT 1 — YOUR FIRST VISUAL BASIC PROGRAM

2 Lesson 1: A First Look at Microsoft Visual Basic

2   Introduction to Microsoft Visual Basic
3   Starting Visual Basic
4   Opening an Existing Visual Basic Project
5   Components of the Compiler
12   Running a Visual Basic Program
13   Positioning a Form in a Visual Basic Program
14   Exiting Visual Basic

18 Lesson 2: Forms, Controls, and Properties

18   Creating a New Project
22   Saving the Project
23   Viewing and Modifying Properties
26   Creating Controls
30   Understanding Focus
32   Setting Additional Properties

38 Lesson 3: Events and Code

38   Events
39   Accessing the Code Window
40   Adding Code to a Command Button
42   Adding an Image to a Form
44   Setting Image Properties
46   Setting Properties from Code
48   Setting the Cancel and Default Command Button Properties
49   Creating a Standalone Program

55 Unit 1 Review

UNIT 2 — CALCULATIONS AND DATA

62 Lesson 4: Mathematical Operators

62   Performing Calculations in Visual Basic
63   Creating Label Controls
64   Using the Addition and Assignment Operators
65   Using Text Boxes and the Val Function
66   Splitting Code Statements Among Lines
69   Using the Subtraction Operator
71   Using Unary Minus
72   Using the Multipication and Division Operators
72   Using Fix
74   Performing Integer Division and Using Modulus

82 Lesson 5: Exponentiation, Order of Operations and Error Handling

82 Exponentiation
82 Order of Operations
86 Using the Visible Property to Enhance Output
87 Using Comments
88 Handling Run-Time Errors
91 Using MsgBox
93 Controlling Program Flow around the Error Handler

100 Lesson 6: Data Types and Variables

100 Data Types
102 Using the AutoSize Property
104 Declaring Variables
105 Using Variables
107 Scope
110 Using the Variant Data Type and Option Explicit

118 Lesson 7: Strings and Decimal Types

118 Declaring String Variables
119 Assigning Text to String Variables
121 Concatenation
125 Using Decimal Types
126 Using the Format Function
128 Using the Enabled Property
130 Using the SelStart and SelLength Properties

137 Unit 2 Review

UNIT 3   DECISION MAKING

144 Lesson 8: If Statements

144 The Building Blocks of Decision Making
145 Using the Conditional Operators
146 Using If Statements
148 Creating and Reading Flowcharts
150 Using If…Else Statements
152 Using Check Boxes
157 Using the Logical Operators

164 Lesson 9: Nested If Statements and Option Buttons

164 Using Nested If Statements
167 Using Option Buttons
173 Using a Form Load Event Procedure
174 Using Select Case

183 Unit 3 Review

UNIT 4   LOOPS, MULTIPLE FORMS, MENUS, AND PRINTING

190 Lesson 10: Do Loops

190 What Are Loops?
190 Using the Do Loops
195 Using the InputBox Function
198 Using the DoEvents Statement
203 Using Nested Loops

210 Lesson 11: For Next Loops and Multiple Forms

210 Using the Print Statement
212 Using For Next Loops
215 Nesting For Next Loops
217 Changing Label Font Settings
219 Using Multiple Forms
226 Adding an About Box

232 Lesson 12: Menus and Printing

232 Creating Menus Using the Menu Editor
235 Writing Code for a Menu Command
237 Using Check Marks in Menus
239 Creating a Submenu
241 Inserting Separator Lines in Menus
242 Printing from Visual Basic

250 Unit 4 Review

UNIT 5   GRAPHICS AND DRAWING

256 Lesson 13: Lines and Shapes

256 Creating Line Controls
258 Creating Shape Controls
258 Changing Properties of Line and Shape
     Controls
260 Manipulating Line and Shape Control
     Properties from Code
263 Drawing Lines from Code
265 Changing the ScaleMode Property
266 Drawing Boxes from Code

**272 Lesson 14: Case Study—
Snake Game**

272 Running the Snake Game
273 Drawing with Pixels and Using
     AutoRedraw
275 How the Snake Game Draws the Snake
277 Analyzing the Snake Game Code

289 Unit 5 Review

LIST OF TABLES

Table 2-1	Object Naming Prefixes	25
Table 4-1	Mathematical Operators	63
Table 6-1	Data Types	101
Table 6-2	Data Type Prefixes	105
Table 7-1	Formatting Symbols	127
Table 7-2	Sample Formats	127
Table 8-1	Conditional Operators	145
Table 8-2	Logical Operators	157
Table 8-3	Order of Operations	158
Table 13-1	Color Values	264

START-UP CHECKLIST

This book has been tested with both Visual Basic 5.0 and Visual Basic 6.0. Microsoft Visual Basic is available for the Microsoft Windows operating system only. The minimum hardware requirements for the two versions appear below.

Visual Basic 5.0—Learning Edition

✓ PC with a 486DX/66 MHz or higher processor (Pentium or higher processor recommended)

✓ Microsoft Windows 95 or later operating system, or Microsoft Windows NT operating system version 4.0 (Service Pack 2 recommended), or Microsoft Windows NT Workstation operating system version 3.51 with Service Pack 5

✓ 8 MB of RAM for Windows 95 or Windows NT Workstation 4.0 or 16 MB of RAM for Windows NT 4.0

✓ Hard-disk space required: 37 MB

✓ CD-ROM drive

✓ VGA or higher-resolution monitor; Super VGA recommended

✓ Microsoft Mouse or compatible pointing device

Visual Basic 6.0—Learning Edition

✓ PC with a 486DX/66 MHz or higher processor (Pentium or higher processor recommended)

✓ Microsoft Windows 95 or later operating system, or Microsoft Windows NT operating system version 4.0 with Service Pack 3 or later

✓ 16 MB of RAM for Windows 95 or later or 24 MB of RAM for Windows NT 4.0

✓ Hard-disk space required: 52 MB

✓ CD-ROM drive

✓ VGA or higher-resolution monitor; Super VGA recommended

✓ Microsoft Mouse or compatible pointing device

For all editions, Internet access and a Web browser are necessary to complete the Internet Activities.

For up-to-date hardware requirements on the latest Visual Basic compiler and for the requirements of other editions of the compiler, go to:

http://www.programvb.com/basics/ aboutvb.htm

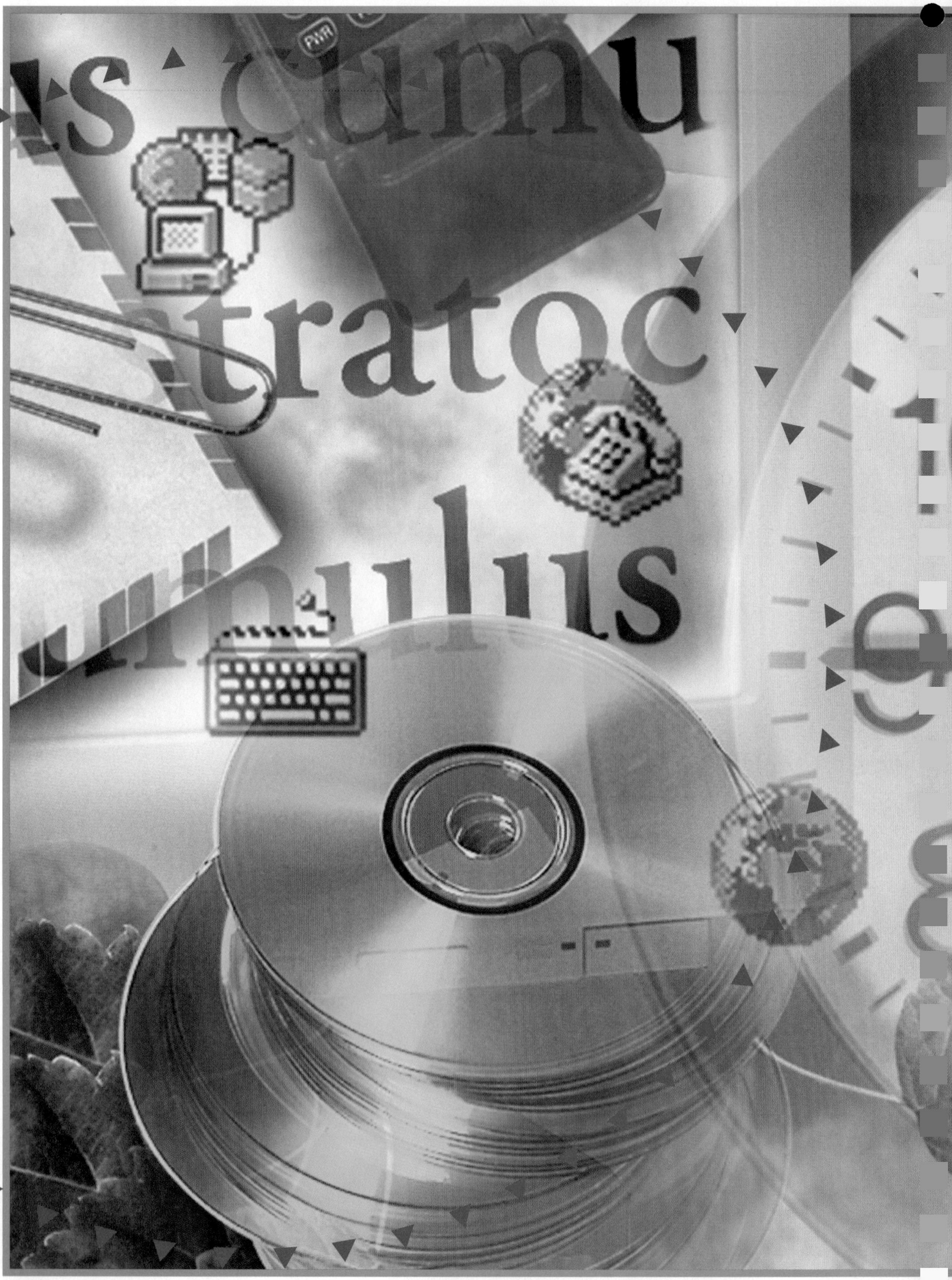

YOUR FIRST VISUAL BASIC PROGRAM

UNIT 1

lesson 1 — 1 hr
A First Look at Microsoft Visual Basic

lesson 2 — 2 hrs.
Forms, Controls, and Properties

lesson 3 — 2 hrs.
Events and Code

Estimated Time for Unit 1: 5 hours

1

A First Look at Microsoft Visual Basic

When you complete this lesson, you will be able to:

- Explain the purpose of Microsoft Visual Basic.
- Start the Visual Basic compiler.
- Open an existing Visual Basic project.
- Explain the purpose of the components on the compiler screen.
- Run a Visual Basic program.
- Position a form in a Visual Basic program.
- Exit Visual Basic.

⏱ Estimated Time: 1 hour

Introduction to Microsoft Visual Basic

Microsoft Visual Basic is a *software development tool*, which means it is a tool that allows you to create programs. One of the reasons that Visual Basic is so popular is because it allows you to easily create complex programs.

Visual Basic combines a graphical interface and programming code to make program development as rapid as possible. With Visual Basic, you use common graphical tools to create the user interface for your program. Then an easy-to-use programming language provides the "behind the scenes" functionality for the program.

You will learn much more about Visual Basic as you progress through the lessons in this book. In this lesson, you will take a quick tour of Visual Basic, identify the components of the Visual Basic environment, and run an existing Visual Basic program.

Starting Visual Basic

Like other Windows programs, Visual Basic can be started from a shortcut on the desktop or from the Start button and Programs menu. Depending on the version of Visual Basic you have installed, the exact name and location of the shortcut or folder containing Visual Basic may vary.

STEP-BY-STEP ➡ 1.1

1. Click the **Start** button.

2. Position the mouse pointer on the **Programs** menu. The Programs menu opens.

3. On the Programs menu, position your mouse pointer on the menu that leads to the Microsoft Visual Basic compiler. This menu may be named Microsoft Visual Basic or Microsoft Visual Studio.

4. When the menu opens, click the **Visual Basic** icon. The Visual Basic compiler starts and the New Project dialog box opens. Your screen should appear similar to Figure 1-1, although your dialog box may be sized differently and may contain fewer items.

5. Leave Visual Basic open for Step-by-Step 1.2. If the New Project dialog box did not appear when Visual Basic started, leave Visual Basic open and proceed.

FIGURE 1-1

The Visual Basic compiler starts with the New Project dialog box.

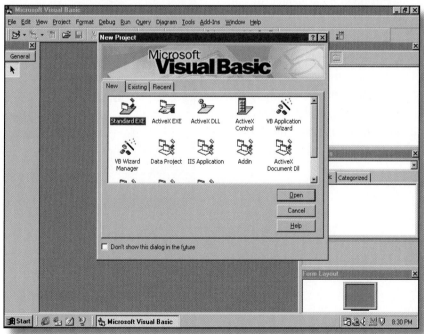

Opening an Existing Visual Basic Project

Visual Basic stores programs in a group of files called a *project*. The main project file has a VBP extension. To open an existing Visual Basic project, click the Existing tab, then open the VBP file that corresponds with the project you wish to open.

1. From the New Project dialog box, click the **Existing** tab.

   NOTE:

   If the New Project dialog box did not appear when you started Visual Basic, choose Open Project from the File menu.

2. Click the **down arrow** in the **Look in** drop down list box to open a list similar to that shown in Figure 1-2.

3. Click the **up** or **down scroll bar arrows** to scroll as needed, then click the item that identifies the disk or drive that holds the data files for this book. A list of files and folders contained on the disk appears in the dialog box.

4. Double-click folders until you see the **SnakeGame** file name.

5. Click **SnakeGame**, then click the **Open** button. Leave the project open for Step-by-Step 1.3.

FIGURE 1-2
The Existing tab from the New Project dialog box allows you to open Visual Basic programs.

Components of the Compiler

W hen you first run the Visual Basic programming environment, it looks similar to other programs you have run in Windows. The screen includes a menu bar, toolbars, and various windows. There is even a toolbox with tools that allows you to draw command buttons, scroll bars, and much more.

Figure 1-3 shows the components of the Visual Basic screen. Do not be concerned if your screen does not show all these components at this time.

FIGURE 1-3
The Visual Basic programming environment has components that are similar to other Windows programs.

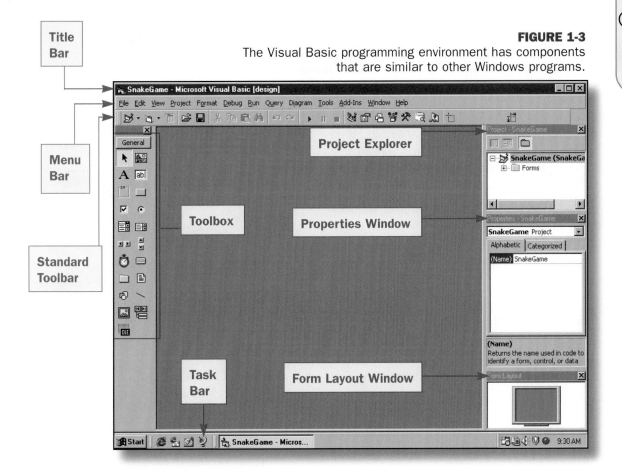

 **NOTE:**

Depending on which version of Visual Basic you have installed, you may see either a blank screen next to the toolbox (as shown in Figure 1-3) or you may see the SnakeGame form. If the SnakeGame form is not displayed, you will learn how to open it later in this lesson.

Menus and Toolbars

The Visual Basic menu bar has some menus found in other Windows programs (such as File and Edit) and some menus that are unique to this programming environment (such as Project and Debug). Like some other Windows programs, Visual Basic has more than one toolbar available. The toolbar that appears by default and that has the standard toolbar buttons is called the *standard toolbar*. Items on the toolbar may vary depending on which version of Visual Basic you have installed.

STEP-BY-STEP ⟹ 1.3

1. Click the **File** menu on the menu bar. The File menu drops down as shown in Figure 1-4 (items shown may vary). Notice that many of the commands in this menu (such as New, Open, Save, and Print) are similar to File menu commands of other Windows programs.

2. Click the **File** menu again. The File menu disappears.

3. Open the other menus from the menu bar and look at some of the commands that are unique to Visual Basic (such as the List Properties/Methods command in the Edit menu).

4. Position the mouse pointer on the first button of the standard toolbar. A tool tip appears below the button with the name of the button as shown in Figure 1-5.

FIGURE 1-4
The File menu has many commands similar to those of other Windows programs.

FIGURE 1-5

The standard toolbar contains buttons for frequently used Visual Basic commands.

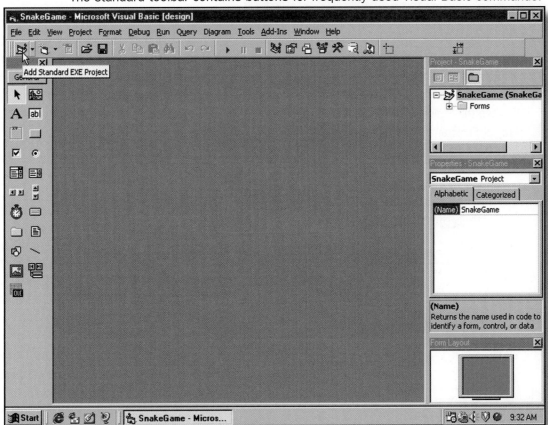

5. Position the mouse pointer on each button on the standard toolbar. Like the menu bar, the standard toolbar contains many common Windows commands.

6. Leave the project open for Step-by-Step 1.4.

The Project Explorer

Another important component of the Visual Basic screen is the Project Explorer. The *Project Explorer* allows you to see the forms and files that make up your program. You will use the Project Explorer to access the forms that you want to work on.

STEP-BY-STEP 1.4

1. Click the title bar of the Project Explorer window, as shown in Figure 1-6. The Project Explorer window becomes active. If you do not see the Project Explorer window, choose Project Explorer from the View menu.

FIGURE 1-6
By default, the Project Explorer window is docked at the upper-right corner of the screen.

If you do not see the Forms folder, click the Toggle Folders button.

2. If a **+** sign appears to the left of the Forms folder in the Project Explorer window, click the **+** sign to open the Forms folder. The Forms folder opens and one form is listed, as shown in Figure 1-7.

FIGURE 1-7
The Project Explorer window organizes the forms used in a Visual Basic program.

3. If the SnakeGame form is not already displayed, double-click the only form in the Project Explorer list (**frmMainForm**). Your screen should look similar to Figure 1-8.

If you cannot see all the command buttons on the form, choose Tile Vertically or Tile Horizontally from the Window menu. If you still do not see all the command buttons on the form, you can resize the form when you run the program later.

4. Double-click the title bar of the Project Explorer window. The Project Explorer window becomes undocked and is moved to the middle of the screen as shown in Figure 1-9.

The position of the Project Explorer window may vary when it is undocked.

5. Position the mouse pointer on the title bar of the Project Explorer window and drag it back to the right side of the screen, just below the toolbar. The Project Explorer window becomes docked again.

6. Leave the project open for Step-by-Step 1.5.

FIGURE 1-8

The form appears when it is double-clicked from the Project Explorer window.

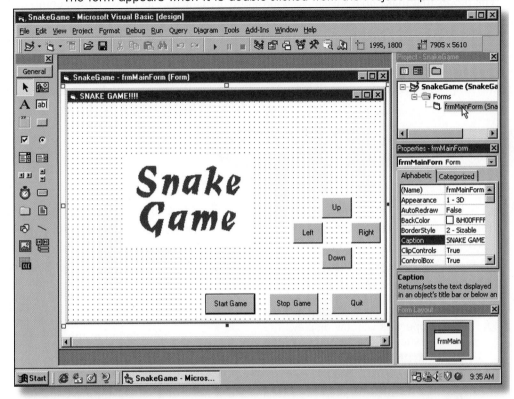

FIGURE 1-9

The windows on the right side of the screen can become undocked by double-clicking the title bar of the window.

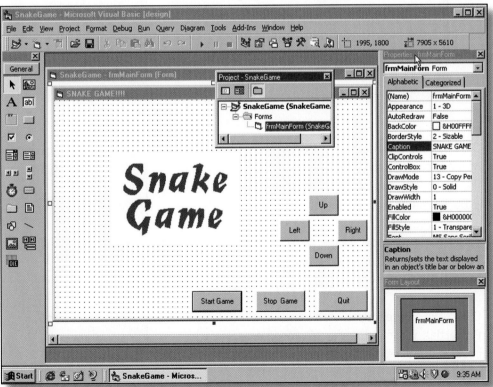

9

The Properties Window

The pieces that make up a Visual Basic program are called *objects*. Windows, command buttons, text boxes, and scroll bars are all examples of objects. Objects placed on forms, such as command buttons and text boxes, are also known as controls. Each object has characteristics that can be customized. These characteristics are called *properties*. To see the properties of an object, select the object and view the properties in the *Properties window*. The properties of the object can also be changed from the Properties window. You will learn how to use the Properties window in the next lesson.

STEP-BY-STEP ⟹ 1.5

1. Click the title bar of the Properties window. The Properties window becomes active, as shown in Figure 1-10. If the Properties window is not displayed, choose Properties Window from the View menu.

FIGURE 1-10
The Properties window displays the characteristics of the selected object.

2. Click the **BackColor** property. A description of the property appears on the bottom of the Properties window as shown in Figure 1-11. Do not change the current setting.

3. Click the **down arrow** on the scroll bar of the Properties window to browse through the list of properties.

4. Click the **Categorized** tab from the **Properties** window. The list of properties becomes grouped by the functions the properties perform, as shown in Figure 1-12.

5. Click the **Alphabetic** tab. The list of properties becomes grouped alphabetically.

6. Leave the project open for Step-by-Step 1.6.

FIGURE 1-11
The bottom of the Properties window displays a description of the selected property.

FIGURE 1-12
Properties can be grouped by function.

The Toolbox

The last part of the Visual Basic screen to visit is the toolbox. The *toolbox* is the collection of tools that allows you to add objects (controls) to the forms you create in Visual Basic. The toolbox has tools for creating objects such as command buttons, text boxes, check boxes, option buttons (also known as radio buttons), picture boxes, and scroll bars. You will use the toolbox in the next lesson to create your first Visual Basic program.

STEP-BY-STEP ⟹ 1.6

1. Position the mouse pointer on the top right tool in the toolbox. The name of the control that the tool creates will appear below the pointer as shown in Figure 1-13.

2. Position the mouse pointer on each of the tools and read the names.

3. Leave Visual Basic open for Step-by-Step 1.7.

FIGURE 1-13
Positioning the mouse pointer on the tools in the toolbox will provide the name of each tool.

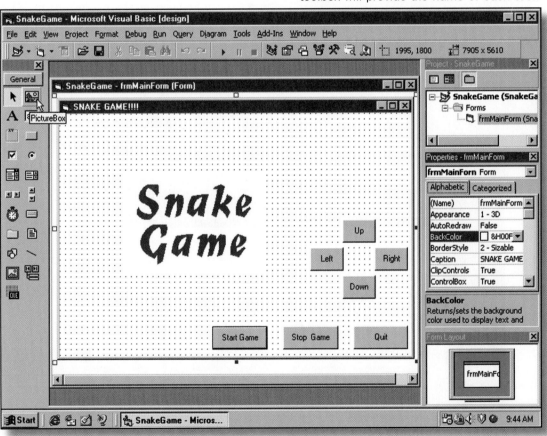

1 1

Running a Visual Basic Program

To run a Visual Basic program, click the Start button from the standard toolbar.

STEP-BY-STEP ⟹ 1.7

1. Click the **Start** button from the standard toolbar. The SnakeGame  program appears on the screen as shown in Figure 1-14. If you cannot see all the command buttons shown in Figure 1-14, drag a corner or side of the SnakeGame window to resize it.

2. Click the **Start Game** button. A box appears on the screen and a line (the snake) begins growing toward the bottom of the box.

3. Before the line reaches the bottom of the box, click the **Right** button. The line will turn to the right and continue toward the right edge of the box.

4. Continue to click the **Up**, **Down**, **Left,** and **Right** buttons to steer the path of the line. When the line hits the edge of the box or crosses its own path, the game is over.

5. When the game is over, click the **OK** button to dismiss the Game Over message.

6. Click the **Quit** button to exit the program. The Visual Basic environment is again active.

7. Leave Visual Basic open for Step-by-Step 1.8.

FIGURE 1-14
The Start button from the standard toolbar runs a program.

Positioning a Form in a Visual Basic Program

FIGURE 1-15
Moving the form changes the position when the program runs.

The *Form Layout window*, which appears in the lower right corner of the screen, shows the position the form will take when the program runs (see Figure 1-15). You can change the position of the form by dragging the form's representation in the Form Layout window.

NOTE:

Only the Form Layout window can change a form's placement when the program runs. Moving the actual form in the Visual Basic environment will not affect the form's placement when the program runs.

STEP-BY-STEP ⇒ 1.8

1. Click the title bar of the Form Layout window. The Form Layout window becomes active. If you do not see the Form Layout window, choose Form Layout Window from the View menu.

2. Position the mouse pointer on the representation of the form in the Form Layout window. The pointer changes to a four-way arrow, as shown in Figure 1-16.

3. In the Form Layout window, drag the form to the bottom right corner of the screen icon.

4. Click the **Start** button on the standard toolbar. Notice that when the program runs, the form appears in the bottom right corner of the screen.

FIGURE 1-16
Moving the form sets the position at which the form will appear.

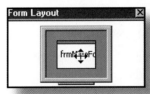

5. Click the **End** button on the standard toolbar. The program ends.

6. Leave the project open for Step-by-Step 1.9.

Exiting Visual Basic

Like other Windows programs, you can exit Visual Basic by choosing Exit from the File menu, or by clicking the Close box at the right end of the Visual Basic title bar.

STEP-BY-STEP 1.9

1. Choose **Exit** from the **File** menu. Because you moved the form in the Form Layout window, you will be asked if you want to save the project and form files.

2. Click **No**. Visual Basic closes.

Summary

■ Microsoft Visual Basic is a tool that allows you to create Windows programs.

■ Visual Basic allows you to easily create complex programs.

■ Visual Basic can be started from a shortcut in the Programs menu or from the desktop.

■ Visual Basic projects are stored in files with a VBP extension. To open a Visual Basic project, you simply have to open the VBP file.

■ Visual Basic has some menus found in other Windows programs and some menus that are unique to Visual Basic.

■ The standard toolbar appears by default and contains buttons for frequently used Visual Basic commands.

■ The Project Explorer allows you to see and open the forms and other files that make up a project.

■ The Properties window lets you view the characteristics, or properties, of the objects that make up a Visual Basic program. The Properties window also allows you to make changes to those properties.

■ The toolbox holds the tools that allow you to add objects such as command buttons to a form.

■ To run a Visual Basic program, click the Start button from the standard toolbar.

■ The Form Layout window allows you to set the position at which the form window will appear when the program runs.

■ Exit Visual Basic by choosing Exit from the File menu or by clicking the Close box on the Visual Basic title bar.

LESSON 1 REVIEW QUESTIONS

TRUE/FALSE

Circle the T if the statement is true. Circle the F if it is false.

T F 1. Microsoft Visual Basic allows you to create programs.

T F 2. Unlike other programs, you cannot start Visual Basic using a shortcut on the desktop.

T F 3. Visual Basic stores programs in groups of files called projects.

T F 4. The Form Layout window allows you to add objects to the forms you create in Visual Basic.

T F 5. The standard toolbar appears by default.

T F 6. Positioning your mouse pointer on a toolbar button will produce a list of properties for that button.

T F 7. You cannot change the properties of an object.

T F 8. An object's properties can be displayed alphabetically and by category.

T F 9. A scroll bar is an example of a property.

T F 10. The Start button on the standard toolbar runs your program.

WRITTEN QUESTIONS

Write your answers to the following questions.

11. What is the purpose of a software development tool?

12. What file extension is given to Visual Basic project files?

13. What is the purpose of the Existing tab of the New Project Dialog Box?

14. Which window lets you modify the characteristics of an object?

15. Which window lets you view the forms and files that make up a project?

16. Which tab shows properties grouped by the functions the properties perform?

17. What is contained in the toolbox?

18. Which command in which menu is used to close Visual Basic?

19. How do you undock a window?

20. What standard toolbar button exits a program that you are running?

LESSON 1 PROJECT

1. Start Visual Basic.

2. Click the **Existing** tab and open the project named **LoanAnalysis**. The project is located in the same folder in which the SnakeGame project is stored.

3. If necessary, click the **+** sign in the Project Explorer to open the Forms folder, then double-click the form.

4. Click some of the objects on the form and view two or three properties of the objects by clicking the property names in the Properties window.

5. Drag the form in the Form Layout window to the upper left corner of the screen icon.

6. Click the **Start** button on the standard toolbar to run the program.

7. Enter the following values in the three fields across the top of the window.
   Loan Amount: **1000**
   Annual Rate (in %): **9**
   Years: **5**

8. Click the **Calculate** button. Values appear in the Payment, Total Interest, and Total of Payments fields at the bottom of the window.

9. Click the **Exit** button.

10. Exit Visual Basic. Click **No** if you are asked to save any changes.

CRITICAL THINKING ACTIVITY

1. Start Visual Basic.

2. Open the **LoanAnalysis** project.

3. View the properties of the **Calculate** button.

4. Move the form in the Form Layout window so that when the program runs, it will be in the upper right corner.

5. Run the program.

6. Suppose you want to buy a new car for $20,000. The loan will be for a period of five years at an interest rate of seven percent. What will the monthly payment be, how much interest will you have paid at the end of the five years, and how much will you actually end up paying for the car?

7. End the program.

8. Exit Visual Basic. Click **No** if you are asked to save any changes.

FORMS, CONTROLS, AND PROPERTIES

OBJECTIVES

When you complete this lesson, you will be able to:

- Create a new Visual Basic project.
- Save a Visual Basic project.
- View and modify form properties.
- Create controls such as command buttons.
- Move, resize, and delete objects.
- Explain the concept of focus.
- Set additional properties (BackColor, Top, and Left).

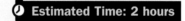 **Estimated Time: 2 hours**

Creating a New Project

In Lesson 1, you started Visual Basic and ran an existing project. To create your own Visual Basic program, however, you must create a new project and begin building your program.

When you start Visual Basic, the New Project dialog box appears, as shown in Figure 2-1. Under the New tab in the New Project dialog box are your options for what kind of project to create. The options visible here may vary, depending on what version of the Visual Basic compiler you have.

For now, we are only interested in the Standard EXE project type. Selecting Standard EXE allows you to create a Windows program from scratch.

 **NOTE:**

The other options in the New Project dialog box allow you to more easily create a variety of specialized programs. For example, the *Application Wizard* helps you create a complete program with standard Windows features already included. On some versions of Visual Basic, other options allow you to create components such as *ActiveX* controls for Web pages.

FIGURE 2-1
The New Project dialog box allows you to choose
what kind of project you want to build.

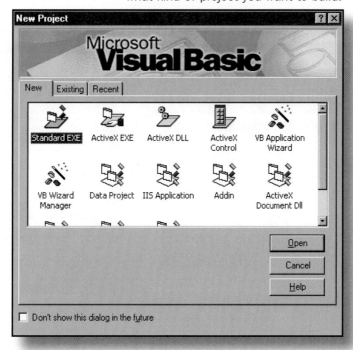

S TEP-BY-STEP ⟹ **2.1**

1. Start **Visual Basic** from the **Programs** menu. After Visual Basic starts, the New Project dialog box will appear.

   NOTE:

   If the New Project dialog box does not automatically appear when you start Visual Basic, choose New Project from the File menu.

2. Click **Standard EXE** to select it, then click the **Open** button (or click the OK button if you opened the New Project dialog box from the File menu). A new project named **Project1** is created. The project includes one blank form by default, as shown in Figure 2-2.

   NOTE:

   If the Project Explorer, Properties, and Form Layout windows are not displayed, click the View menu and click the appropriate window names. If the Forms folder is not displayed in the Project Explorer, click the Toggle Folders button. If a form and a list of properties are not displayed, click the + sign next to the Forms folder in the Project Explorer, then double-click the form icon.

3. Leave the project open for Step-by-Step 2.2.

   (continued on next page)

FIGURE 2-2

A standard new Visual Basic project includes one blank form.

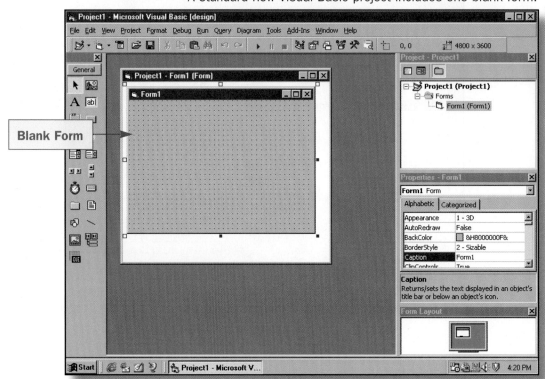

Forms

The project created by selecting the Standard EXE option consists of only one object: a blank form. Remember that objects are the pieces that make up a Visual Basic program. In Visual Basic, *forms* become the windows and dialog boxes when the program runs. Every program has at least one form because all other objects must be contained within forms. For example, a program cannot consist of a command button alone. The command button must be on a form.

There is no functionality in our program, except for the functions common to all forms. In the case of the default blank form, the window displayed when the program runs will have the ability to be moved, resized, maximized, minimized, and closed.

STEP-BY-STEP ⟶ 2.2

1. Click the **Start** button from the standard toolbar. A blank window  appears as shown in Figure 2-3. This blank window is created as a result of the blank form in your project.

2. Click the Maximize button on the form. The form fills the screen as shown in Figure 2-4.

3. Click the **Restore** button. The window returns to its original position on the screen.

4. Position the mouse pointer on the title bar and drag the window to the upper left corner of the screen below the standard toolbar.

5. Position the mouse pointer in the lower right corner of the window. The pointer becomes a double-headed arrow.

6. Drag the corner of the form until it is approximately 2 inches from the right edge of the screen and 2 inches from the bottom of the screen (exact sizing of the form is not important).

(continued on next page)

FIGURE 2-3
The form appears when the Start button is clicked.

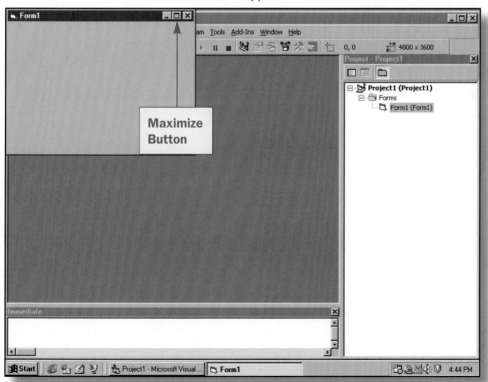

21

FIGURE 2-4
The window generated by your program can be maximized like most windows.

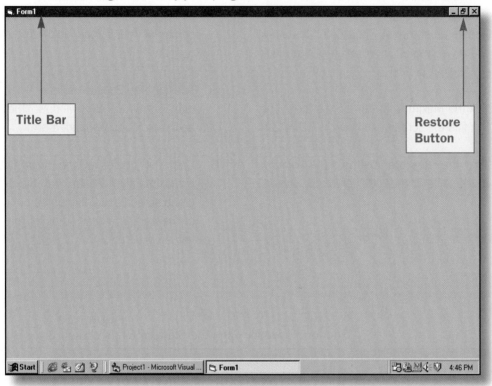

7. Click the **Close** button in the upper right corner of the Form1 window. The form closes and the Visual Basic compiler with the default blank form is active again.

8. Leave the project open for Step-by-Step 2.3.

Saving the Project

When saving a project, you actually save the forms of the project and then the project itself. The most convenient way to accomplish this is to use the Save Project button on the toolbar. First, a dialog box will appear for saving the form. Once the form is saved, another dialog box will appear, allowing you to save the project.

S TEP-BY-STEP 2.3

1. Click the **Save Project** button from the standard toolbar. The Save File As dialog box appears. You will first save the form.

2. Change the drive and folder to the location where your instructor would like you to save your files.

3. Click in the File name box and change the file name to **frmMyForm**, then click the

Save button. The Save Project As dialog box appears. This time you will save the project information.

4. Click the File name box and change the file name to **MyVBProgram**.

5. Click the **Save** button.

6. Leave the project open for Step-by-Step 2.4.

 **NOTE:**

If you need to close Visual Basic at any point after this in the lesson, click the Save Project button on the standard toolbar to save your work, then exit Visual Basic. To reopen the project, click the Existing tab in the New Project dialog box, change drives and folders until you locate *MyVBProgram*, then double-click it. If necessary, click the + sign next to the Forms folder in the Project Explorer and double-click the form icon.

Viewing and Modifying Properties

As you saw in Step-by-Step 2.2, a form has certain characteristics. One of the advantages of programming in Visual Basic is that so much functionality can be achieved without writing programming code. These characteristics of Visual Basic objects are called properties. Every object in Visual Basic has properties. You learned in Lesson 1 that the properties of objects can be viewed in the Properties window.

The Properties window allows you to easily alter the properties of objects. For example, you can alter the property that controls whether the window has Minimize and Maximize buttons.

S TEP-BY-STEP 2.4

1. Click on **Form1** to select it, if it is not already selected. Handles will appear around the border of the form when it is selected and the title bar will be darkened,

as shown in Figure 2-5. (Do not be concerned if you see fewer than eight handles, you could resize the form to see more handles but it is not necessary now.)

(continued on next page)

FIGURE 2-5
An object must be selected in order to alter the object's properties.

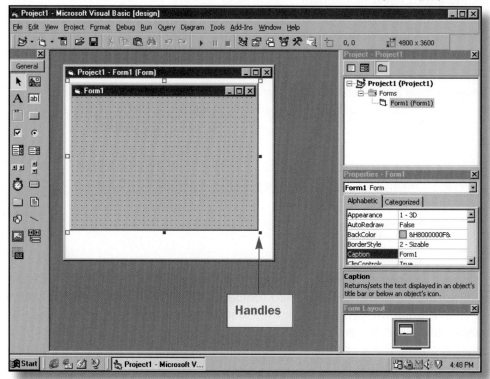

Handles

NOTE:

If the Properties box is empty, click the + sign next to the Forms folder in the Project Explorer, then double-click the Form1 icon.

2. Click the down scroll bar arrow in the Properties window until you see the MaxButton property. Click the **MaxButton** property. A down arrow appears at the right edge of the MaxButton property field. An arrow at the right edge of a field indicates that there are predefined options from which to choose.

3. Click the **down arrow** at the right edge of the MaxButton property field and select **False** from the drop down menu. Notice that the Maximize button on the form becomes inactive (dimmed).

4. Click the **MinButton** property from the Properties window and set its value to **False**. Notice that the Maximize and Minimize buttons on the form disappear.

5. Click the **Moveable** property and set it to **False**.

6. Click the **Start** button from the standard toolbar to run the program.

7. Position the mouse pointer on the title bar of the window and attempt to drag it to the lower right corner of the screen. The form remains in its original position because the Moveable property is set to False.

8. Click the **End** button from the standard toolbar.

9. Click the **Save Project** button (no dialog box will appear since the project has already been named).

10. Leave the project open for Step-by-Step 2.5.

Two of the most important properties of a form are the Caption and Name properties. The Caption property allows you to specify the text that appears in the title bar of the form. The Name property has a less visible, but very important, purpose. Each object has a name. The name of the object becomes very important when you begin writing Visual Basic code to manipulate the objects.

When naming objects, you should use names that are meaningful and describe the object you are naming. Many programmers use names that specify the type of object, as well as describing the object. To identify the type of object, a prefix is added to the name of the object. Table 2.1 shows some of the common prefixes and sample names.

TABLE 2-1

OBJECT NAMING PREFIXES

Prefix	Type of Object	Example
cmd	Command button	cmdClose
frm	Form	frmPrintDialogBox
img	Image	imgLogo
lbl	Label	lblPrompt
txt	Text box	txtWidth

STEP-BY-STEP ➤ 2.5

1. Click on **Form1** to select it. Handles will appear around the border of the form when it is selected.

2. Scroll up in the Properties window and click the **Caption** property.

3. Key **My VB Program** as the new caption. The title bar of the form changes as each letter is keyed as shown in Figure 2-6 (the caption shown in Figure 2-6 is not completely keyed).

(continued on next page)

FIGURE 2-6
The title bar of the form changes as the caption is typed.

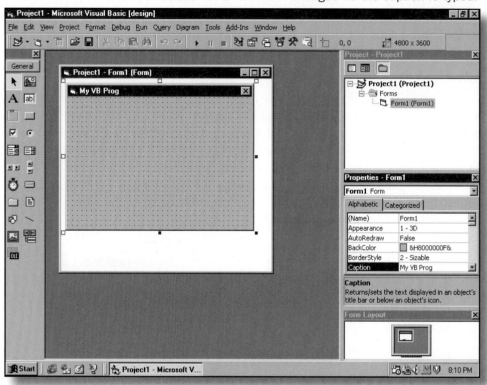

4. Press the **Enter** key to exit from the Caption text box.

5. Click the **(Name)** property from the top of the Properties window.

6. Key **frmMyForm** as the new name, then press the **Enter** key to exit from the Name text box.

7. Save the changes but leave the project open for Step-by-Step 2.6.

NOTE:

The Name property appears in parentheses to force it to appear at the top of the alphabetical list of properties.

Creating Controls

A blank form is not very exciting. To transform a blank form into a custom program, the first step is to add controls to the form. *Controls* are the command buttons, text boxes, scroll bars, and other objects that make up the user interface. Like forms, controls have properties that can be customized to suit your needs.

2 6

One of the most common controls is the command button. A *command button* is a standard pushbutton control. The OK and Cancel buttons that appear in many dialog boxes are examples of command buttons.

To create a command button, use the CommandButton tool on the toolbox (see Figure 2-7). You can double-click the tool to create a command button on the form or click the tool once and draw a command button on the form by dragging the mouse pointer in the area you want the command button to appear. The command button you create can be moved and resized if necessary.

FIGURE 2-7
The CommandButton tool
is used to create
command button controls.

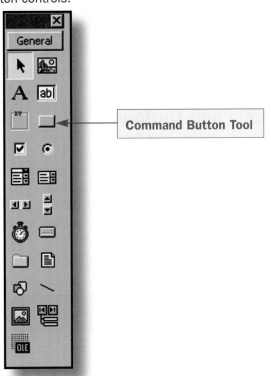

Command Button Tool

 (arrow pointing to Command Button Tool)

![STEP-BY-STEP 2.6]

1. Double-click the **CommandButton** tool on the toolbox. A command button appears in the center of the form.

2. To create another command button, click the **CommandButton** tool on the toolbox one time to select it.

(continued on next page)

NOTE:

Command buttons are named automatically as they are created. Generic names such as Command1 and Command2 will appear on newly created command buttons.

3. Position the mouse pointer in the lower right corner of the form. Notice that the pointer changes from an arrow to a cross.

4. Drag the mouse pointer to create a second command button that is approximately the same size as the first command button as shown in Figure 2-8.

5. Save the changes but leave the project open for Step-by-Step 2.7.

Setting Properties of the Command Buttons

Command buttons may seem simple at first. Like other objects, however, command buttons have many properties that can be set. The Name and Caption properties are among the most important. Be sure to name command buttons with meaningful names. The Caption property of a command button specifies the text that the user sees on the command button.

FIGURE 2-8
A control can be added to a form by double-clicking the control on the toolbox or by manually drawing the object to the desired size.

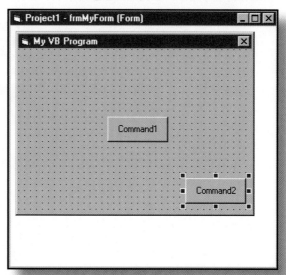

S TEP-BY-STEP ⟹ 2.7

1. Click the **Command1** button to select it (handles will surround it).

2. From the **Properties** window, click the **Caption** property and key **Show Image**, then press the **Enter** key.

3. Click the **(Name)** property and key **cmdShow**, then press the **Enter** key.

4. Click the **Command2** button.

5. Change the caption to **Exit** and change the name to **cmdExit**.

6. Save the changes but leave the project open for Step-by-Step 2.8.

Moving, Resizing, and Deleting Objects

Command buttons can be moved and resized easily. The objects in Visual Basic can be moved and resized using techniques that are common to most Windows programs. You can delete an object by selecting the object and pressing the Delete key.

TIP

Visual Basic allows you to be imaginative with the size and position of objects. However, keep the Microsoft Windows standards in mind. Your programs will have a more professional appearance if the command buttons and other objects in your programs have a similar size and placement as those in other Windows programs.

S TEP-BY-STEP ⟹ 2.8

1. Drag the **Show Image** button towards the upper right corner of the form.

✓ **NOTE:**

If any of the eight handles are missing, you can drag to reposition the Show Image button again.

2. Click the **Exit** button that you created. Handles appear around the border of the command button to indicate that it is selected.

3. Position the mouse pointer on the top middle handle bar and drag it up until it forms a box as shown in Figure 2-9.

4. If it is not already selected (surrounded by handles), click the **Exit** button that you created.

5. Press the **Delete** key. The Exit button disappears.

6. Double-click the **CommandButton** tool from the toolbox.

FIGURE 2-9
The handles are used to resize controls.

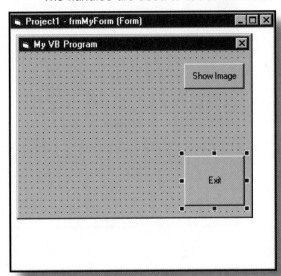

7. Change the name of the button you just created to **cmdExit** and change the caption to **Exit**.

8. Drag the **Exit** button to the bottom right corner of the form. Your form should appear similar to Figure 2-10.

9. Save the changes but leave the project open for Step-by-Step 2.9.

(continued on next page)

FIGURE 2-10
Command buttons can be resized and moved on the form.

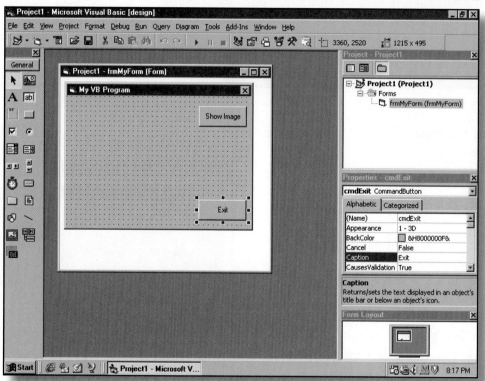

Understanding Focus

As you create programs that consist of controls (command buttons, scroll bars, and other objects) in windows, the concept of focus becomes an important one. As you have used programs, you have probably noticed that only one window at a time is active on the screen. You may have also noticed that within the window, only one control is active. For example, the cursor (blinking line) can only be in one text box. The object that is currently active is said to have the *focus*.

To see the focus move from one control to another, you can repeatedly press the Tab key while a dialog box is active. Each object in the window will get the focus in a sequence called the *tab order*.

STEP-BY-STEP 2.9

1. Choose the **Print** command from the **File** menu. The Print dialog box opens.

2. Press the **Tab** key. Notice how the focus moves from one control to another.

3. Press the **Tab** key repeatedly until the Cancel button is selected and press the **Enter** key. The Print dialog box disappears. Pressing the Enter key activated the command button with the focus.

4. Save the changes but leave the project open for Step-by-Step 2.10.

The project you are working on has two command buttons on the form. When the program runs, the focus will alternate between the two command buttons as the Tab key is pressed.

STEP-BY-STEP ⇒ 2.10

1. Click the **Start** button to run the program. The form, including the two command buttons you created is active on the screen, as shown in Figure 2-11.

2. Press the **Tab** key. The focus moves from the Show Image button to the Exit button.

3. Click the **Show Image** button. The focus moves to the Show Image button.

4. Click the **Exit** button you created. The focus moves to the Exit button.

(continued on next page)

FIGURE 2-11
When the program starts, the Show Image button has focus.

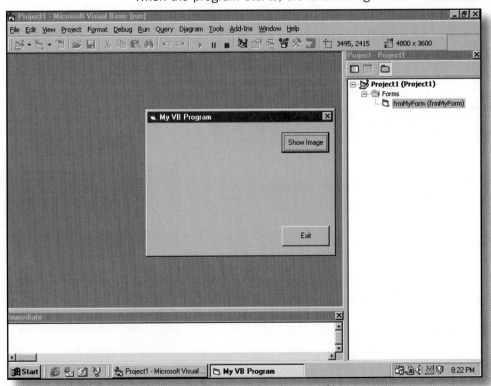

5. Click the **End** button from the standard toolbar. The program ends.

6. Save the changes but leave the project open for Step-by-Step 2.11.

In Step-by-Step 2.10, you clicked the Show Image button and the Exit button. Activating those command buttons, however, produced no action. Creating a command button is only the first step. Giving a command button the caption *Exit* will not make the command button have the function of an Exit button. In the next lesson, you will learn how to write programming code to give these command buttons functionality.

Setting Additional Properties

Other properties that are commonly set when creating Visual Basic programs are the BackColor property and the properties that accurately set the position and size of objects.

Setting the BackColor Property

By default, forms have a gray background. The BackColor property can be changed to display a color other than gray. When setting the BackColor property, you can select from a palette of colors which is accessible from the Properties window.

TIP

Color should be used sparingly in your programs. The more your programs have the color and appearance of standard Windows programs, the more professional your work will appear. Overusing colors can also make text in your programs harder to read.

FIGURE 2-12
The BackColor property can be easily altered from the Properties window.

S TEP-BY-STEP 2.11

1. If **frmMyForm** is not already selected (surrounded by handles), click on it.

2. Click the **BackColor** property from the **Properties** window.

3. Click the **down arrow** at the right edge of the BackColor property field. A window of color options appears below the BackColor property as shown in Figure 2-12.

4. Click the **Palette** tab. A selection of colors appears.

5. Click the white box located at the upper left corner of the color palette. The form changes from gray to white.

6. Save the changes but leave the project open for Step-by-Step 2.12.

Setting the Top and Left Properties

Often, you can use the mouse to size and position objects such as command buttons. However, if you want precise placement, you can use the Top and Left properties to specify the location of the command buttons. The Top property specifies the distance the top left corner of the command button will appear from the top edge of the form. The Left property specifies the distance the top left corner of the command button will appear from the left edge of the form. By default the unit of measure for the Top and Left properties is *twips*. With twips, you can specify very precise measurements. There are 1440 twips in one inch.

NOTE:

There is no Right property. To specify how far a command button will appear from the right edge of a form, you must specify how far the command button is to appear from the left edge.

STEP-BY-STEP ▷ 2.12

1. Click the **Exit** button to select it.

2. In the Properties window, scroll down, click the **Top** property and key **2500**, then press the **Enter** key.

3. Scroll up, click the **Left** property and key **3200**, then press the **Enter** key.

4. Click the **Show Image** button to select it.

5. Change the **Top** property to **250**, then press the **Enter** key.

6. Change the **Left** property to **3200**, then press the **Enter** key.

7. Save your changes, then choose **Exit** from the **File** menu to exit Visual Basic.

NOTE:

If your buttons are no longer visible when you change the measurements in these steps, experiment with smaller measurements or drag to resize the form.

Summary

■ To create your own Visual Basic program, you must create a new project. The Standard EXE project type allows you to create a program from scratch.

■ Projects created using the Standard EXE option begin with one blank form. Forms become the windows and dialog boxes when the program runs.

■ Every program has at least one form. All other objects must be contained within forms.

■ A window created from a Visual Basic form has certain functionality by default, such as the ability to be moved, resized, maximized, minimized, and closed.

■ Properties are the characteristics of Visual Basic objects. Properties can be modified in the Properties window.

■ The Caption and Name properties are two of the most important properties. The Caption controls what the user sees in the title bar of a form and other objects such as command buttons. When we add programming code later, the Name property allows us to refer to the object using a meaningful name. Programmers often use a naming standard when naming objects.

■ Controls are the command buttons, text boxes, scroll bars, and other objects that make up the user interface.

■ A command button is a standard pushbutton control that commonly appears in dialog boxes.

■ Command buttons can be moved, resized, and deleted like other Windows objects.

■ The term focus refers to the active status of one of the objects in a window. Only one object can have the focus.

■ The BackColor property controls the background color of a form.

■ The Top and Left properties can be used to accurately position objects. By default, the Top and Left properties use a measurement called twips. There are 1440 twips in one inch.

■ When saving a Visual Basic project, the forms are saved first, followed by the project information.

LESSON 2 REVIEW QUESTIONS

TRUE/FALSE

Circle the T if the statement is true. Circle the F if it is false.

T F 1. The ActiveX option helps you create a complete program with standard Windows features already included.

T F 2. Every program must have at least one form.

T F 3. Visual Basic programs have some functionality without writing any code.

T F 4. The btn prefix is commonly used when naming command buttons.

T F 5. The OK and Cancel buttons that appear in dialog boxes are examples of command buttons.

T F 6. A text box in a dialog box is an example of a control.

T F 7. An object can be deleted by selecting the object and pressing the Delete key.

T F 8. The inactive controls on a form are said to have focus.

T F 9. Selecting the Background property will allow you to change the background color of a form.

T F 10. When saving a project, you actually save the forms of the project and then the project itself.

WRITTEN QUESTIONS

Write your answers to the following questions.

11. What appears when the Standard EXE option is selected from the New Project dialog box?

12. A project created by the Standard EXE option consists of one object by default. What is that object?

13. What appears when an object is selected?

14. What term describes the characteristics of Visual Basic objects?

15. How do you specify the text that will appear in the title bar of a form?

16. What naming prefix is generally used when naming a form?

17. List three examples of controls.

18. What unit of measurement does Visual Basic use for the Top and Left properties?

19. What term describes the sequence in which the controls in a window become active as the Tab key is pressed?

20. What button on the standard toolbar is used to save a program?

LESSON 2 PROJECT

1. Start Visual Basic and create a new project.

2. Change the (**Name**) property of the form to **frmMyForm**.

3. Change the **Caption** property of the form to **Lesson 2 Project**.

4. Save the project with a form name of **frmMyForm2** and a project name of **MyVBProgram2**.

5. Add a command button to the form.

6. Change the **Caption** property of the command button to **Exit**.

7. Change the (**Name**) property of the command button to **cmdExit**.

8. Drag the Exit button to the lower right corner of the form.

9. Draw a new command button on the form that is approximately the same size as the Exit button.

10. Change the **Caption** property of the new command button to **Go** and change the (**Name**) property of the command button to **cmdGo**.

11. Resize the Go button so it is approximately half as wide and twice as tall as the Exit button.

12. Click the **Start** button on the standard toolbar to run the program (the Exit button will have the focus).

13. Press the **Tab** key to switch the focus between the command buttons.

14. End the program.

15. Select and delete the Go button from the form.

16. Move the Exit button to the center of the form.

17. Click on the form and position the pointer on the lower right corner. Resize the form so the Exit button appears in the lower right corner.

18. Save the changes, then exit Visual Basic.

CRITICAL THINKING ACTIVITY

1. Start Visual Basic and create a new project.

2. Give the form a caption and a descriptive name property.

3. Add an Install button and a Cancel button to the form, giving each a caption and a descriptive name property.

4. Move and resize each object so the form looks similar to Figure 2-13.

5. Save the project with an appropriate form name and project name, then exit Visual Basic.

FIGURE 2-13
Add an Install button and a Cancel button as shown here.

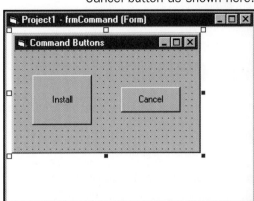

EVENTS AND CODE

When you complete this lesson, you will be able to:

- Describe events and how events are key to Windows programs.

- Access the Code window.

- Add code to a command button.

- Add an image to a form.

- Set image properties.

- Set properties from code.

- Set the Cancel and Default command button properties.

- Create a standalone Windows program.

⏱ **Estimated Time: 2 hours**

Events

Windows is an event-driven environment. In an *event-driven* system, the computer is constantly waiting for the user to take some action with the mouse, keyboard, or other device. That action triggers an *event*, and the software in the computer attempts to find something to do with that action.

Each object has a set of events that are supported by the object. When you create an object, such as a command button, it is up to you to write the code that will handle the events. That code is written in Visual Basic.

You only have to write code for the events you are interested in. For example, a command button supports events called Click, MouseDown, and MouseUp. The Click event occurs when the user clicks a command button. To be more specific, the MouseDown event occurs when the user presses the mouse button and holds it down over the command button. The MouseUp event occurs when the user releases the mouse button. Normally, you only need to write code for the Click event. The added control provided by MouseDown and MouseUp is not normally needed.

The code you write to handle a specific event is called an *event procedure*. You will write event procedures for events that you want to handle. For events you wish to ignore, you don't have to write anything.

In Lesson 2, you created two command buttons on a form and then ran the program. Recall that you clicked the command buttons, but nothing happened. When you clicked the Exit button that you created, a Click event was generated. Because your mouse pointer was over the Exit button, that command button was given the Click event to process. However, since you had not written any code for the command button, it did not know how to process the Click event and the event was ignored.

In this lesson, you will add code for handling the Click event to the command buttons you created in the previous lesson. As you progress through the lessons in this book, you will learn about additional events and how to write code for those events.

Accessing the Code Window

The first step in adding code to an object is to access the Code window. To add code to a command button, open the form that contains the command button and double-click the command button. The Code window will appear.

STEP-BY-STEP ⟹ 3.1

1. Start Visual Basic and click the **Existing** tab (or choose **Open Project** from the **File** menu).

2. Change drives and folders as necessary, then double-click **MyVBProgram** that was created in Lesson 2 (not MyVBProgram2).

3. If necessary, use the View menu to open the Project Explorer, Properties, and Form Layout windows.

4. If necessary, click the **+** sign to open the Forms folder from the Project Explorer window. If the form is not already on your screen, double-click **frmMyForm**. The form appears in the middle of the screen.

5. Double-click the **Exit** button. The Code window appears. Your screen should appear similar to Figure 3-1.

6. Leave the project open for Step-by-Step 3.2.

(continued on next page)

FIGURE 3-1

The Code window allows you to enter code for an object or control.

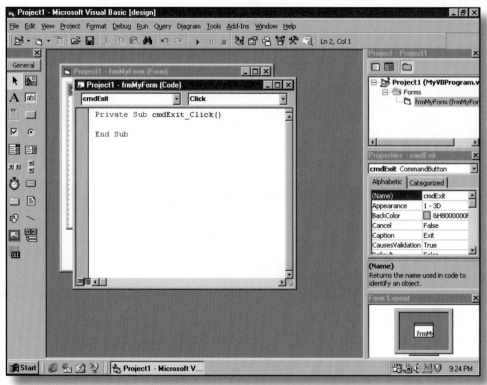

Notice that the Code window already has some code written in it. A *subroutine* (a section of code to perform a specific task) has been set up for you. The name of the subroutine indicates that the routine is to handle the Click event of the cmdExit button. The code for the Exit button will be added at the location where the cursor is blinking.

Adding Code to a Command Button

To add code to the Code window, you simply enter the code from the keyboard much like you would use a word processor. You can insert and delete text, and use cut, copy, and paste.

The Code window, however, has special features that automatically format your code and help you enter code more easily and more accurately. For example, using a technology called *Intellisense®*, it will anticipate what you are about to key and complete your statements for you.

Visual Basic is not *case-sensitive*, meaning capitalization of key words and other elements of the code is not critical. Keying a command in all caps, all lowercase, or a combination of case has no effect on the functionality. However, to keep things neat, the Code window editor will standardize the case of much of your code.

NOTE:

The Code window does not automatically wrap text like a word processor. Each line of code should be complete on one line. Press the Enter key at the end of each line of code. Press the Backspace key to delete blank lines. You can resize the Code window to make seeing your code easier.

Let's begin by adding code for the Exit button. The Visual Basic command to end a program is the End statement.

STEP-BY-STEP 3.2

1. Press the **Tab** key to indent the line. It is common practice to use indention to improve the readability of programming code. The usefulness of indenting code will become more apparent in later lessons when the code is more complex.

2. Key **end** and press the **Enter** key. Notice that Visual Basic capitalizes the word *end* and changes the color to blue. Your Code window should appear similar to Figure 3-2.

(continued on next page)

NOTE:

The color in which the key words in the Code window appear may vary.

FIGURE 3-2
Visual Basic automatically formats key words.

41

3. Press the **Backspace** key twice to remove the blank line below the code you just keyed.

4. Click the **Close** button from the Code window. The Code window closes and the form becomes active.

5. Click the **Start** button from the standard toolbar to run the program.

6. Click the **Exit** button. The event procedure you wrote is activated and the program ends.

7. Click the **Save Project** button on the standard toolbar to save the changes but leave the project open for Step-by-Step 3.3.

Adding an Image to a Form

Visual Basic allows you to easily add graphics to your programs. One of the easiest ways to add an image to a form is to use the Image tool (located towards the bottom of the toolbox). The Image tool creates an object called an *image control*. An image control provides a framework for displaying an image on a form.

Like the CommandButton tool, the Image tool can be double-clicked to place an object of a default size on the form. You can also click the Image tool once and then drag to draw an image control. The image control can be moved and resized like other controls.

NOTE:

The Picture Box tool at the top of the toolbox creates a control similar to an image control. A picture box control is more flexible, but slightly less efficient than an image control.

STEP-BY-STEP ⇒ 3.3

1. Double-click the **Image** button from the toolbox. An image control appears in the center of the form.

2. Position the mouse pointer in the center of the image control and drag it to the upper left corner. Drag the lower right corner of the image control to resize it. Your form should look similar to Figure 3-3.

3. While the image control is selected (surrounded by handles), click the **Picture** property from the **Properties** window. A button with three tiny dots, called an ellipsis, appears in the Properties field, as shown in Figure 3-4. The *ellipsis*, in this case, indicates that you can browse your hard drive for a file that will serve as the source of the image.

FIGURE 3-3
The image control allows graphics
to be shown in a program.

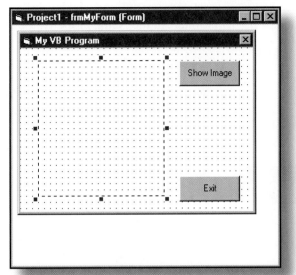

FIGURE 3-4
The ellipsis shown
indicates that you can
browse for a value.

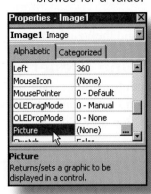

4. Click the ellipsis at the end of the Picture property field. The Load Picture dialog box appears on the screen as shown in Figure 3-5.

5. From the **Look in** box, select the drive and folder where your template files are located. A list of picture files appears in the Load Picture dialog box (depending on how your template files are organized on your system, there may be only one picture file listed for this lesson).

6. Click **VBasic** from the list of picture files and click the **Open** button. A picture of the cover of this textbook appears within the image control. Notice how the image control resizes itself to fit the size of the picture.

7. Save the changes but leave the project open for Step-by-Step 3.4.

FIGURE 3-5
The Load Picture dialog box allows you to select a
picture that will be the source of the image.

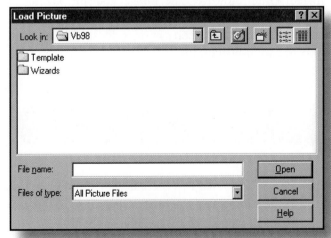

Setting Image Properties

Like other objects, image controls have an extensive set of properties that can be changed. For our purposes, there are three properties that are of particular interest: the Name property, the Stretch property, and the Visible property.

The Name Property

Naming an image control is as important as naming other objects. The name you give the image control will be the name you use when you refer to the control in your Visual Basic code. The *img* prefix is often used when naming image controls.

STEP-BY-STEP ⟶ 3.4

1. If necessary, click on the image control to select it.

2. Scroll up and click the **(Name)** property. Remember, the Name property appears in parentheses at the top of the Properties list.

3. Change the name of the image control to **imgMyImage** and press the **Enter** key.

4. Save the changes but leave the project open for Step-by-Step 3.5.

The Stretch Property

When you selected the image for the image control, the image control resized itself to fit the image. Often, however, the image you are placing on the form is not the size you would like displayed. The *Stretch property* allows the image to be resized to fit the size of the image control. By default, the Stretch property is set to False. Setting the Stretch property to True will allow the image to resize to fit the control.

STEP-BY-STEP ⟶ 3.5

1. If necessary, click on the image control to select it. Resize the image control so it appears similar to Figure 3-6. Notice that the image control resizes, but the image itself remains the original size. The image does not resize because the Stretch property is set to False.

2. Change the **Stretch** property to **True** from the **Properties** window. The image stretches to fit inside the image control as shown in Figure 3-7.

3. Click the **Start** button on the standard toolbar to run the program. Notice the image appears in the window.

4. Click the **Exit** button to end the program.

5. Save the changes but leave the project open for Step-by-Step 3.6.

FIGURE 3-6
When the Stretch property is set to False, the image control can be resized, but the image will not stretch to fit the control.

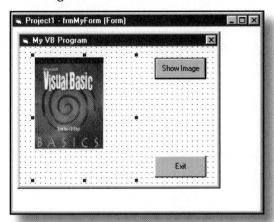

FIGURE 3-7
Changing the Stretch property to True causes the image to resize to fit the control.

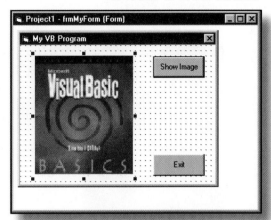

The Visible Property

The Visible property gives you control over when an image is visible to the user. Setting the Visible property to False makes the image invisible to the user. As you will see when you write the code for the Show Image button, the Visible property can be changed from code.

 **NOTE:**

In the Snake Game you played in Lesson 1, the large words "Snake Game" that appear when you first run the program are actually in an image control. The program uses the Visible property to make the words disappear when the game is started.

STEP-BY-STEP ▷ 3.6

1. Click on the image to select the image control.

2. Change the **Visible** property of **imgMyImage** to **False**.

3. Click the **Start** button on the standard toolbar. The program begins, but because the Visible property of the image control is set to False the image does not appear on the form. Your screen should appear similar to Figure 3-8.

(continued on next page)

4. Click the **Exit** button to end the program.

5. Save the changes but leave the project open for Step-by-Step 3.7.

FIGURE 3-8
The Visible property allows the image to be hidden.

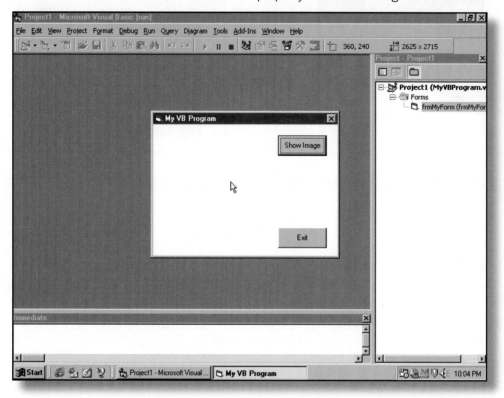

Setting Properties from Code

One of the most common tasks for Visual Basic code is setting properties of objects such as controls and forms. While it is true that the properties of objects can be set when the object is created, you will often want to manipulate those properties while the program runs.

Visual Basic allows you to change a property by specifying the name of the control, the property, and the value you want to give the property. Figure 3-9 shows a line of code that changes an image control's Visible property to False.

The period (usually referred to as a dot) separates the object from the property. The item to the right of the dot is called a *method*. The term method is common to object-oriented programming languages. In Figure 3-9, the word *Visible* is actually a method for changing the Visible property. There are other methods used in Visual Basic programming that do not relate to a property.

The image control object knows how to set its own Visible property, and it provides the Visible method for doing so. When you write the Visual Basic code, you are sending a message to the imgMyImage object, telling it to change its Visible property using the Visible method. *Message* is another object-oriented programming term. In object-oriented programming, you don't actually set the property—you ask the object to set its own property by sending it a message.

FIGURE 3-9
Properties can be changed from code.

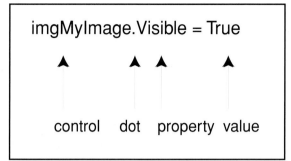

STEP-BY-STEP ⟹ 3.7

1. Double-click the **Show Image** button. The Code window appears on the screen.

2. Press the **Tab** key.

3. Key **imgMyImage.Visible = True** as shown in Figure 3-10 (ignore the drop down boxes that appear as you key).

4. Close the Code window.

5. Click the **Start** button from the standard toolbar. The program becomes active on the screen. Notice that the image is not visible.

(continued on next page)

FIGURE 3-10
The code in the Show Image button asks the image control to set its Visible property to True.

4 7

6. Click the **Show Image** button on the form. The image appears on the screen. Your screen should appear similar to Figure 3-11.

7. Click the **Exit** button.

8. Save the changes but leave the project open for Step-by-Step 3.8.

FIGURE 3-11
The image appears on the screen after
the Show Image button is clicked.

Setting the Cancel and Default Command Button Properties

You have probably noticed in most windows that include command buttons, there is a command button that will be selected when you press the Enter key and a command button that will be selected when you press the Esc key. Often, the Enter key will select the OK button, and the Esc key will select the Cancel button.

There are two command button properties involved in adding this functionality to your programs: the Default property and the Cancel property. The command button with the *Default property* set to True will be activated when the user presses the Enter key. The command button with the *Cancel property* set to True will be activated when the user presses the Esc key.

Only one command button on a form can have the Cancel property set to True. The same is True for the Default property.

STEP-BY-STEP 3.8

1. Click the **Show Image** button and set the **Default** property to **True**.

2. Click on the **Exit** button and set the **Cancel** property to **True**.

3. Click the **Start** button on the standard toolbar to run the program.

4. Press the **Enter** key. The Show Image button is activated and the image appears.

5. Press the **Esc** key. The Exit button is activated and the program ends.

6. Save the changes but leave the project open for Step-by-Step 3.9.

Creating a Standalone Program

Running programs from within the Visual Basic environment with the Start button from the standard toolbar is fine when you are developing a program. When you have a finished product, however, you will want to make a program file that can be run like other Windows programs, without Visual Basic being loaded.

By creating a *standalone program*, you can distribute a program you have written to anyone who is running Windows—whether they have Visual Basic or not.

To create a standalone program from your Visual Basic project, choose the Make command from the File menu. The Make command will show the name of your program in the menu, so it will vary depending on the project you have opened.

 **NOTE:**

Some editions of Visual Basic may not have the feature for creating standalone programs.

STEP-BY-STEP 3.9

1. Choose **Make MyVBProgram** from the **File** menu. The Make Project dialog box appears as shown in Figure 3-12.

2. Use the dialog box to locate the folder where you intend to save the standalone program. Your instructor may have special instructions for saving.

3. Change the file name within the Make Project dialog box to **VBStandalone** and click the **OK** button.

4. After the EXE file is created, exit Visual Basic. If necessary, save any changes that were made to your files.

(continued on next page)

FIGURE 3-12
The Make Project dialog box allows you to select the location for your standalone program.

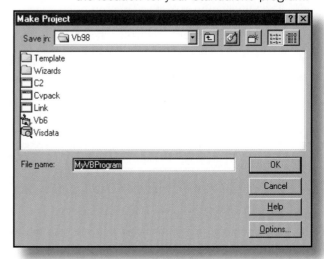

4 9

5. Double-click the **My Computer** icon on your desktop (or click the Windows **Start** button, position the mouse pointer on **Programs**, and click **Windows Explorer**). Double-click drives and folders to locate the VBStandalone file.

6. Double-click the program named **VBStandalone.** The program starts.

7. Click the **Show Image** button on the form (or press the **Enter** key). The program runs exactly the same as it did within the Visual Basic compiler.

8. Click the **Exit** button (or press the **Esc** key). Close all the My Computer or Windows Explorer windows.

Summary

- Windows is an event-driven environment. In an event-driven system, the user triggers events that control the work.

- To control what happens when an event occurs, you must write event procedures for each event that you want to handle.

- To access the Code window, double-click an object such as a command button.

- The code you write in Visual Basic is written in sections called subroutines.

- Adding code is much like working in a word processor. The basic text-editing features are available. In addition, Visual Basic has *Intellisense®* features to help format your program code.

- The End statement ends a program.

- The Image tool allows you to add an image control to a form.

- Using the Name property, you can give an image control a name. That name will be used when you refer to the control in code.

- The Stretch property set to True causes an image to resize to fit the dimensions of the image control.

- The Visible property controls whether an object is showing or hidden.

- Setting properties from code is one of the most common uses for Visual Basic code. Setting properties from code allows you to change properties while a program runs.

- To change an object's properties from code, you send a message to the object. The object uses a method to change the property.

- A command button with the Default property set to True will be activated when the user presses the Enter key.

- A command button with the Cancel property set to True will be activated when the user presses the Esc key.

- A standalone program is one that will run without any special programming language software being loaded. Visual Basic creates standalone Windows programs using the Make command from the File menu.

LESSON 3 REVIEW QUESTIONS

TRUE/FALSE

Circle the T if the statement is True. Circle the F if it is False.

T F **1.** Microsoft Windows is an event-driven environment.

T F **2.** An event can be triggered only by the mouse.

T F **3.** Double-clicking a command button control brings up the Code window.

T F **4.** In Visual Basic, exact capitalization of all of the key words is critical.

T F **5.** An image control provides a framework for an image.

T F **6.** The Stretch property set to True allows an image to resize to fit the image control.

T F **7.** When setting properties from code, every property of the object must be specified.

T F **8.** The command button with the Default property set to False will be activated when the user presses Esc.

T F **9.** Only one command button can have the Default property set to True.

T F **10.** A standalone program can run on a computer that does not have Visual Basic installed.

WRITTEN QUESTIONS

Write your answers to the following questions.

11. What is the term for code that handles a specific event?

12. What is the term for the section of code that is set up for you when you access the Code window?

13. What is Intellisense®?

14. What does an ellipsis (…) at the edge of a Properties field indicate?

15. Why is it important to give a meaningful name to an image control?

16. What is the purpose of the Visible property?

17. When setting a property from code, what is the item that immediately follows the dot in the line of code and what does it do?

18. Write a line of code that will cause the image held in an image control named imgLogo to be hidden.

19. What is the name of the command button property that causes the button to be activated when the Esc key is pressed?

20. Why would you want to create a standalone program?

LESSON 3 PROJECTS

PROJECT 3A

In this project, you will use the Top property of an image control to move an image on the form while the program is running.

1. Start Visual Basic and create a new project.

2. Give the form the name **frmHighLow** and the caption **High Low**.

3. Use the **Properties** window to set the **Height** property of the form to **3750** and the **Width** property to **4500**.

 **NOTE:**

Height and Width properties are measured in twips, just like the Top and Left properties.

4. Add a **Cancel** button to the form with the caption **Cancel**. Name it **cmdCancel**. Drag the command button to the lower right corner of the form.

5. Write an event procedure that will cause the program to end when the Cancel button is clicked.

6. Run the program to test it.

7. Add an image control to the form and drag it to the upper left corner of the form.

8. Load the VBasic image into the image control and set the **Stretch** property to **True**. Name the image **imgVBasic**.

9. Set both the **Height** and **Width** properties of the image control to **1500**.

10. Set the **Top** property of the image control to **200**.

11. Set the **Left** property of the image control to **400**.

12. Add a command button with the caption **High** to the form. Name it **cmdHigh** and drag it to the upper right corner of the form. (If it overlaps the image, click on the form and drag handles to resize it, then drag the command button again.)

13. Add a command button with the caption **Low** to the form. Name it **cmdLow** and place it below the High button.

14. Add the following code to the **High** command button Click event procedure.

```
imgVBasic.Top = 200
```

15. Add the following code to the **Low** command button Click event procedure.

```
imgVBasic.Top = 1500
```

16. Make the **Cancel** button the command button that will be activated when the Esc key is pressed.

17. Save the project with a form name of **frmHighLow** and a project name of **HighLow**.

18. Run the program and test the command buttons (remember to press the **Esc** key to test the Cancel button).

19. Exit Visual Basic.

PROJECT 3B

A command button's Enabled property can be used to disable a command button so that it can no longer be clicked. This is commonly used to prevent a user from selecting an option that is not currently available. In this project, you will open the project you created in the lesson and disable the Show Image button after the image is visible.

1. Start Visual Basic, click the **Existing** tab, and open the **MyVBProgram** project (not MyVBProgram2).

2. If necessary, open the form.

3. Double-click the **Show Image** button to access its event procedure.

4. Press the **End** key to move to the end of the code that makes the image visible, then press the **Enter** key.

5. Add the following line of code.

```
cmdShow.Enabled = False
```

6. Close the Code window.

5 3

7. Run the program to see the Show Image button become disabled after it is clicked. (When you run the program the image is invisible, then when you click the Show Image button, the image appears and the button is disabled.)

8. Press the **Esc** key to end the program.

9. Make a standalone program named **VBStandalone2** that includes the new functionality, then exit Visual Basic (saving the changes).

10. Double-click the **My Computer** icon on the desktop, locate the new standalone file, and start the program.

11. Test the buttons, then close all the My Computer windows.

CRITICAL THINKING ACTIVITY

Open the MyVBProgram project again (not the standalone program) and make the following modifications. (If you did not complete the steps in Project 3B, perform those steps before making the modifications below.) Run the program to test the modifications, then exit Visual Basic, saving the changes.

1. Create a command button with the caption **Hide Image**. Give the command button an appropriate name and position it below the Show Image button.

2. From the Properties window, set the **Enabled** property of the Hide Image button to **False**.

3. Add code to the **Show Image** button event procedure that will enable the Hide Image button after the Show Image button is disabled.

4. Write an event procedure for the **Hide Image** button that hides the image, disables the Hide Image button, and enables the Show Image button.

UNIT 1 REVIEW QUESTIONS

MATCHING

Write the letter of the description from Column 2 that best matches the term or phrase in Column 1.

Column 1	Column 2
_____ 1. form	**A.** objects that make up the user interface.
_____ 2. properties	**B.** capitalization of key words and other elements of the code is critical.
_____ 3. event procedure	**C.** the window that shows the position the form will take when the program is run.
_____ 4. Form Layout Window	**D.** objects that become the windows and dialog boxes when the application is run.
_____ 5. focus	**E.** the window that allows you to see the forms that you want to work on.
_____ 6. toolbox	**F.** the technology used in Visual Basic that will anticipate what you are about to key and will complete your statements for you.
_____ 7. case-sensitive	**G.** the characteristics of an object.
_____ 8. controls	**H.** the code written to handle a specific event.
_____ 9. IntelliSense®	**I.** the collection of tools that allows you to add objects to the forms you create in Visual Basic.
_____ 10. Project Explorer Window	**J.** the object that is currently active.

WRITTEN QUESTIONS

Write your answers to the following questions.

11. What appears when a command button on a form is double-clicked?

12. What is the purpose of the End button located on the standard toolbar?

13. What key activates the Cancel property of an object?

14. What are the two tabs for displays in the Properties window?

15. What are two examples of command buttons found in other Windows programs?

16. What property controls whether an object is shown or hidden?

17. What key moves the focus from one control to another?

18. What kind of program can be run without the Visual Basic compiler?

19. What contains the collection of tools that allows you to add objects to the forms you create in Visual Basic?

20. What property allows you to specify the text that appears in the title bar of a form?

UNIT 1 APPLICATIONS

Estimated Time: 1 hour

APPLICATION 1-1

Write the name of the screen components from Figure U1-1 here.

A. _____

B. _____

C. _____

D. _____

E. _____

F. _____

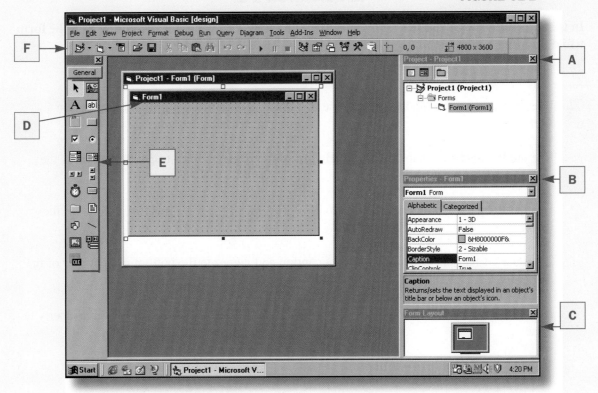

APPLICATION 1-2

Start Visual Basic and create a new project. Position the mouse pointer on each of the toolbox tools shown in Figure U1-2 and write the name of the tool in the spaces provided.

A. _____

B. _____

C. _____

D. _____

E. _____

F. _____

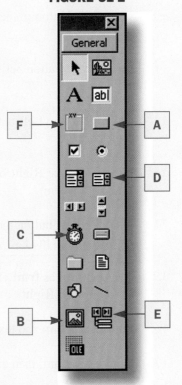

APPLICATION 1-3

In this project, you will use the Left property of an image control to move an image on the form while the program is running.

1. If necessary, start Visual Basic and create a new project.

2. Use the **Properties** window and give the form the name **frmLeftRight** and the caption **LeftRight**.

3. Use the **Properties** window to set the **Height** property of the form to **3400**, then press the **Enter** key.

4. Use the **Properties** window to set the **Width** property of the form to **4700**, then press the **Enter** key.

5. Add an **Exit** button (with an appropriate caption and name) to the bottom right corner of the form. Add code to make the program end when the button is active.

6. Add the VBasic image to the form with the name **imgVBasic** and set the **Stretch** property to **True**.

7. Set both the **Height** and **Width** properties of the image control to **1500**.

8. Set the **Top** property of the image control to **200**.

9. Set the **Left** property of the image control to **400**.

10. Add a **Left** button to the lower left corner of the form and give it an appropriate caption and name.

11. Add a **Right** button between the Left and Exit buttons and give it an appropriate caption and name.

12. Add code to the **Left** button that will position the image as close as possible to the left side of the form.

13. Add code to the **Right** button that will position the image as close as possible to the right edge of the form.

14. Make the **Exit** button the button that will be activated when the Esc key is pressed.

 **NOTE:**

15. Save the form as **frmLeftRight** and save the project as **LeftRight**.

16. Run the program and test all of the buttons.

17. End the program, then exit Visual Basic.

If your Left and Right buttons did not place the image correctly when you ran the program, double-click the command buttons, change the measurements in the Code window, then run the program again.

INTERNET ACTIVITY

In this activity, you will use the Internet to learn more about Microsoft Visual Basic.

1. Open your Web browser.

2. Go to the Web address below.

   `http://www.programvb.com/basics`

3. On the home page, click the link called **Information about Microsoft Visual Basic**.

4. Browse the information and links that appear on your screen.

5. When you have finished investigating the links, close your Web brower.

CALCULATIONS AND DATA

UNIT 2

lesson 4   2 hrs.
Mathematical Operators

lesson 5   2 hrs.
Exponentiation, Order of Operations and Error Handling

lesson 6   2 hrs.
Data Types and Variables

lesson 7   2 hrs.
Strings and Decimal Types

Estimated Time for Unit 2: 8 hours

MATHEMATICAL OPERATORS

OBJECTIVES

When you complete this lesson, you will be able to:

- Describe the purpose of operators and how calculations are performed in Visual Basic.

- Create label controls.

- Use the addition and assignment operators.

- Use text boxes to get data from the user and use the Val function to extract a numeric value from a text box.

- Split code statements among lines in the Code window.

- Use the subtraction operator.

- Use unary minus.

- Use the multiplication and division operators with the Fix function to remove the fractional portion of numbers.

- Perform integer division and use the modulus operator.

⏱ **Estimated Time: 2 hours**

Performing Calculations in Visual Basic

It is no secret that computers are well-suited for math. In fact, most of the tasks a computer performs can be reduced to some mathematical function. Like other programming languages, Visual Basic allows you to use mathematical equations in your programs. In this lesson, you will learn how to perform the basic mathematical functions using the mathematical operators.

Operators are symbols that perform specific operations in Visual Basic statements. As you will learn in later lessons, there are operators that are not strictly mathematical. But for now, we will only be concerned with performing basic math operations using the common operators.

Since you began learning basic math, you have been using operators such as + and − to add and subtract values. To make Visual Basic statements as easy to read as possible, symbols were selected that are similar or identical to the symbols you are accustomed to using. Table 4-1 shows the mathematical operators you will use in this lesson.

TABLE 4-1

MATHEMATICAL OPERATORS

Operator	Description
=	Assignment
+	Addition or unary plus
-	Subtraction or unary minus
*	Multiplication
/	Division
\	Integer division
Mod	Modulus

NOTE:

There may be a couple of operators in Table 4-1 that are new to you. Don't worry, in this lesson you will learn all about them and put each of them to work in a program.

Creating Label Controls

The *Label control* is used to place text on a form. Sometimes a label is used to identify a text box or to add a title or message to a form. The Caption property of a label specifies what text will appear on the label. The text that appears on the label cannot be directly changed by the user. Labels can also be used to provide output. To provide output, you write code for the desired calculation. The result of the calculation is then assigned to the Caption property of the label and the result also appears on the label on the form.

In Step-by-Step 4.1, you will open a Standard EXE project and create some labels.

1. Start Visual Basic and open a new Standard EXE project. If necessary, open the Forms folder in the Project Explorer and double-click the Form icon.

2. In the **Properties** window, give the new form the name **frmAddition** and the caption **Addition**.

3. Double-click the **Label** tool, which is found in the toolbox. A label appears on the form. The caption of the label is Label1.

4. Click the **Caption** property from the **Properties** window.

5. Key your name as the caption for the label and press the **Enter** key. Notice that the caption changes on the label as you key the caption in the Properties window.

6. Click the **(Name)** property, key **lblMyName** and press the **Enter** key.

7. Position the mouse pointer in the center of the label and drag it to the upper left corner of the form.

8. Save the project with the form named **frmAddition** and project named **Addition**. Leave Visual Basic open for Step-by-Step 4.2.

TIP

Remember that another way to place controls such as labels on a form is to click the tool once, then drag to draw the control. You can then move, resize, or delete the control as needed.

Using the Addition and Assignment Operators

The addition operator (+) and *assignment operator* (=) perform just as you would expect. For example, in the statement below, the values 16 and 8 are added, and the result is placed in the caption of the label named lblAnswer. The assignment operator changes the value of the item on the left of the assignment operator to the value to the right of the assignment operator. After the statement is executed, the label will display the result of the addition (24).

NOTE:

The term *hard-coded* refers to information that is entered directly into the source code and cannot change while the program runs. Values that are keyed directly into source code are also called *literals*.

```
lblAnswer.Caption = 16 + 8
```

The statement above is not very realistic, however. In most cases, rather than writing code that adds two hard-coded values, you will be adding values that may be entered by a user or other values that may change each time the program is run.

S TEP-BY-STEP ⇒ 4.2

1. Click the **Label** tool from the **Toolbox** to select it.

2. Draw a label in the center of the form that is about half the size of the other label.

3. Change the caption of the new label to the number zero (**0**) and press the **Enter** key.

4. Change the name of the new label to **lblAnswer**.

5. Click the **CommandButton** tool and create a command button near the bottom center of the form. Name the button **cmdCalculate** and change the button's caption to **Calculate**.

6. Double-click the **Calculate** button, press the **Tab** key, and add the code in CODE Step 6 in the Click event procedure.

   CODE Step 6

   ```
   lblAnswer.Caption = 16 + 8
   ```

7. Close the Code window. Click the **Start** button on the standard toolbar to run the program. The Answer label in the center of the form currently has a caption of 0.

8. Click the **Calculate** button. The caption for the Answer label changes to 24, the result of adding 16 and 8, as shown in Figure 4-1. Your screen should show your name in the top left corner of the form.

FIGURE 4-1
The Caption property of the label was changed by the code in the Calculate button.

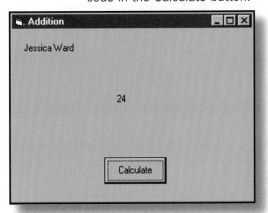

9. Click the **End** button on the Standard toolbar to end the program.

10. Save the changes to your form.

11. Choose **Remove Project** from the **File** menu to close the project.

12. Leave Visual Basic open for Step-by-Step 4.3.

Using Text Boxes and the Val Function

*T*ext boxes are the fields placed on dialog boxes and in other windows that allow the user to enter a value. You have seen and used text boxes in the previous lessons. In this lesson, you will learn how to extract the value from a text box and use it in a mathematical operation. Figure 4-2 shows an example of a text box (the File name box). The Text property of a text box specifies what text will appear on the text box.

How Text Differs from Numeric Data

Text boxes accept data from the user. This data comes in the form of text. In a computer, text, which can include letters, symbols, and numbers, is treated differently than strictly numeric information. For example, if the user enters 234 in a text box, the computer treats that entry as three characters—a 2, a 3, and a 4. It does not automatically treat the entry as two-hundred and thirty-four. Therefore, numbers in a text box must be converted to a true numeric value before they can be used in a calculation.

FIGURE 4-2
Text boxes are fields that get input from the user.

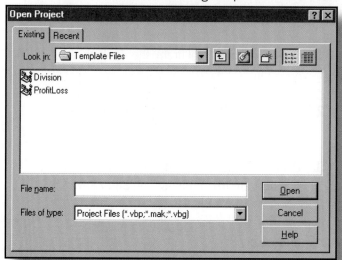

When a computer stores text, it uses a numeric value to represent each allowable character. For example, to your computer, the character "A" is represented by the value 65. The system of codes that the computer uses to represent characters is called the ASCII code. For now, just understand that the characters entered in text boxes need a conversion from numeric text to a numeric value before mathematical operations can be performed.

Using the Val Function

The conversion necessary to convert the numeric text characters in a text box to numeric values is done by the Val function. The *Val function* takes numbers that are in a text format and returns a numeric value that can be used in calculations. The statement below is an example of how the Val function is used. The items in parentheses are the text boxes.

```
lblTotal.Caption = Val(txtPrice.Text) + Val(txtSalesTax.Text)
```

In the statement above, notice that the text boxes (txtPrice and txtSalesTax) begin with the txt prefix. This makes it clear that the controls are text boxes. (Remember that controls are the objects you insert from the toolbox.) The *Text* following the period accesses the values entered by the user in the textboxes. The *Caption* following the period indicates that the answer of the calculation will be assigned to the Caption property of the label. The statement is instructing the computer to take the value in the txtPrice text box, add the value in the txtSalesTax text box to it, and assign the sum of the values to the Caption property of the label named lblTotal.

Splitting Code Statements Among Lines

When you begin writing code that includes calculations, the lines of code often become long. Visual Basic provides a way to split a line of code among two or more lines. Within a line of code, you can key an underscore (_), known as the *line-continuation character*. The line-continuation character tells the compiler to skip to the next line and treat the text there as if it were a part of the same line. In Step-by-Step 4.3, you will use the line-continuation character to break a long line of code into two lines.

STEP-BY-STEP 4.3

1. Choose **Open Project** from the **File** menu.

2. Change to the drive and folder where your template files are located, then open the **ProfitLoss** project.

3. If the form is not displayed, open the **Forms** folder from the Project Explorer window and double-click the form **frmProfitLoss.** Your screen should appear similar to Figure 4-3.

4. Double-click the **Calculate** button. The Code window appears.

5. Add a blank line below the cmdCalculate_Click() line, then position the cursor on the blank line.

6. Press the **Tab** key to indent the line.

(continued on next page)

FIGURE 4-3
The Profit & Loss form appears on your screen.

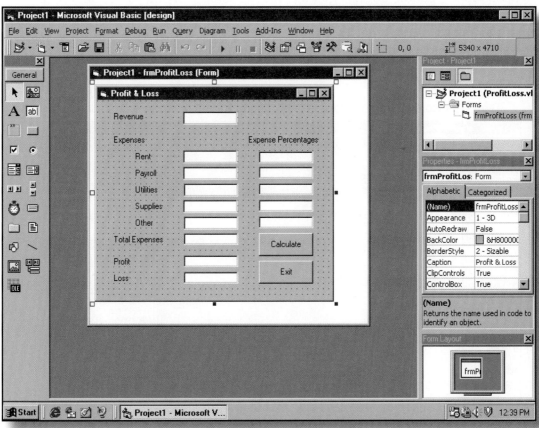

6 7

7. Add the code in CODE Step 7 to total the expenses.

```
'Calculate Total Expenses
lblTotalExp.Caption = Val(txtRent.Text) + Val(txtPayroll.Text) + _
Val(txtUtil.Text) + Val(txtSupp.Text) + Val(txtOther.Text)
```

 **IMPORTANT:**

Always key a space before the line-continuation character to avoid errors.

NOTE:

The apostrophe (') at the beginning of the code for step 7 allows you to enter text into the code that the compiler will ignore. Everything from the apostrophe to the end of the line will be ignored. These notes in the code are called *comments*. You will learn more about comments in the next lesson.

FIGURE 4-4
The underscore character allows a line of code to be broken into multiple lines.

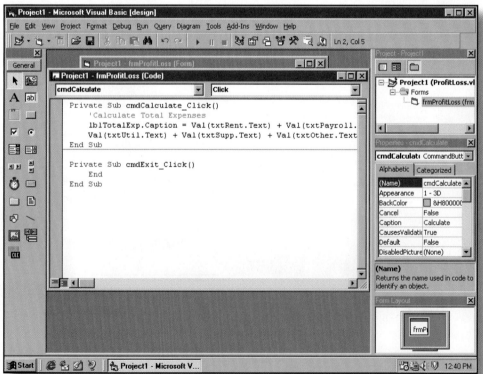

This code will add the values in the Rent, Payroll, Utilities, Supplies, and Other text boxes and assign the sum of the values to the Caption property of the label named lblTotalExp. The Code window should appear similar to Figure 4-4.

 TIP

When you use parentheses in code, count to be sure you have an equal number of left (and right) parentheses.

8. Close the Code window and click the **Start** button on the standard toolbar to run the program.

9. Key the following data into the corresponding text boxes on the form.

Rent	**350**
Payroll	**600**
Utilities	**200**
Supplies	**100**
Other	**50**

10. Click the **Calculate** button. The expenses are totaled and the results are stored in the Total Expenses Field as shown in Figure 4-5.

11. Click the **Exit** button. The Profit & Loss program closes.

12. Save the changes but leave the project open for Step-by-Step 4.4.

FIGURE 4-5
The Calculate button totals the data on the form.

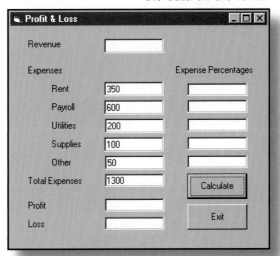

Using the Subtraction Operator

The subtraction operator subtracts the value to the right of the operator from the value to the left of the operator. In other words, it works just the way you learned in elementary school.

In Step-by-Step 4.4, notice that profit is calculated by subtracting the value in a label from the value in a text box. You extract the value from a label using the Caption property.

STEP-BY-STEP 4.4

1. Double-click the **Calculate** button.

2. Click at the end of the second line of code and press the **Enter** key twice to create a blank line.

(continued on next page)

NOTE:

In the following code for the profit calculation, the Val function is not necessary in order to extract the value from the lblTotalExp caption. Because earlier code set the caption to a numeric value, we could assume that the caption is still a numeric value. However, using the Val function in cases like these is good practice.

3. Add code in CODE Step 3 to calculate the profit.

CODE Step 3

```
'Calculate Profit
lblProfit.Caption = Val(txtRev.Text) - Val(lblTotalExp.Caption)
```

This code will subtract the value in the label named lblTotalExp from the value in the text box named txtRev and assign the result to the Caption property of the label named lblProfit. Your screen should appear similar to Figure 4-6.

FIGURE 4-6
The subtraction operator subtracts one value from another.

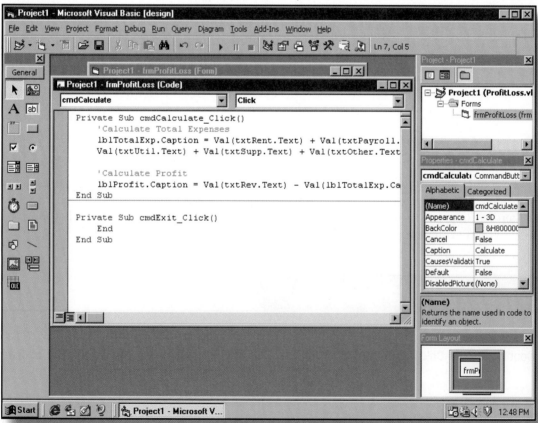

4. Close the Code window and run the program.

5. Key the same data for expenses that you keyed in Step-by-Step 4.3. Key **1200** in the Revenue field.

6. Click the **Calculate** button. Both the Profit field and the Total Expenses field store the results of the calculation as shown in Figure 4-7.

7. Click the **Exit** button to close the program.

8. Save the changes but leave the project open for Step-by-Step 4.5.

FIGURE 4-7
The Calculate button figures the profit.

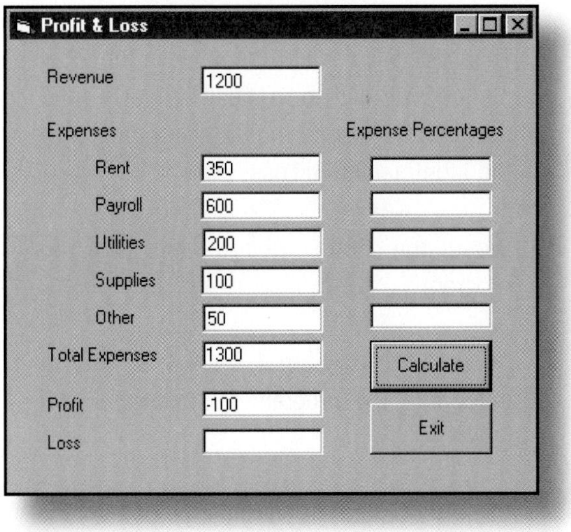

Using Unary Minus

You can use the subtraction operator as *unary minus* to perform negation, which means making a positive value negative or making a negative value positive. For example, the statement below takes the value in the label named lblAnswer and changes the sign of the value. If lblAnswer is holding a negative number, the unary minus will make it positive. If the value in the label is already positive, the unary minus will make it negative.

```
lblNegatedAnswer.Caption = -Val(lblAnswer.Caption)
```

The addition operator can be used as a unary plus. The unary plus is rarely used, however, because it has little practical value. Values in Visual Basic are assumed to be positive unless they are specifically signed as negative.

STEP-BY-STEP ▷ 4.5

1. Double-click the **Calculate** button.

2. Add the code in CODE Step 2 beneath the code that calculates the profit.

CODE Step 2

```
'Calculate Loss
lblLoss.Caption = -Val(lblProfit.Caption)
```

(continued on next page)

7 1

This code will convert the value in the label named lblProfit to a positive value and assign the result to the Caption property of the label named lblLoss.

3. Close the Code window and run the program.

4. Refer to Step-by-Step 4.3 – 4.4 for data to enter into the program for expenses and revenue.

5. Click the **Calculate** button. The loss is now calculated as well as the total expenses and profit as shown in Figure 4-8.

6. Click the **Exit** button.

7. Save the changes but leave the project open for Step-by-Step 4.6.

FIGURE 4-8
The negated profit represents the loss.

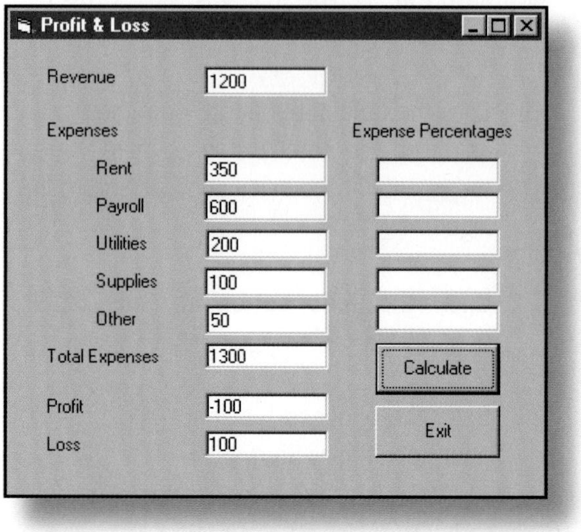

Using the Multiplication and Division Operators

Multiplication and division are represented by symbols that are slightly different from those used in standard mathematics. An asterisk (*) represents multiplication and a forward slash (/) represents division. These symbols are used for multiplication and division in most programming languages because they are available on a standard computer keyboard.

Using Fix

There are times when you are interested in only whole numbers after a calculation is performed. Most programming languages include a function that drops the fractional part of a number. In other words, the function removes everything to the right of the decimal point. This process is called *truncation*. In Visual Basic, the *Fix function* returns the truncated whole number.

In the program you have been creating in the step-by-steps of this lesson, we need to calculate the percentage of the total expenses which are allocated to each of the expense categories. For example, in the case of the Rent expense, the amount spent on rent must be divided by the total expenses and then multiplied by 100 in order to have a percentage. Using the multiplication and division operators, that calculation can be performed with the following code.

```
Val(txtRent.Text) / Val(lblTotalExp.Caption) * 100
```

The result of this calculation will commonly have a fractional part. If all we are interested in is the whole number percentage, the Fix function can be used to truncate the result.

```
Fix(Val(txtRent.Text) / Val(lblTotalExp.Caption) * 100)
```

By placing the entire expression in parentheses, the Fix function is applied to the result of the entire expression.

STEP-BY-STEP 4.6

1. Double-click the **Calculate** button to open the Code window.

2. Add the code in CODE Step 2 beneath the code that calculates the loss.

3. Close the Code window and run the program.

4. Enter **1500** for Revenue, **350** for Rent, **700** for Payroll, **250** for Utilities, **100** for Supplies, and **60** for Other on the form.

5. Click the **Calculate** button. Each of the percentages is calculated, as well as the total expenses, profit, and loss, as shown in Figure 4-9.

6. Click the **Exit** button.

7. Save the changes to the project, then choose **Remove Project** from the **File** menu.

8. Leave Visual Basic open for Step-by-Step 4.7.

FIGURE 4-9
The program calculates the percentage of the total that each expense represents.

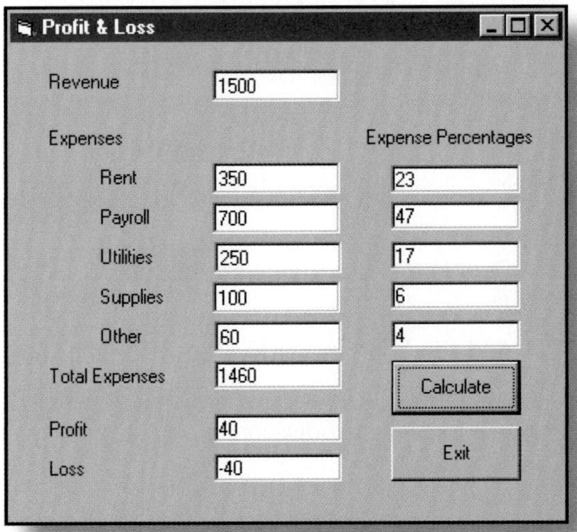

CODE Step 2

```
'Calculate Expense Percentages
lblRentPerc.Caption = Fix(Val(txtRent.Text) / _
Val(lblTotalExp.Caption) * 100)
lblPayrollPerc.Caption = Fix(Val(txtPayroll.Text) / _
Val(lblTotalExp.Caption) * 100)
lblUtilPerc.Caption = Fix(Val(txtUtil.Text) / _
Val(lblTotalExp.Caption) * 100)
lblSuppPerc.Caption = Fix(Val(txtSupp.Text) / _
Val(lblTotalExp.Caption) * 100)
lblOtherPerc.Caption = Fix(Val(txtOther.Text) / _
Val(lblTotalExp.Caption) * 100)
```

Performing Integer Division and Using Modulus

In computer programming, there are times when you want to work exclusively with whole numbers, called *integers*. When performing division, however, the results are often fractional, even when you begin with whole numbers. For example, 5 and 3 are both integers, but when you divide 5 by 3, the result is fractional (1.666667).

For cases where you want to work strictly with integers, Visual Basic provides two special operations: integer division and modulus. *Integer division* returns only the whole number portion of the division of integers. *Modulus* returns the remainder of integer division.

Performing Integer Division

Integer division is performed using the backward slash (\), often called simply a back slash. This operation returns a whole number. For example, 5 \ 3 returns 1 as the result.

STEP-BY-STEP ⟹ 4.7

1. Choose **Open Project** from the **File** menu. Open the **Division** project from your template files.

2. If necessary, open form **frmDivision.** Your screen should appear similar to Figure 4-10.

3. Double-click the **Calculate** button.

4. Add the code in CODE Step 4 to calculate the quotient. Be sure to use the backslash (\) for integer division when keying the code below.

5. Close the Code window and run the program.

6. Enter **6** in the field outside the division bar (the divisor) and **10** inside the division bar (the dividend).

7. Click the **Calculate** button. The quotient is calculated and the results are displayed to the left of the r as shown in Figure 4-11.

8. Click the **Exit** button. The program closes.

9. Save the changes but leave the project open for Step-by-Step 4.8.

CODE Step 4

```
'Calculate Quotient
lblQuotient.Caption = Val(txtDividend.Text) \ Val(txtDivisor.Text)
```

FIGURE 4-10

The Division form appears on your screen.

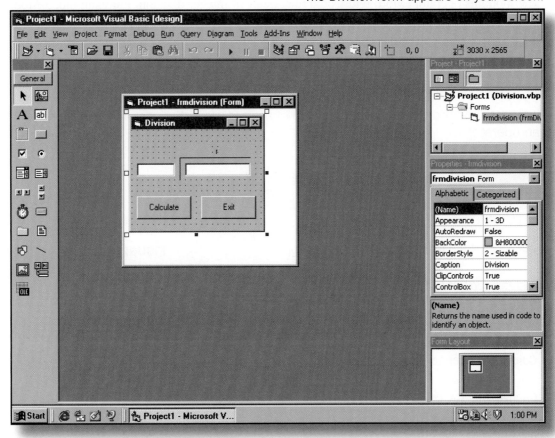

FIGURE 4-11

The Calculate button
calculates the quotient.

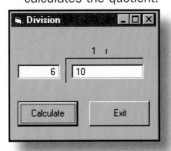

Using the Modulus Operator

The modulus operator (Mod) returns the remainder of integer division. For example, 5 Mod 3 returns the result 2 because 5 divided by 3 is 1 remainder 2.

NOTE:

Unlike other operators, Mod is not a single character. Nevertheless, Mod functions as an operator.

STEP-BY-STEP 4.8

1. Double click the **Calculate** button.

2. Add the code in CODE Step 2 to calculate the remainder.

3. Change the **Default** property of the **Calculate** button to **True.**

4. Change the **Cancel** property of the **Exit** button to **True.**

5. Close the Code window.

6. Run the program. Enter **5** in the field outside the division bar (the divisor) and **27** inside the division bar (the dividend).

7. Click the **Calculate** button. The quotient and remainder are calculated and the results are displayed above the division bar as shown in Figure 4-12.

FIGURE 4-12
The Calculate button calculates the quotient and remainder.

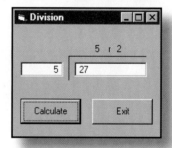

8. Click the **Exit** button. The program closes.

9. Save the changes to the project and form, then exit Visual Basic.

CODE Step 2

```
'Calculate Remainder
lblRemainder.Caption = Val(txtDividend.Text) Mod Val(txtDivisor.Text)
```

Summary

- Visual Basic allows you to use mathematical equations in your programs.

- Operators are symbols that perform specific operations in Visual Basic statements.

- The addition operator (+) adds values.

- The assignment operator (=) assigns the result of the expression on the right of the operator to the item to the left of the operator.

- Values keyed directly into Visual Basic code are called hard-coded values or literals.

- Text boxes are the fields placed on dialog boxes and in other windows that allow the user to enter a value.

- The numbers in a text box are considered to be text characters. To use the numbers as actual values in a calculation, the Val function must be used to convert the numeric text to a numeric value.

- When a line of code is long, you can split the code into two lines in the Code window by keying an underscore at the end of the line and continuing the statement on the next line. The underscore is called the line-continuation character.

- Placing an apostrophe in code allows you to enter text (called a comment) into the code. Everything from the apostrophe to the end of the line will be ignored.

- The subtraction operator (-) subtracts the value to the right of the operator from the value to the left of the operator.

- The subtraction operator can be used to perform negation. When used in this way, the subtraction operator is called the unary minus.

- Multiplication is represented by an asterisk (*).

- Division is represented by a forward slash (/).

- The Fix function removes the fractional portion of a number. The Fix function performs an operation called truncation.

- Integer division returns only the whole number portion of the division of integers.

- Integer division is represented by a backward slash (\).

- The modulus operator (Mod) returns the remainder of integer division.

TRUE/FALSE

Circle the T if the statement is true. Circle the F if it is false.

T   F   1. Operators are symbols that perform specific operations in Visual Basic statements.

T   F   2. Values entered directly into Visual Basic code are called hard-coded or literals.

T   F   3. Text boxes are fields on a form that allow the user to enter a value.

T   F   4. Text boxes store user input in a numeric format.

T   F   5. The subtraction operator and the unary minus operator are two different characters.

T   F   6. The addition operator cannot be used as a unary plus.

T   F   7. The backslash character is used for integer division.

T   F   8. The result of integer division is the remainder of the division.

T   F   9. The Val function truncates the fractional part of a number.

T   F   10. In Visual Basic an expression cannot take up more than one line.

WRITTEN QUESTIONS

Write your answers to the following questions.

11. List the seven mathematical operators covered in this lesson.

12. What are the differences between the forward slash and the backslash?

13. Which operator returns the remainder of integer division?

14. Which character is used as the line-continuation character?

15. Which character is used to begin comment statements?

16. What is the purpose of the Fix function?

17. What prefix commonly begins text box names?

18. What must you do in order to use information stored in the Text property of a text box in numeric calculations?

19. Write the code for a command button that will calculate the result of multiplying values in two text boxes, *num1* and *num2*, and display the result in a label called *lblResult*.

20. The following code appears in the *cmd_Click* subroutine of a command button. What will happen when the button is clicked?

```
lblResult.Caption = 12 \ 7
```

LESSON 4 PROJECTS

PROJECT 4A

Your local high school is having a bake sale to raise money for a local charity. You have been asked to write a program that will calculate the total sales and show the percentages of each item sold during the bake sale. The program's user interface should look similar to Figure 4-13. The form and each item on the form should be given a caption (use Figure 4-13 as your guide). Use the following names for the form and the items on the form: **frmBakeSale, lblSalesPercent, lblCakes, lblPies, lblMuffins, txtCookies, txtCakes, txtPies, txtMuffins, lblCookiesPerc, lblCakesPerc, lblPiesPerc, lblMuffinsPerc, lblTotalSalesLabel, lblTotalSales, cmdExit,** and **cmdCalculate.** For the four bake sale item text boxes, delete the text in the Text property box. For the four percent labels and the total sales label, delete the text in the Caption property and use the BackColor property and the Palette tab to change the labels to a white background and change the Border property to Fixed Single. You will need to align and resize items on the form by either dragging them or using the Top, Left, Height, and Width properties.

FIGURE 4-13

Create a program with a user interface like the one shown here.

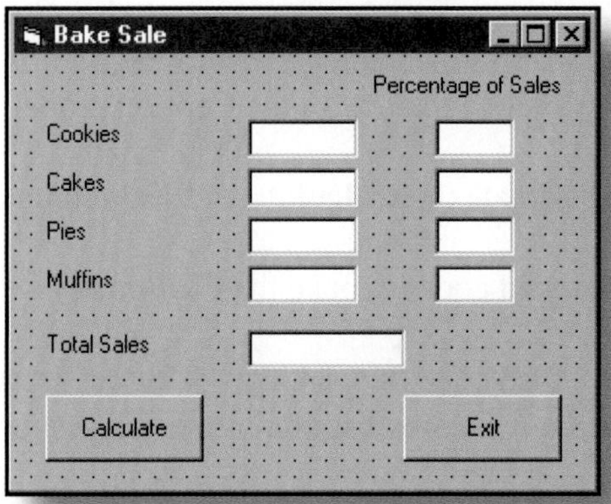

1. Start Visual Basic and open a new Standard EXE project.

2. Create the form on Figure 4-13 using the guidelines given above.

3. Save your program with an appropriate form and project name.

4. Add code so the **Exit** button will end the program.

5. Add code so the amounts in the four text boxes will be added and the result assigned to the Caption property of the label named lblTotalSales.

6. Add code so that the percent of total sales will be calculated for Cookies, Cakes, Pies, and Muffins. (Hint: Use the Fix function.)

7. Close the Code window, run the program, enter appropriate values, click the **Calculate** button to test the output labels, then end the program.

8. Save the changes to your program and remove the project from the screen.

PROJECT 4B

A local jewelry company has asked you to write a program that will calculate sales commission for their employees. The business gives their employees 4% of their total sales. Create the form similar to Figure 4-14.

1. Open a new project. Give your form an appropriate name and caption.

2. Create the labels for **Employee** and **Total Sales** with appropriate names and captions. Align the labels at the left.

3. Use the TextBox tool to create the textboxes to the right of Employee and Total Sales with appropriate names. Align them with the associated labels to the left. Delete the text for the Text property boxes for the two textboxes.

4. Create the label for **Commission Earned** and name it **lblCommissionLabel** (don't forget the caption). Create a label to the right of Commission Earned with the name **lblCommission** (delete the text in the Caption property box).

5. Create the **Calculate** and **Exit** command buttons with appropriate names and captions.

6. Add code to make the **Exit** button end the program.

7. Add code to calculate 4% of the amount entered in the Total Sales text box and assign the result to the caption of the label named lblCommission.

8. Close the Code window, run the program, enter appropriate values, click the **Calculate** button to test the Commission Earned box, then click the **Exit** button.

9. Save your program with an appropriate form and project name, then exit Visual Basic.

FIGURE 4-14
Create a program with a form
similar to the one shown here.

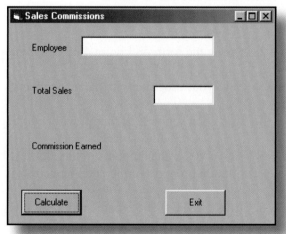

CRITICAL THINKING ACTIVITY

Write a program to calculate the number of buses needed to transport a specified number of people to summer camp. Policy states that you can only order as many buses as you can completely fill. The remaining campers will ride in vans and cars. The program should prompt the user to input the number of people needing transportation and the number of people that can fit on a single bus. The program should calculate the number of buses that must be ordered and the number of people who will need to ride in vans and cars. (Hint: Use integer division and the modulus operator to calculate the outputs.)

EXPONENTIATION, ORDER OF OPERATIONS AND ERROR HANDLING

OBJECTIVES

When you complete this lesson, you will be able to:

■ Use the exponentiation operator to raise numbers to a power.

■ Describe the order of operations.

■ Use the Visible property to enhance output.

■ Describe the purpose of comments in programs.

■ Handle run-time errors using Debug and the On Error GoTo statement.

■ Display messages using the MsgBox function.

■ Control program flow using the Exit Sub statement.

⏱ **Estimated Time: 2 hours**

Exponentiation

In Lesson 4, you learned about the basic mathematical operators. There is one more operator required to complete the set of math operators: exponentiation. *Exponentiation* is the process of raising a number to a power.

The symbol that represents exponentiation is the caret (^). The operator raises the number to the left of the operator to the power that appears to the right of the operator. For example, to raise 2 to the 16th power, the Visual Basic code would appear as shown below.

```
2^16
```

Order of Operations

From your math classes, you may recall the rules related to the order in which operations are performed. These rules are called the *order of operations*. Visual Basic uses the same set of rules for its calculations.

Ask yourself, what is the result of the calculation below?

```
1 + 2 * 3
```

Is it 9? Not if you follow the rules of the order of operations. The order of operations states that multiplication is performed before addition, so the calculation is performed as shown in Figure 5-1, resulting in the correct answer, which is 7.

The basic order of operations follows:

1. Exponentiation

2. Unary plus and minus

3. Multiplication, division, integer division, Mod

4. Addition and subtraction

Operations are performed from left to right. For example, if a formula includes three addition operators and two multiplication operators, the multiplication operators are applied from left to right, then the addition operators are applied from left to right.

Visual Basic allows you to use parentheses to override the order of operations. If you intend for 1 + 2 * 3 to result in 9, then you can use parentheses to force the addition to be performed first, as shown in Figure 5-2.

FIGURE 5-1
The order of operations causes multiplication to be performed before addition.

$$X = 1 + 2 * 3$$
$$X = 1 + \quad 6$$
$$X = 7$$

FIGURE 5-2
Parentheses can be used to override the order of operations.

$$X = (1 + 2) * 3$$
$$X = 3 \quad * \ 3$$
$$X = 9$$

NOTE:

Operations within parentheses are performed first. But within the parentheses, the order of operations still applies. You can, however, place parentheses inside of parentheses.

STEP-BY-STEP ▷ 5.1

1. Start Visual Basic.

2. Open the **Interest** project from your template files. The Interest project, when completed, will calculate the amount of money you will have in a savings account in the future if a specified amount of money is put into a savings account today.

3. If necessary, open the **Forms** folder from the Project Explorer window and double-click the form **frmInterest.** Your screen should appear similar to Figure 5-3.

4. Double-click the **Calculate** button.

(continued on next page)

FIGURE 5-3

The Interest Calculation form appears on your screen.

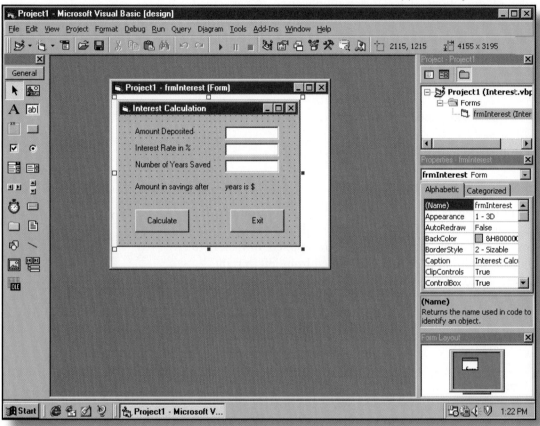

5. Add the code in CODE Step 5 to calculate the total in the account at the end of the savings period, and to show the number of years entered by the user in the output. Your screen should appear similar to Figure 5-4.

CODE Step 5

```
'Calculate future value
lblTotal.Caption = Fix(Val(txtDeposit.Text) * _
(1 + (Val(txtInterest.Text) / 100)) ^ Val(txtYears.Text))

'Repeat the number of years saved in the output
lblYearsSaved.Caption = Val(txtYears.Text)
```

When calculating the future value, the Val function is used to extract the numeric values from the text boxes. The multiplication, addition, division, and exponentiation operators are used to perform the required calculation. The Fix function truncates the result to round it down to the nearest whole number. The truncated result is assigned to the Caption property of the label named lblTotal.

FIGURE 5-4

The formula that calculates the future value of the saved money uses exponentiation.

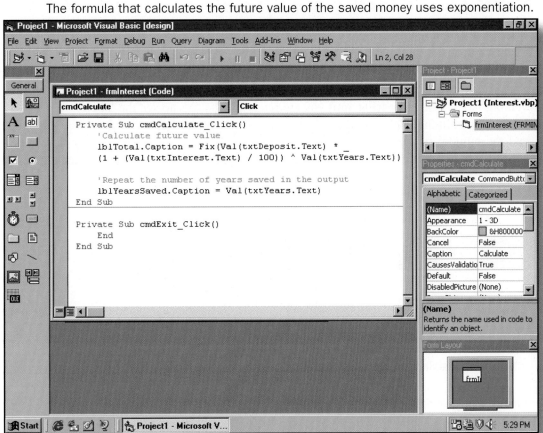

6. Close the Code window and run the program.

7. Enter the following data into the form.

Amount Deposited	**1500**
Interest Rate in %	**8**
Number of Years Saved	**15**

8. Click the **Calculate** button. The data is calculated and displayed on the form as shown in Figure 5-5.

9. Click the **Exit** button. The program closes.

10. Save the changes to the project but leave it open for Step-by-Step 5.2.

FIGURE 5-5

The Calculate button calculates the data and displays it on the form.

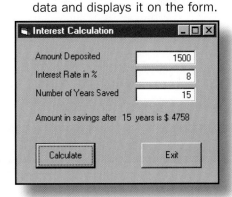

Using the Visible Property to Enhance Output

You have used the Visible property to make an image appear and disappear. There are many more uses for the Visible property. Another example of a useful application of the Visible property is preventing labels from appearing until you are ready for the user to see the label.

For example, in the Interest project, the user enters an amount of money deposited, the interest rate, and the number of years the money will be in the account. The program may have a better appearance if the line that displays the output is not visible until the output has been calculated.

By initially setting the Visible property of the output labels to False, the output will remain invisible until you make the labels visible in the code.

STEP-BY-STEP ▷ 5.2

1. Click the bottom left label with the caption "Amount in savings after".

2. Change the **Visible** property to **False**.

3. Click the bottom right label with the caption "years is $".

4. Change the **Visible** property to **False**.

5. Run the program to see that the labels do not appear, as shown in Figure 5-6.

6. Click the **Exit** button.

7. Save the changes to the project but leave it open for Step-by-Step 5.3.

FIGURE 5-6
The Visible property is used to hide the output labels.

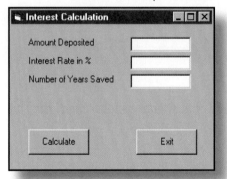

The code to make the labels visible can be placed in the Calculate button's Click event procedure.

STEP-BY-STEP ▷ 5.3

1. Double-click the **Calculate** button. The Code window appears.

2. Add the code in CODE Step 2 at the bottom of the procedure to set the Visible property of the two hidden labels to True when the Calculate button is clicked.

CODE Step 2

```
'Make output visible
lblLabel1.Visible = True
lblLabel2.Visible = True
```

3. Close the Code window and run the program.

4. Enter the following values in the input fields.

FIGURE 5-7
The Calculate button sets
the bottom two labels'
Visible properties to True.

Amount Deposited	**2500**
Interest Rate in %	**7.5**
Number of Years Saved	**10**

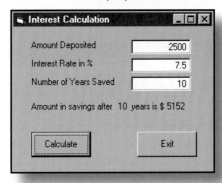

5. Click the **Calculate** button. The output labels appear as shown in Figure 5-7.

6. Click the **Exit** button.

7. Save the changes to the project but leave it open for Step-by-Step 5.4.

Using Comments

In the previous lesson, and in the Interest project you have been working on, you used the apostrophe to create comments in your code. Whenever you want to add a note or comment to a program, you can key an apostrophe, followed by any text you want to add to the line. The compiler will ignore everything from the apostrophe to the end of that line.

Comments can appear on their own line, like the comments you entered in the previous lesson. Comments can also be added to the end of a line of code. For example, the code below has a comment attached to the end of the statement.

```
lblAnswer.Visible = False   'Hide lblAnswer
```

IMPORTANT:

Remember, the compiler will ignore everything on the line that follows the apostrophe. Therefore, you can add a comment to the right of a code statement, but code added to the right of a comment will not execute.

When writing a program, you may think that you will always remember what you did and why. Most programmers, however, eventually forget. But more importantly, others may need to make changes in a program you wrote. They probably will be unaware of what you did when you wrote the program. That is why comments are important.

You can use comments to:

■ explain the purpose of a program

■ keep notes regarding changes to the source code

■ store the names of programmers for future reference

■ explain the parts of your program

Comments added to programs are often called *internal documentation*.

Handling Run-Time Errors

The programs you have written up to this point have assumed that the user will always enter valid data and that nothing will go wrong with the calculations. In the real world, however, users will enter all kinds of unexpected data, or fail to enter required data. These error conditions are sometimes called *exceptions*. The term exception comes from the idea that normally things will go smoothly, with the *exception* of certain instances.

Exceptions are also called *run-time errors*. A run-time error is any error that occurs when the program is running. Run-time errors are not detectable at the time the program is compiled because the error is caused by conditions that do not exist until the program is running. A common run-time error is division by zero. Division by zero is not a legal mathematical operation. So if conditions are such that division by zero occurs while a program is running, a run-time error or exception occurs.

Let's take a look at an example of what happens when an error occurs in a Visual Basic program. The Interest project should still be open on your screen.

STEP-BY-STEP ▭▷ 5.4

1. Run the program.

2. Enter **999999** for Amount Deposited and for Number of Years Saved and enter **99** for Interest Rate.

3. Click the **Calculate** button. An error dialog box appears in the middle of the screen as shown in Figure 5-8.

4. Click the **Debug** button on the error dialog box. The Code window becomes active and the line of code where the error occurred becomes highlighted. Your screen should appear similar to Figure 5-9.

FIGURE 5-8
An error dialog box appears when the Calculate button is clicked and inaccurate data has been entered.

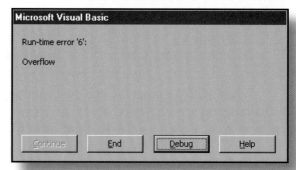

FIGURE 5-9
The Debug button highlights the failed code.

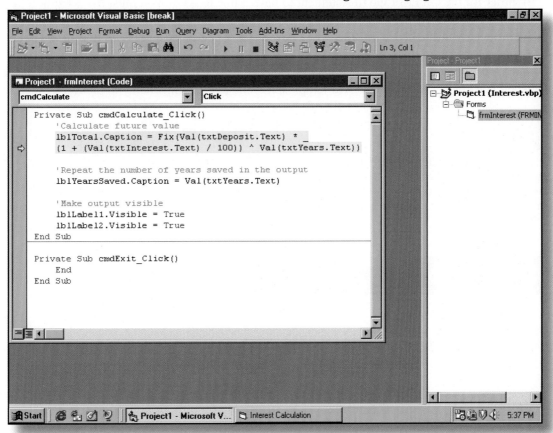

5. Close the Code window and click the **End** button on the standard toolbar. The program ends and the form becomes active on the screen.

6. Save the changes to the project but leave the project open for Step-by-Step 5.5.

Trapping Run-Time Errors with the On Error GoTo Statement

When an error or exception does occur, you would rather your program handle the situation gracefully, rather than halt with some standard error message like the one in Step-by-Step 5.4.

Visual Basic allows you to write code that will be executed when a run-time error occurs. To specify what code will execute when an error occurs, you must turn on *error trapping*. Error trapping is the process of interrupting the normal chain of events that occurs when an error is encountered and replacing that chain of events with your own code.

To turn on error trapping, use the On Error GoTo statement above the code that might generate a run-time error. The On Error GoTo statement specifies the line of code that the program should jump to if an error occurs. The code that will be executed if an error occurs is often called an *error handler* or *error-handling routine*.

Using Code Labels

In order for the On Error GoTo statement to have a line to go to, you must use what is called a *code label* to create a spot to which the program can jump if an error occurs. A code label is just a name that appears in the code, followed by a colon. The code label marks the line in the code to which you want to jump if an error occurs.

The Code window will force code labels to appear against the left margin. If you indent a code label when you key it, the code label will jump back to the left margin when you press the Enter key.

TIP

Code labels have uses other than in error trapping. There are ways to make execution jump to a specific portion of a program, even when no error occurs. However, forcing execution to jump to other parts of the code should only be done in extreme circumstances, such as error condition.

STEP-BY-STEP ⟹ 5.5

1. Double-click the **Calculate** button.

2. Add the code in CODE Step 2 above the code that calculates the future value.

TIP

The code label used for an error handler does not have to be named ErrorHandler. Any descriptive code label could be used.

CODE Step 2

```
'If error occurs, go to end of the routine to print error message
On Error GoTo ErrorHandler
```

3. Add the code in CODE Step 3 at the end of the event procedure, but before the End Sub. Your screen should appear similar to Figure 5-10.

CODE Step 3

```
'Error handler
ErrorHandler:
```

4. Close the Code window and run the program.

5. Enter **99** for Interest Rate and **999999** for the other two values.

6. Click the **Calculate** button. Notice that this time the error dialog box does not appear. When an error occurs, the execution simply jumps to the end of the event procedure and the procedure ends. In essence, the error is simply ignored.

7. Click the **Exit** button.

8. Save the changes to the project but leave it open for Step-by-Step 5.6.

FIGURE 5-10
The On Error GoTo statement causes the execution to jump to the ErrorHandler code label if an error occurs.

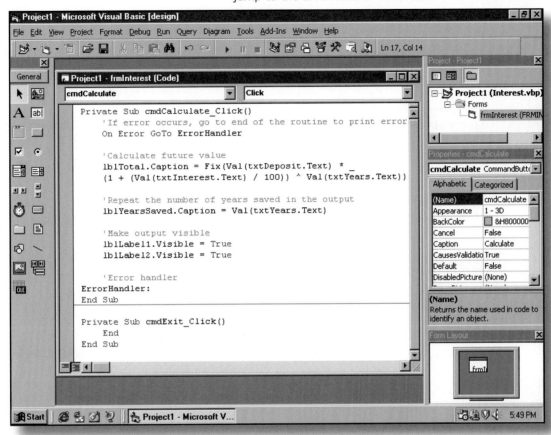

Using MsgBox

One of the easiest ways to display a message of your own, such as an error message, is to use the MsgBox function. The *MsgBox function* causes a dialog box to pop up, displaying a message that you specify. Besides being easy to use, the MsgBox function gives your programs a more professional look and feel.

The MsgBox function provides a convenient way to display an error message when you trap an error with the On Error GoTo statement. You can add the code for the MsgBox function after the ErrorHandler code label to cause a dialog box to appear, explaining the error to the user.

An example of how to use the MsgBox function appears below. In the parentheses that follow the MsgBox keyword, you can place a custom message that you want to appear in the dialog box. The message must appear in quotation marks.

```
MsgBox("Illegal entry. Please try again.")
```

9 1

STEP-BY-STEP ⟹ 5.6

1. Double-click the **Calculate** button.

2. Add the code in CODE Step 2 just below the ErrorHandler code label to display a message box when an error occurs.

3. Close the Code window and run the program.

4. Enter **99** for Interest Rate and **999999** for the other two values.

5. Click the **Calculate** button. A message box appears explaining that incorrect values were entered as shown in Figure 5-11.

6. Click the **OK** button to dismiss the message box.

7. Click the **Exit** button.

8. Save the changes to the project but leave it open for Step-by-Step 5.7.

CODE Step 2

```
MsgBox ("The values you entered resulted in an error. Try Again.")
```

FIGURE 5-11
A message box appears when an error occurs.

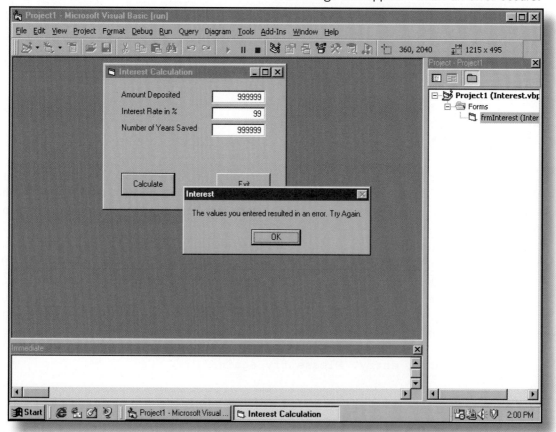

Controlling Program Flow around the Error Handler

The program appears to be trapping errors correctly. However, further use of the application will reveal that the program does not operate correctly. Even when no error occurs, the error message is displayed.

STEP-BY-STEP ⟹ 5.7

1. Run the program again.

2. Enter **1500**, **8**, and **15** in the three fields, then click the **Calculate** button. The output is displayed correctly, and the error message still appears.

3. Click the **OK** button to dismiss the message box.

4. End the program.

5. Save the changes to the program but leave it open for Step-by-Step 5.8.

The reason the error message always appears is because the code for the error handler appears at the bottom of the same event procedure that calculates the output. Therefore, when the code that generates the output is complete, execution continues right into the error handler. So even though the On Error GoTo statement did not force the flow of execution to the error handler, the flow of execution reached the error handler in its normal progress through the event procedure.

You can use the *Exit Sub statement* to prevent this from occurring. The Exit Sub statement forces the event procedure to end, regardless of whether there is more code in the procedure. By placing the Exit Sub statement *above* the error handler, you can cause the procedure to end before the error handler code is executed. The error trapping that you activated with the On Error GoTo statement will still be able to force the flow of execution to jump to the error handler. However, when no error occurs, the procedure will end when the flow of execution reaches the Exit Sub statement.

It is also a good idea to place an Exit Sub statement at the end of the error handler. Even though the procedure will terminate when the Exit Sub statement is reached, placing an Exit Sub at the end of the error handler will prevent problems in the future if an additional code label and code is placed below the error handler.

Figure 5-12 shows the revised event procedure code, with error handling and the Exit Sub statements in place.

FIGURE 5-12
The Exit Sub statements ensure proper program flow.

```
Private Sub cmdCalculate_Click()
    'If error occurs, go to end of the routine to print error message
    On Error GoTo ErrorHandler

    'Calculate future value
    lblTotal.Caption = Fix(Val(txtDeposit.Text) * _
    (1 + (Val(txtInterest.Text) / 100)) ^ Val(txtYears.Text))

    'Repeat the number of years saved in the output
    lblYearsSaved.Caption = Val(txtYears.Text)

    'Make output visible
    lblLabel1.Visible = True
    lblLabel2.Visible = True

    'End procedure
    Exit Sub

    'Error handler
ErrorHandler:
    MsgBox ("The values you entered resulted in an error. Try Again.")
    Exit Sub
End Sub
```

S TEP-BY-STEP ⟹ 5.8

1. Double-click the **Calculate** button.

2. Modify the code in the cmdCalculate_Click event procedure to match the code shown in Figure 5-12 (note that there are two places for the Exit Sub code).

3. Close the Code window.

4. Run the program, enter **99** for the Interest Rate and **999999** for the other two values and click the **Calculate** button to generate the error.

5. Click the **OK** button to dismiss the dialog box.

6. Enter **2500**, **7.5**, and **10** in the input fields and calculate again. When no error occurs, the message box is not displayed.

7. End the program.

8. Save the changes to the project and exit Visual Basic.

Summary

- The exponential operator (^) raises a number to a power.

- The rules that dictate the order that math operators are applied in a formula are called the order of operations.

- Parentheses can be used to override the order of operations.

- The Visible property can be used to hide a label until you are ready for the user to see it.

- The apostrophe is used to add comments to Visual Basic code.

- Comments allow you to keep track of changes in code and explain the purpose of code.

- Comments are often called internal documentation.

- Errors that occur while a program is running are called run-time errors or exceptions.

- Visual Basic allows you to trap errors, using On Error GoTo, directing program execution to code that you specify when an error occurs.

- A code label is a name that appears in code, followed by a colon. You can direct program execution to jump to the code label.

- The MsgBox function pops up a dialog box, delivering a message to the user.

- When you redirect the flow of execution using On Error GoTo, you must use the Exit Sub to end the event procedure before the error handler code is reached.

TRUE/FALSE

Circle the T if the statement is true. Circle the F if it is false.

T F   1. Exponentiation is the process of raising a number to a power.

T F   2. Addition and subtraction are evaluated before multiplication and division.

T F   3. Exponentiation will be evaluated first since it appears first in the order of operations.

T F   4. Parentheses can appear within another set of parentheses.

T F   5. You cannot override the order of operations in Visual Basic.

T F   6. The Visible property can be used on labels as well as images.

T F   7. Visual Basic code will be executed if it appears to the right of comment statements.

T F   8. A program will not compile if it contains a run-time error.

T F   9. The Exit Sub statement can appear more than once in a subroutine.

T F   10. You can use the MsgBox function to display custom error messages.

WRITTEN QUESTIONS

Write your answers to the following questions.

11. Which symbol is used for the exponentiation operator?

12. Why is it important that programmers be aware of the order of operations?

13. Why might parentheses be used in an expression?

14. What symbol indicates a comment?

15. What is internal documentation?

16. What statement is used to trap exceptions?

17. Why are code labels important in error trapping?

18. What is an error-handling routine?

19. What happens when an Exit Sub statement is executed?

20. What is another name for run-time errors?

LESSON 5 PROJECTS

PROJECT 5A

Evaluate the following expressions.

Expression	Result
2 * 3 + 1	_____
1 + 2 * 3	_____
4 / 2 + 6 * 2	_____
4 / (2 + 6) * 2	_____
4 * 4 + 2 − 1	_____
7 + 2 * 3 − 2	_____
1 + 2 * 3 − 9 / 3	_____
12 / 3 + 1 + 12 * 2 − 5	_____
(5 + 7) / 3 + 7 * 2 − 5	_____
5 + 8 / 2 − 16 / 2 + 3 * 6	_____

PROJECT 5B

Write a program that prompts the users for two values, as shown in Figure 5-13. The program should use the exponential operator to calculate the result of raising the first number to the second.

1. Start Visual Basic and open a new project.

2. Use the TextBox tool to insert two textboxes with one slightly above and to the right of the other one as shown in Figure 5-13. The lower textbox should be named **txtBase** and the upper textbox should be named **txtExponent**. Change the Text property for both textboxes to **0**.

3. Use the label tool to add the label for the equal sign. It should be named **lblEqual** and the caption should be the = sign. Change the **Font** property to **14 point**.

4. Use the label tool to add a blank label to the right of the equal sign. It should be named **lblResult** and the caption should be deleted. The font should also be 14 point.

FIGURE 5-13
Create a program with a form like the one shown below.

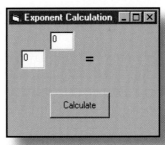

9 7

5. Add a **Calculate** command button.

6. Give your form an appropriate name and caption.

7. Add code to the **Calculate** button so the caption of the label named lblResult will contain the answer of the number entered for txtBase raised to the number entered for txtExponent.

8. Close the Code window, run the program, enter a value for the base (the lower textbox) and a value for the exponent (the upper textbox) and click the **Calculate** button.

9. End the program, save your form and project with an appropriate name, and remove the project from the screen.

PROJECT 5C

1. Open the **Division** project you worked with in Lesson 4.

2. Add code to the **Calculate** button for **On Error GoTo ErrorHandler** and **ErrorHandler:** including comments for both lines.

3. Add code for a message of your choice.

4. Close the Code window and run the program with no values, then click the **OK** button to dismiss the error message.

5. Test again with valid entries (you should still get the error message). Click the **OK** button to dismiss the message, then end the program.

6. Add the **Exit Sub** statement to the code and test the program again with valid entries.

7. End the program, save the changes to your project, and remove the project from the screen.

PROJECT 5D

1. Open the **Buses** project created from the Critical Thinking activity in Lesson 4.

2. Your project should have two labels at the top of the form with text boxes to their right and below those four items your form should have two additional labels with blank labels to their right. Change the Visible property of the bottom four labels to False so they won't display when you first run the program.

3. Modify the code for the **Calculate** button so the four labels whose Visible property you changed to False will be displayed when you run the program with valid entries to calculate.

4. Run the program to verify that it works (the bottom four labels should be invisible until you enter numbers in the top two text boxes and click the Calculate button).

5. Save the changes to the project.

6. Exit Visual Basic.

CRITICAL THINKING ACTIVITY

The National Weather Service at your local airport measures rainfall by taking readings from three rain gauges at different locations on the airport property. These three readings are averaged to determine the official rainfall total. Write a program that will accept the rainfall amounts from three rain gauges and output an average of the three readings.

DATA TYPES AND VARIABLES

OBJECTIVES

When you complete this lesson, you will be able to:

- Describe the purpose of data types and variables.
- Use the AutoSize property.
- Declare and use variables.
- Describe the scope of variables.
- Use the Variant data type and the Option Explicit statement.

🕐 **Estimated Time: 2 hours**

Data Types

Computers are all about data. Practically all useful programs are involved in collecting, processing, storing, and delivering data. There are many kinds of data. You might first think of numbers when you hear the word data. Of course, data can be in the form of text, dates, sounds, and pictures.

 **NOTE:**

You already have some experience with data types. The Val function converts one type of data (text) to another (a numeric value).

All data in a computer is actually stored numerically. As you learned in an earlier lesson, even text is stored as numbers. When you program, however, it is often important to know what type of data you are working with and to specify types of data.

Visual Basic supports a certain set of data types. There are data types for whole numbers, floating-point numbers (decimals), text, dates, and more. Table 6-1 shows the ten most common Visual Basic data types.

The integer data types are used when you need to use whole numbers (numbers without a decimal point). There are three integer data types. The most common integer data type is the one named Integer. But if the values you intend to store might be outside of the range of an Integer, use the Long data type instead.

The decimal types are Single, Double, and Currency. The Single data type can store data with up to seven digits of precision. If you need more precision than that, use the Double data type. For dollar amounts, use the Currency data type.

The other types of data are for storing text, dates, and True or False values. You will learn more about these data types in later lessons.

TABLE 6-1

DATA TYPES

Data Type	Range
Integer Data Types	
Byte	0 to 255
Integer	-32,768 to 32,767
Long	-2,147,483,648 to 2,147,483,647
Decimal Types	
Single	-3.402823E+38 to 3.402823E+38
Double	-1.79769313486232E+308 to 1.79769313486232E+308
Currency	-922,337,203,685,477.5808 to 922,337,203,685,477.5807
Other Types	
String	1 to about 65,000 characters
Date	January 1, 100 to December 31, 9999
Boolean	True or False
Variant	Varies

You can choose to store data in memory locations called *variables*. Variables are a common feature of programming languages. Variables can be used to store and manipulate all kinds of data. For example, you can have a variable of the Integer data type that can store numbers from –32,768 to 32,767. Variables get their name from the fact that the value can vary as the program runs.

Using the AutoSize Property

The *AutoSize property* will adjust the size of a control to fit its contents. In the case of a label, the AutoSize property will shrink the label to fit the caption.

To learn about AutoSize and how variables can be used in a program, we are going to create a program that calculates your age in months.

STEP-BY-STEP ⟩ 6.1

1. Start Visual Basic and create a new Standard EXE project.

2. Add five label controls to the form. Position them as shown in Figure 6-1.

3. Set the Name properties of the label controls to **lblAgeYears**, **lblMonths**, **lblYou**, **lblOutputMonths**, and **lblAgeMonths**.

FIGURE 6-1
Position five labels on the form as illustrated here.

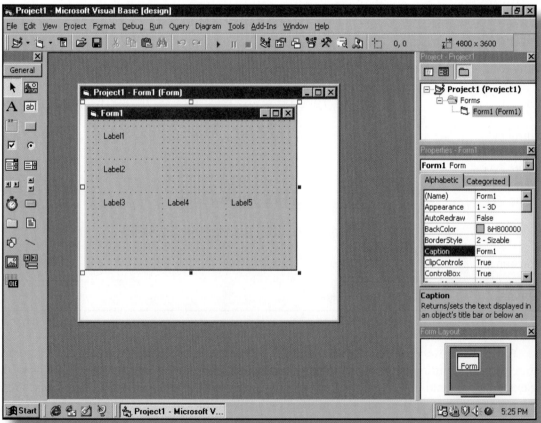

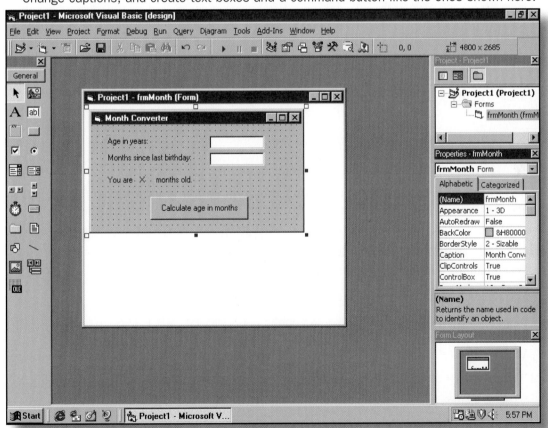

4. Set the Name property of the form to **frmMonths** and the caption to **Month Converter**.

5. Save the form as **frmMonthConverter** and the project as **MonthConverter**.

6. Select all of the labels by positioning the pointer in the lower right corner of the form and dragging up to the upper left corner of the form.

7. From the **Properties** window, change the **AutoSize** property to **True**. The AutoSize of each of the selected labels is changed.

8. Set the captions of the five labels to **Age in years:**, **Months since last birthday:**, **You are**, **X**, and **months old.**, as shown in Figure 6-2. The size of each label changes as you key the captions.

9. Create two textboxes and one command button. Position and size the controls on the form as shown in Figure 6-2.

10. Set the name of the command button to **cmdMonths** and set the caption to **Calculate age in months**.

(continued on next page)

FIGURE 6-2

Change captions, and create text boxes and a command button like the ones shown here.

1 0 3

11. Change the names of the two textboxes to **txtYears** and **txtMonths** and delete the text in the Text property of the two textboxes. Your screen should appear similar to Figure 6-2.

12. Change the **Visible** properties of lblYou, lblOutputMonths, and lblAgemonths to **False**. The output will not be visible when the program first runs.

13. Save the changes but leave the form open for Step-by-Step 6.2.

Declaring Variables

The first step to using a variable in your programs is to let the compiler know that you want to set up a memory location as a variable, what you want to call the variable, and what data type you want the variable to have. This process is called *declaring* a variable. To declare a variable, use the Dim statement as shown below.

```
Dim VariableName As DataType
```

For example, the following statement declares a variable named intAnswer with the Integer data type.

```
Dim intAnswer As Integer
```

NOTE:

Notice in the Dim statement example that the variable name is preceded by the int prefix. It is common to use naming prefixes with variables, as with controls.

Rules for Naming Variables

When naming variables, keep the following rules in mind.

1. Variable names must begin with an alphabetic character (a letter).

2. Following the first character, letters, numbers, and the underscore (_) are allowed.

3. Variable names cannot include any spaces. Some programmers use the underscore in places where you might want a space.

4. Variable names can be up to 255 characters long.

In the same way that a prefix can be used to identify a control's type, prefixes should be used to identify the data type of a variable. Table 6-2 shows the commonly-used variable naming prefixes.

In Step-by-Step 6.2, you will declare a variable in a command button's Click event procedure. Later in this lesson, you will learn that where you declare a variable affects the usage of the variable.

TABLE 6-2

Lesson ⑥ Data Types and Variables

DATA TYPE PREFIXES

Prefix	Data Type	Example
byt	Byte	bytCount
int	Integer	intPeople
lng	Long	lngInches
sng	Single	sngWeight
dbl	Double	dblMass
cur	Currency	curSalary
str	String	strName
dte	Date	dteAnniversary
bln	Boolean	blnSold
vnt	Variant	vntValue

STEP-BY-STEP 6.2

1. Double-click the **Calculate age in months** button. The Code window opens.

2. Key **Dim intMonths As Integer** at the top of the event procedure and press the **Enter** key twice. The intMonths variable will be used to store the user's age in months once that value is calculated.

3. Leave the Code window open for Step-by-Step 6.3.

Using Variables

Variables can be used in the same way you have been using labels and text boxes. Use the assignment operator to assign a value to a variable. For example, the code below assigns the value in the txtMonths text box to an Integer variable named intMonths.

```
intMonths = Val(txtMonths.Text)
```

You can also assign hard-coded values to a variable. For example, the code below assigns a value to a variable of type Double.

```
dblMass = 3.4568973
```

You can use the mathematical operators to perform calculation with numeric variables, as shown in the example below.

```
sngTotalWeight = sngProductWeight + sngPackagingWeight
```

To output the value in a variable, you can assign the value in a variable to a label, as shown in the example below.

```
lblTotalWeight.Caption = sngTotalWeight
```

Because variables have a specific data type, you do not have to use the Val function on a variable unless the variable is holding text (a string variable). Numeric variables cannot hold data that does not match the data type. Therefore, you can safely assume that the value in a numeric variable (such as sngTotalWeight) is a number.

STEP-BY-STEP ➯ 6.3

1. Below the variable declaration, add the code in CODE Step 1 to calculate the number of months.

2. Add the code in CODE Step 2 to display the results. Your screen should appear similar to Figure 6-3.

3. Close the Code window and run the program.

4. Enter **5** in the **Age in years** text box and enter **4** in the **Months since last birthday** text box.

5. Click the **Calculate age in months** button. The three labels become visible and display the results as shown in Figure 6-4.

6. Click the **Close** button on the Month Converter program's title bar. The program closes.

CODE Step 1

```
'Calculate Months
intMonths = (Val(txtYears.Text) * 12) + Val(txtMonths.Text)
```

CODE Step 2

```
'Display Number of Months Old
lblOutputMonths.Caption = intMonths
lblYou.Visible = True
lblOutputMonths.Visible = True
lblAgeMonths.Visible = True
```

FIGURE 6-3
The intMonths variable holds the results of the calculation.

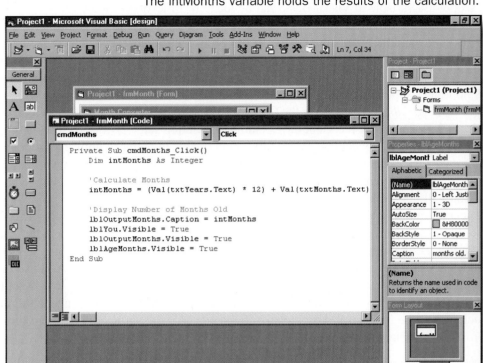

7. Save the changes to the project.

8. Leave the project open for Step-by-Step 6.4.

FIGURE 6-4

The Calculate age in months command button calculates the results and displays them on the form.

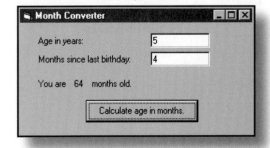

Scope

The term *scope* refers to the reach of a variable. In other words, a variable's scope indicates which procedures can use the variable. Where you declare a variable determines the scope of a variable.

Three Levels of Scope

The scope of a variable in Visual Basic can be local, form-level, or global.

A *local variable* is declared within an event procedure, like the intMonths variable you declared in this lesson. The variable is only accessible to the code within that event procedure. In fact, the variable does not even exist outside of that procedure. The memory space is reserved for a local variable at the time the variable is declared in the event procedure. When the procedure ends, the variable is no longer kept in memory.

A *form-level variable* is declared in the General Declarations section of a form's Code window. You will learn how to access the General Declarations section later in this lesson. A form-level variable is accessible to all procedures in the form and remains in memory until the program ends.

A *global variable* is declared in a code module's General Declarations section. Global variables are primarily used in programs that involve multiple forms where data must be exchanged between the forms. You will not work with global variables in this textbook.

As a general rule, you should declare variables as locally as possible. For example, if a variable is needed only inside a particular event procedure, the variable should be declared locally. The more global a variable is, the more likely it is that programming errors will occur. When a variable is declared locally, it is easier to trace all of the code that might affect the variable. A global or form-level variable could be affected by code in many procedures. Therefore, if the variable is not needed outside of the local event procedure, declare the variable locally. If a variable is needed throughout a form, declare it at the form level. Use global variables only if the variable is required throughout all of the forms of a program.

FIGURE 6-5

You can access the General Declarations section of the Code window by selecting (General) from the Object list.

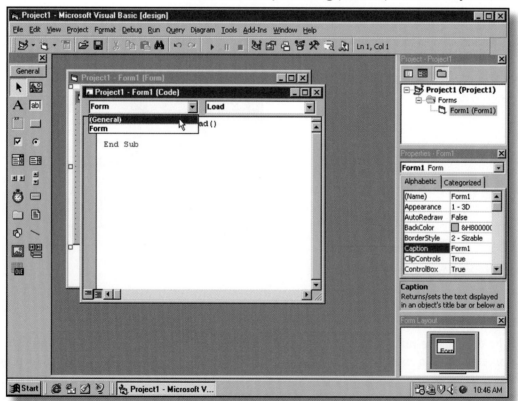

The General Declarations Section

You just learned that you can make a variable accessible to an entire form by declaring the variable in the General Declarations section of a form's Code window. To access the General Declarations section, select (General) from the Object list that appears at the top of the Code window, as shown in Figure 6-5.

In the next lesson, we are going to extend the month converter project to calculate the user's age in dog years, cow years, and mouse years. In order to calculate the dog years, cow years, and mouse years, we need the intMonths variable to be a form-level variable. As a form-level variable, we will be able to access intMonths from other event procedures on the form.

In Step-by-Step 6.4, you will move the intMonths variable declaration to the General Declarations section to make it have a form-level scope.

S TEP-BY-STEP ⟩ 6.4

1. Double-click the **Calculate age in months** button. The Code window opens.

2. Select **(General)** from the **Object** list at the top of the Code window (currently showing cmdMonth). The Code window should appear similar to Figure 6-6.

(continued on next page)

FIGURE 6-6
The General Declarations section is where you declare variables that need to be accessible to the whole form.

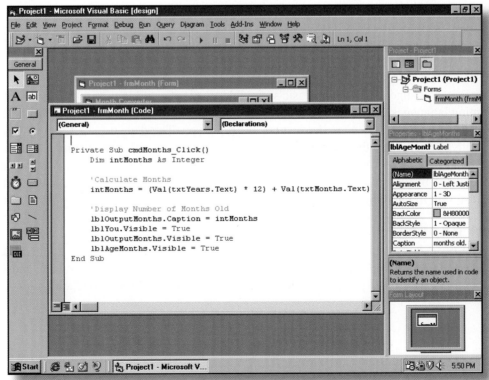

3. Key **Dim intMonths As Integer** and press the **Enter** key. A line appears below the General Declarations section.

4. Delete the intMonths declaration statement and the blank line below it from the Click event procedure.

5. Close the Code window.

6. Run the program and test with values to verify that the program still works.

7. Click the Close button on the corner of the Month Converter program.

8. Save the changes but leave the project open for Step-by-Step 6.5.

Using the Variant Data Type and Option Explicit

In Visual Basic, you should always declare your variables before you attempt to use them. However, if you fail to declare a variable before you use it, Visual Basic creates the variable for you and gives it the Variant data type. There is, however, a way to prevent variables from being used before they are declared.

The Variant Type

The *Variant* data type is very flexible. It can store many different types of data. It can store a number or text. A Variant is similar to a cell in a spreadsheet. When entering data in a spreadsheet, you don't have to declare a data type for each cell. If you key text in a spreadsheet cell, it will hold text. If you key an integer, it will hold an integer. If you key a dollar amount, it will hold that, too. The Variant type is not very efficient and should not be used unless you really need that flexibility. Whenever possible, you should select a specific data type for your variables.

There is a danger in Visual Basic's flexible way of working with variables. In most programming languages, if you try to use a variable that has not been declared, you will get an error message. In Visual Basic, the compiler just creates it for you. The danger is that you may declare a variable with one name and then attempt to use the variable with a different or misspelled name. For example, suppose you declared a variable named blnAllowed but when you use it, you accidentally key blnAlowed. Instead of giving an error, an additional variable named blnAlowed would be created, resulting in unpredictable results.

Option Explicit

Visual Basic has an option that prevents you from using variables that have not been declared. By entering the *Option Explicit* statement in the General Declarations section, you can cause Visual Basic to generate an error if you attempt to use a variable that has not been declared.

1. Double-click the **Calculate age in months** button to access the Code window.

2. Move the cursor to the top line of the General Declarations section.

3. Press the **Enter** key to create a blank line above the intMonths declaration line.

4. Press the **up arrow** to move the cursor to the blank line you just created.

5. Key **Option Explicit** on the blank line. Your screen should appear similar to Figure 6-7.

6. Close the Code window and run the program to test it, then end the program.

7. Save your changes and exit Visual Basic.

FIGURE 6-7

The Option Explicit statement will prevent you from using undeclared variables.

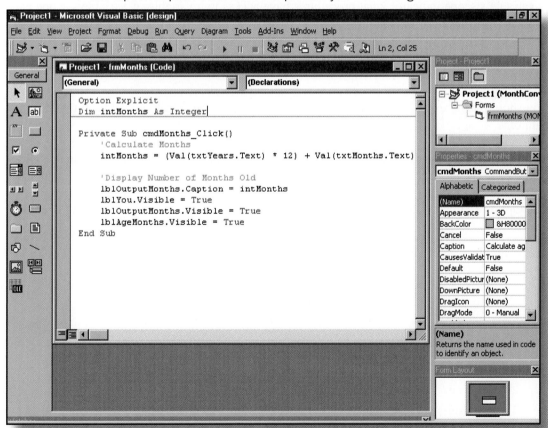

Summary

- Data can be in the form of numbers, text, dates, pictures, and even sound.

- Visual Basic supports a set of data types. There are data types for whole numbers, floating-point numbers (decimals), text, dates, and more.

- You can choose to store data in memory locations called variables.

- The AutoSize property will adjust the size of a control to fit its contents.

- The first step to using a variable is to declare it using the Dim statement.

- When naming variables, keep the naming rules in mind. It is also a good idea to use naming prefixes to identify the data type of the variable.

- You can assign values to variables using the assignment operator. You can also use the other mathematical operators with numeric variables.

- A variable's scope indicates what procedures have access to a variable. A variable's scope can be local, form-level, or global.

- The General Declarations section of a form's Code window allows you to declare form-level variables.

- You should declare variables before you use them. Undeclared variables will have the Variant data type.

- The Variant data type can hold many different kinds of data, but is less efficient than specific data types.

- The Option Explicit statement prevents variables from being used without first being declared.

LESSON 6 REVIEW QUESTIONS

TRUE/FALSE

Circle the T if the statement is true. Circle the F if it is false.

T F 1. The AutoSize property will adjust the value of a number so that it will be in the range of a Visual Basic data type.

T F 2. All data in a computer is stored numerically.

T F 3. A variable name can begin with any alphanumeric character.

T F 4. In order to do calculations with variables, you must first convert them to hard-coded values.

T F 5. The position in which you declare a variable affects the usage of the variable.

T F 6. Variable scope refers to the range of the values a data type can hold.

T F 7. You can assign the value of a numeric variable to a label or textbox without using the Val function.

T F 8. Visual Basic will always generate an error if you use a variable before it is declared.

T F 9. By declaring a variable in the General Declarations section of a form's Code window, you can make the variable accessible to an entire program.

T F 10. Using the Variant data type is much more efficient than using any of the other Visual Basic data types.

WRITTEN QUESTIONS

Write your answers to the following questions.

11. What are the three common integer data types?

12. What are the three common decimal data types?

13. What is the Dim statement used for?

14. Write Visual Basic code to declare an Integer variable called intNumber.

15. List three commonly used prefixes for naming variables.

16. Which operator assigns a value to a variable?

113

17. List the three levels of variable scope and give a brief description of each.

18. What type of data can be stored in a Variant variable?

19. What data type is given by default to undeclared variables?

20. What is the purpose of the Option Explicit statement?

LESSON 6 PROJECTS

PROJECT 6A

1. Start Visual Basic and open the **Interest** program you worked with in Lesson 5.

2. Add the following code to the beginning of the Calculate button to declare three variables.

```
'Declare Variables
Dim intDeposit As Integer
Dim intInterest As Integer
Dim intYears As Integer
```

3. Just below the OnError GoTo statement, add code to set the values of the variables equal to the values in the corresponding textboxes. Example: **intDeposit = Val(txtDeposit.Text)**

4. Modify the code that calculates the future value so the three variables you added in step 2 are used in the calculation instead of the values in the textboxes. (Hint: Replace *txt* with *int* and delete the *.Text*. You can also delete the Val because the int variable always means numeric data. Do not delete the Fix. A left parenthesis follows Fix and precedes the number 1 and a right parenthesis follows 100 and intYears.)

5. Set the lblYearsSaved caption equal to the variable Years (intYears).

6. Run the program and verify that it works (do not use fractional interest rates such as 2.5).

7. Save the changes to the program.

8. Exit Visual Basic.

PROJECT 6B

A railroad company has asked you to write a program to calculate the number of cars on a train and the total weight of the train when the cars are empty. The user interface of the program has already been created and saved as Train Template. The owner has given you the data in the following chart to use in each calculation.

Type of Car	Weight of Car
Box Car	65000
Caboose	48000
Refrigerated Car	59400
Tank Car	45200
Hopper Car	51300

1. Start Visual Basic and open **Train Template** from your template files.

2. Create two variables in the General Declarations section that stores the number of cars and the total weight of the train:

   a. Double-click any of the car command buttons and select **General** from the **Object** list box at the left.

   b. Key **Option Explicit** and press the **Enter** key.

   c. Key **Dim intTotalWeight As Long** and press the **Enter** key. (This variable will increment the caption for the lblWeight label each time you click a car command button when you run the program.)

   d. Key **Dim intCounter As Integer** and press the **Enter** key. (This variable will increment the caption for the lblNumber label each time you click a car command button when you run the program.)

   e. Close the Code window.

3. Add code (and comments) to each command button that adds the weight of the car named on the command button to the total weight of the train. Also add code to each button that adds 1 to the number of cars on the train. Display the results on the screen:

    a. Double-click the **Box Car** button.

    b. Key **'Add weight of car to total weight of train** and press the **Enter** key.

    c. Key **intTotalWeight = intTotalWeight + 65000**, then press the **Enter** key twice.

    d. Key **'Count total number of cars** and press the **Enter** key.

    e. Key **intCounter = intCounter + 1** and press the **Enter** key twice.

    f. Key **'Display Results** and press the **Enter** key.

    g. Key **lblNumber.Caption = intCounter** and press the **Enter** key.

    h. Key **lblWeight.Caption = intTotalWeight** and press the **Enter** key.

    i. Close the Code window, then repeat steps a-h for each of the car's command buttons, using the appropriate weight from the chart. (Hint: You can copy the code from one car's event procedure to another, then change the weight.)

4. Add code to the **Exit** button to end the program.

5. Run the program and test it by clicking car command buttons at random. Each time you click a command button, the number of cars should increment by 1 and the total weight should increase by the weight of the car whose command button you clicked.

6. End the program and save your changes but leave the project open.

CRITICAL THINKING ACTIVITY

The railroad company has asked you to modify the program you created in Project 6B. The railroad would like the program to calculate the total length of the train as well as the total weight. Use the values in the following chart for the length of each car. Add labels for the total length on the form under the total weight, then add code for the length of each car. (Hint: Don't forget to add a line of code in the General Declarations section.)

Type of Car	Length of Car in Feet
Box Car	55
Caboose	36
Refrigerated Car	39
Tank Car	35
Hopper Car	46

STRINGS AND DECIMAL TYPES

Declaring String Variables

In previous lessons, you have learned that Visual Basic has a special data type for working with text. Text is often called *alphanumeric* data because text can include letters or numbers. Text can also include other characters, such as periods, commas, and other symbols.

In computer programming, data types that hold text are usually referred to as *strings*. The term string is used because text is a series of characters that have been strung together.

Visual Basic has a data type named String. When you declare a string using a statement like the one below, the resulting variable can hold a string of any practical length. The length of the string can also change as the program runs. The memory space required for the string is allocated as needed.

```
Dim strFirstName As String
```

 **NOTE:**

Visual Basic does provide a way to create strings of fixed length. You will not use fixed-length strings in this book. However, information about fixed-length strings can be found in the online help.

Assigning Text to String Variables

When assigning text to a string variable, you must place the text in quotation marks, as shown in the code below.

```
strFirstName = "Kaley"
```

Hard-coded text, like the name *Kaley* in the example above, is called a *string literal*. You can also assign the text from a textbox to a string variable, as shown in the example below.

```
strFirstName = txtFirstName.Text
```

Often, you will assign the text from one string variable to another, as shown below.

```
strFirstName = strMyName
```

Actually, any expression that results in a string value can be assigned to a string variable. You will see other examples later.

Like a numeric variable, a string variable can only hold one string. Each time you assign a string to a string variable, the existing data in the variable is replaced.

STEP-BY-STEP ⇨ 7.1

1. Start Visual Basic.

2. Open **StringCopy** from your template files and if necessary, open the **frmCopy** form. Your screen should appear similar to Figure 7-1.

3. Double-click the **Copy Text** button. The Code window opens.

4. Select **General** from the **Object** list box (currently showing **cmdCopy**), then add the code in CODE Step 4 for the **General Declarations** section (press the **Enter** key after each line).

CODE Step 4

```
Option Explicit
Dim strText As String
```

5. If necessary, select **cmdCopy** from the **Object** list box, then move the cursor just above the **End Sub** statement and press the **Tab** key.

6. Add the code in CODE Step 6 to copy the text in the first textbox to a string variable and then copy the variable to the second textbox.

CODE Step 6

```
'Copy txtText1 to txtText2
strText = txtText1.Text
txtText2.Text = strText
```

(continued on next page)

FIGURE 7-1
This program will provide you with some practice declaring and using strings.

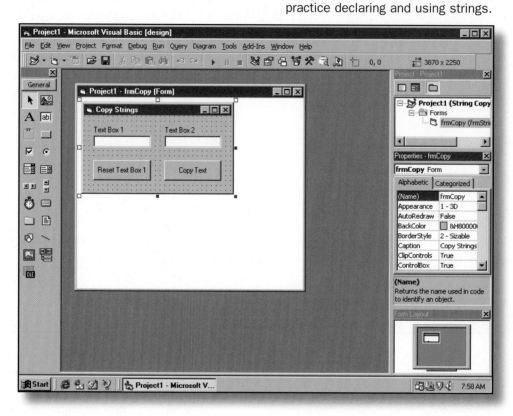

7. Select **cmdReset** from the Object list box. A new section of code for the Reset Text Box 1 button appears in the Code window as shown in Figure 7-2.

8. Add the code in CODE Step 8 to clear the text in the first textbox and reset the strText variable.

9. Close the Code window and run the program.

10. Key **Visual Basic** in the first textbox.

11. Click the **Copy Text** button. The words *Visual Basic* are copied to Text Box 2.

12. Click the **Reset Text Box 1** button. The first text is cleared.

13. Click the **Copy Text** button again. The contents of the strText variable (now blank) are copied to the second textbox.

CODE Step 8

```
'Reset the string variable and txtText1
strText = " "
txtText1.Text = strText
```

120

FIGURE 7-2
The Object list box generates the beginning code for an existing control.

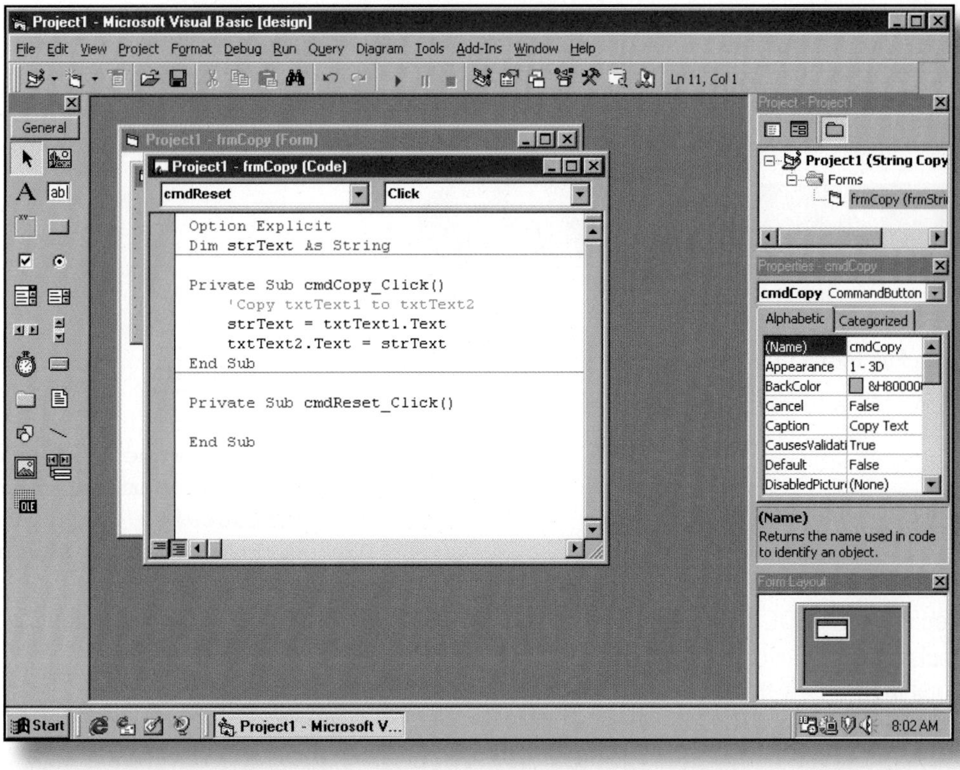

14. End the program and save the changes to the project.

15. Choose **Remove Project** from the **File** menu. The project closes.

16. Leave Visual Basic open for Step-by-Step 7.2.

Concatenation

Just before Step-by-Step 7.1, you learned that each time you assign text to a string, the text already in the string is replaced. There are times, however, when you would like to add text to the existing string. In other words, you would like to "string" on more characters. Visual Basic allows you to do just that using an operation called *concatenation*.

Concatenation appends one string to the end of another. The ampersand (&) is used for concatenation. For example, the code below concatenates two string literals, resulting in a compound word, *bookkeeper*.

```
strCompoundWord = "book" & "keeper"
```

You can concatenate more than two strings in one expression. In addition, the strings can come from other variables or can be string literals. In the example below, the first, middle, and last name are merged. String literals (in this case a pair of quotation marks with a blank space between them) are used to place a blank space between the names.

```
strFullName = strFirstName & " " & strMiddleName & " " & strLastName
```

The first, middle, and last names could just as easily come from textboxes.

```
strFullName = txtFirstName.Text & " " & txtMiddleName.Text & _
    " " & txtLastName.Text
```

S TEP-BY-STEP 7.2

1. Open **Full Name** from your template files and if necessary, open the **frmName** form. Your screen should appear similar to Figure 7-3.

2. Double-click the **OK** button.

3. Select **General** from the **Object** list box, then add the CODE in Step 3 in the **General Declarations** section to create four String variables.

CODE Step 3

```
Option Explicit
Dim strFirstName As String
Dim strMiddleName As String
Dim strLastName As String
Dim strFullName As String
```

4. Select **cmdOk** from the **Object** list box.

FIGURE 7-3

This program will use concatenation to create a string of your full name.

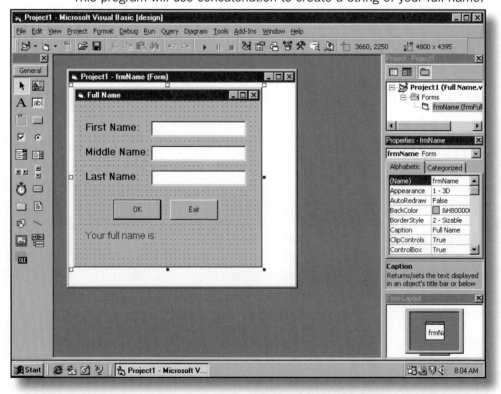

5. Add the code in CODE Step 5 to set the variables equal to their corresponding textbox.

6. Press the **Enter** key twice, then add the code in CODE Step 6 to concatenate the First, Middle, and LastName variables into the FullName variable.

7. Press the **Enter** key twice, then add the code in CODE Step 7 to display the string on the form.

8. Close the Code window and run the program.

9. Key your first, middle, and last names into the appropriate textboxes.

10. Click the **OK** button. Your name appears at the bottom of the form as shown in Figure 7-4.

11. End the program and save the changes to the project.

FIGURE 7-4
The concatenated string appears at the bottom of the form.

12. Choose **Remove Project** from the **File** menu. The project closes.

13. Leave Visual Basic open for Step-by-Step 7.3.

CODE Step 5

```
'Initialize Variables
strFirstName = txtFirstName.Text
strMiddleName = txtMiddleName.Text
strLastName = txtLastName.Text
```

CODE Step 6

```
strFullName = strFirstName & " " & strMiddleName & " " & strLastName
```

CODE Step 7

```
lblFullName.Caption = strFullName
lblFullName.Visible = True
```

You can also use concatenation when creating the caption for a label. In Step-by-Step 7.3, you will use concatenation to create a single label to provide the user with the necessary output.

1. Open the **Dog Years** program from your template files. The program is similar to the program you created earlier that calculates the number of months you have lived. By the end of this lesson, this program will convert your age into dog years. First, however, we will use concatenation to output your age in months.

2. If necessary, open the form **frmDogYears**. Your screen should appear similar to Figure 7-5.

3. Double-click the **Calculate age in months** button. The Code window appears.

4. Add blank lines below the intMonths code, then add the code in CODE Step 4 to create a string that will display the results.

5. Close the Code window and run the program.

6. Key **634** in the **Age in years** textbox.

CODE Step 4

```
'Display Number of Months Old
lblOutputMonths.Caption = "You are " & intMonths & " months old."
lblOutputMonths.Visible = True
```

FIGURE 7-5
This program will convert your age into dog years.

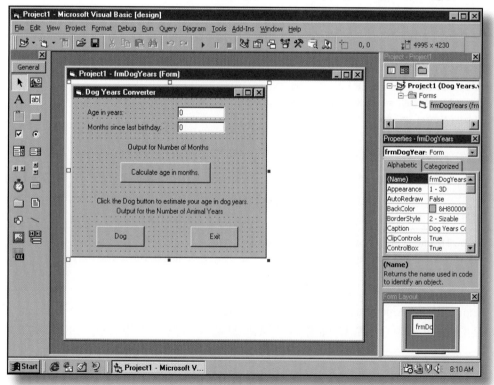

7. Click the **Calculate age in months** button. The answer is displayed above the command button. Your screen should appear similar to Figure 7-6.

8. End the program and save your changes but leave the project open for Step-by-Step 7.4.

FIGURE 7-6
The label shows the concatenated string.

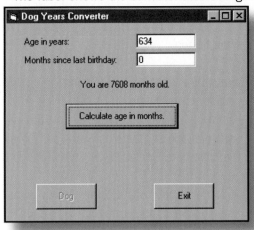

Using Decimal Types

The programs you have worked with up to this point have involved integer values. However, as you learned in Lesson 6, there are three data types for handling decimal data, also known as floating-point numbers.

The Single and Double data types are used for general decimal values. The *Single data type* is used for decimal values that will not exceed six or seven digits. The *Double data type* is used for decimal values with more than six or seven digits.

When you are working with dollars and cents, the *Currency data type* is ideal. It is specially designed to be precise in calculations involving money.

TIP

The Double data type uses more memory than the Single type. Therefore, you should use the Single data type, except in cases where the extra capacity of the Double type is needed.

STEP-BY-STEP ▷ 7.4

1. Double-click the **Calculate age in months** button.

2. Add the code in CODE Step 2 to the end of **cmdMonths** (just above **End Sub**) to make

the instructions for the program visible after the Calculate age in months button is clicked. (The instructions are the line that reads "Click the Dog button to estimate your age in dog years.")

(continued on next page)

CODE Step 2

```
'Display Instructions
lblInstructions.Visible = True
```

3. Close the Code window and double-click the **Dog** button.

4. Key **Dim strYears as String** and **Dim sngYears As Single** at the beginning of the cmdDog event procedure to declare strYears and sngYears as String and Single variable data types.

5. Add the code in CODE Step 5 to calculate the number of dog years and set it equal to the variable years. Remember that the sng (Single) variable allows for your answer to contain a value of up to six or seven decimal places.

6. Add the code in CODE Step 6 so that the instructions will be hidden after the Dog button has been clicked when you run the program.

CODE Step 6

```
'Hide Instructions
lblInstructions.Visible = False
```

7. Leave the Code window open for Step-by-Step 7.5.

CODE Step 5

```
'Calculate Dog Years
sngYears = (7 * intMonths) / 12
```

Using the Format Function

When you provide the result of a calculation as output, it is important for the data to appear in a format that is attractive and useful to the user. The *Format function* allows you to apply custom formatting to a number before displaying the value. The Format function can be used to format decimal values, phone numbers, and more.

 **NOTE:**

The Format function can also be used to apply formatting to strings, dates, and times. The Visual Basic online help has additional information about how to format these data types.

You specify the format you want using special symbols. For example, the code below formats the value 1234.56 to appear as $1,234.56.

```
strAmount = Format(1234.56, "$#,###.00")
```

The Format function can take a little getting used to. The first step is to learn the most common symbols used to apply formatting to numbers. Table 7-1 shows the symbols you will use when formatting numeric values. All of these are used in the code above except the % sign.

TABLE 7-1

FORMATTING SYMBOLS

Symbol	Description
0	The 0 symbol causes a digit to appear in the space. If the data has no value for that digit, a zero appears.
#	The # symbol is similar to the 0 symbol. The difference is that nothing appears in the space if the number being formatted does not require that digit to be used.
.	The period is used to specify where you want the decimal point to appear in the format.
,	By placing commas in the format in the usual places, commas will appear in the output.
%	The percent sign causes a number to be multiplied by 100 and a percent sign to be placed at the end of the number.

Use the symbols in Table 7-1 to create formats for your values. Let's take a look at some examples in Table 7-2.

TABLE 7-2

SAMPLE FORMATS

Code	Result
Format(12345.67, "000000.000")	012345.670
Format(12345.67, "######.000")	12345.670
Format(12345.67, "######.###")	12345.67
Format(12345.67, "###,###.##")	12,345.67
Format(12345.67, "$###,###.##")	$12,345.67
Format(0.89, "##%")	89%

1. Add the code in CODE Step 1 to the end of the cmdDog Click event procedure to display the results and format the lblOutputAnimalYears label to display up to three digits followed by one required decimal place.

2. Close the Code window and run the program.

3. Enter **15** in the **Age in years** textbox and enter **4** in the **Months since last birthday** textbox.

4. Click the **Calculate age in months** button. Your age in months appears and the instructions for the Dog button appear.

5. Click the **Dog** button. The Visible property of lblOutputAnimalYears is set to True, the instructions disappear, and the results are displayed as shown in Figure 7-7.

6. End the program.

7. Save the changes to your project but leave the project open for Step-by-Step 7.6.

FIGURE 7-7
The Dog button displays the results on the form.

CODE Step 1

```
'Display Results
strYears = Format(sngYears, "###.0")
lblOutputAnimalYears.Caption = "In dog years, you are " & _
    strYears & " years old."
lblOutputAnimalYears.Visible = True
```

Using the Enabled Property

You have used the Visible property to make command buttons and other controls appear and disappear from a form. The Enabled property performs a similar function. Using the *Enabled property*, you can make a control, such as a command button, take on a grayed appearance, making it inactive but still visible.

By default, objects are enabled. To disable an object, set the Enabled property to False using a statement like the one below.

```
cmdCalculate.Enabled = False
```

S TEP-BY-STEP ⟹ 7.6

1. Click the **Dog** button and change its **Enabled** property to **False**.

2. Double-click the **txtYears** textbox. The Code window appears, showing an event procedure for the Change event.

3. Add the code in CODE Step 3 to disable the Dog button when the data in the textbox is changed, hide the existing results on the form, and to enable the Calculate age in months button.

4. Select **txtMonths** from the **Object** list box at the top of the Code window.

5. Add the code in CODE Step 5 just above the End Sub statement to disable the Dog button when the data in the textbox is changed, hide the existing results on the form, and to enable the Calculate age in months button.

6. Select **cmdMonths** from the **Object** list box.

CODE Step 3

```
'Enable Human Months Button
cmdMonths.Enabled = True

'Disable Dog Command Button
cmdDog.Enabled = False
lblOutputAnimalYears.Visible = False
```

CODE Step 5

```
'Enable Human Months Button
cmdMonths.Enabled = True

'Disable Dog Command Button
cmdDog.Enabled = False
lblOutputAnimalYears.Visible = False
```

7. Add the code in CODE Step 7 to enable the Dog button when the human months are calculated.

CODE Step 7

```
'Enable Dog Command Button
cmdDog.Enabled = True
```

8. Close the Code window and run the program. Notice that the Dog button is disabled when the program starts.

9. Enter **21** in the **Age in years** textbox and enter **1** in the **Months since last birthday** textbox.

10. Click the **Calculate age in months** button. The Dog button becomes enabled and the instructions appear as well as the age in months.

(continued on next page)

11. Click the **Dog** button. The results for the number of dog years are displayed on the form.

12. Change the **Age in years** textbox to **30**. The Dog button becomes disabled and the previous results for the number of dog years disappear as shown in Figure 7-8.

13. Click the **Calculate age in months** button to recalculate the number of human months. The Dog button becomes enabled.

14. Click the **Dog** button. The recalculated results for the number of dog years appear on the form.

15. End the program.

FIGURE 7-8
The Dog button becomes disabled when new data is entered.

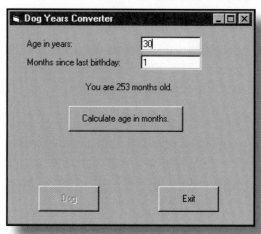

16. Save the changes but leave the project open for Step-by-Step 7.7.

Using the SelStart and SelLength Properties

In the dialog boxes of various programs you have used, you may have noticed that when a textbox gets focus, the text in the box is automatically highlighted. The advantage of this feature is that replacing the value in the textbox with new characters requires only that you begin keying. You can add this functionality to your programs using the SelStart and SelLength properties.

The *SelStart property* specifies the location where the insertion point will be inserted when the textbox gets the focus. The *SelLength property* specifies how many characters should be selected to the right of the cursor. So to select the text in the textbox, SelStart is set to zero to place the cursor at the far left of the textbox. Then SelLength is set to the length of the text in the textbox.

Because the length of the text in the textbox will vary, we will use a new function. The *Len function* determines the length of the text in the textbox. The code below shows the code required to select the text in a textbox named txtFirstName.

```
txtFirstName.SelStart = 0
txtFirstName.SelLength = Len(txtFirstName.Text)
```

The first line of the code above positions the cursor before the first character in the txtFirstName textbox. The second line of code uses the Len function to determine the length of the text in the textbox. The value returned by the Len function is the number of characters currently in the textbox. Setting the SelLength property to the length of the text in the textbox causes all of the characters in the textbox to be highlighted, as if you selected them with the mouse.

STEP-BY-STEP ➤ 7.7

1. Double-click the **txtYears** textbox.

2. The list box on the top right of the Code window is the Procedure list box. Select **GotFocus** from the **Procedure** list box. An event procedure for the GotFocus event is added to the Code window.

3. Add the code in CODE Step 3 to highlight the text in the txtYears textbox when it receives the focus.

Your screen should appear similar to Figure 7-9.

(continued on next page)

CODE Step 3

```
'Select Text
txtYears.SelStart = 0
txtYears.SelLength = Len(txtYears.Text)
```

FIGURE 7-9
The code in the GotFocus procedure will automatically select the text in the txtYears textbox when the cursor is placed in the textbox.

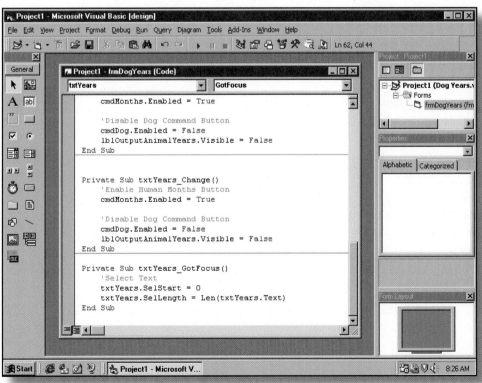

1 3 1

4. Select **txtMonths** from the **Object** list box and select **GotFocus** from the **Procedures** list box.

5. Add the code in CODE Step 5 to highlight the text in the txtMonths textbox when it receives the focus.

6. Close the Code window and run the program.

7. Enter **49** in the **Age in years** textbox and enter **7** in the **Months since last birthday** textbox.

8. Click the **Calculate age in months** button.

9. Click the **Dog** button. The results are displayed on the form.

10. Click the **Age in years** textbox. Notice that the number 49 becomes highlighted as shown in Figure 7-10.

11. Change the number to **24** and click the **Calculate age in months** button.

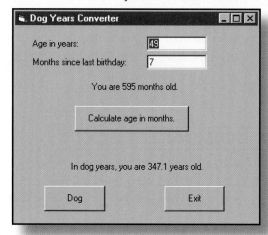

FIGURE 7-10
The contents in the Age in years textbox become highlighted when you click in the textbox.

12. Click the **Dog** button. The results are again displayed on the form.

13. End the program. Save the changes to the project and exit Visual Basic.

CODE Step 5

```
'Select Text
txtMonths.SelStart = 0
txtMonths.SelLength = Len(txtMonths.Text)
```

Summary

■ Strings hold text or alphanumeric data.

■ Visual Basic has a data type for strings.

■ Text assigned to a string variable must be placed in quotation marks.

■ You can use the assignment operator to assign text from a textbox to a string variable or from a string variable to another string variable.

■ Concatenation is the process of appending one string to the end of another.

■ The ampersand (&) is the symbol used for concatenation.

■ The Single, Double, and Currency data types hold decimal data.

■ The Currency data type is specially designed for handling dollars and cents.

■ The Format function can be used to format decimal values, phone numbers, and more.

■ The Format function uses a string of symbols to specify a format for data.

■ The Enabled property is used to make a control inactive or active.

■ The SelStart and SelLength properties and the Len function can be used together to highlight the text in a textbox.

TRUE/FALSE

Circle the T if the statement is true. Circle the F if it is false.

T   F   **1.**   Visual Basic contains a built in data type for working with strings.

T   F   **2.**   The length of a string cannot change as a program runs.

T   F   **3.**   The assignment operator can be used to assign text to a string.

T   F   **4.**   You cannot assign text from one string variable to another.

T   F   **5.**   Concatenation appends one string to the end of another.

T   F   **6.**   You can concatenate more than two strings in one expression.

T   F   **7.**   The Single data type uses less memory than the Double data type.

T   F   **8.**   The Format function cannot be used on strings.

T   F   **9.**   The Enabled property behaves the same as the Visible property.

T   F   **10.**   The SelLength property alone can be used to select the text in a textbox.

WRITTEN QUESTIONS

Write your answers to the following questions.

11. What term describes a series of characters that have been strung together?

12. Explain the difference between a string variable and a string literal.

13 What characters must a string literal be enclosed in?

14. Which operator is used for concatenation?

15. What are the differences between the Single and Double data types?

16. Which floating-point data type allows you to do calculations with money?

17. What is the Format function used for?

18. What is the purpose of the # symbol when used with the Format function?

19. What property allows you to disable a control, making it inactive, but still visible?

20. Which two properties allow you to select text in a textbox?

LESSON 7 PROJECTS

PROJECT 7A

1. Start Visual Basic and open **Interest Calculation** from your template files. The program is similar to the Interest program you worked with in Lessons 5 and 6.

2. Add code for the **GotFocus** procedure for the three textboxes so the text will be highlighted when the textbox is selected.

3. Close the Code window, then double-click the **Calculate** button.

4. Create a String variable named **strOutput** and a Single variable named **sngTotal**.

5. Under the Calculate future value comment, delete lblTotal.Caption and change it to **sngTotal**.

6. Add the following code to store the output in the strOutput variable and display it on the form.

```
'Make output visible
strOutput = "Amount in savings after " & txtYears.Text & _
    " years is $" & Format(sngTotal, "###.00")
lblOutput.Caption = strOutput
lblOutput.Visible = True
```

7. Close the Code window and run the program.

8. Enter data into the textboxes to verify that everything works correctly (you can use interest rates that are not whole numbers).

9. End the program and save the changes to your project, but leave Visual Basic open.

PROJECT 7B

Your school library has asked you to create a program that will calculate late fees students owe on overdue books. Your school charges $.05 per week each book is late.

1. Open **Library** from your template files.

2. Add code to each textbox that will highlight the text when the textbox is selected.

3. Double-click the **Calculate** button.

4. Create a String variable named **strFullName** and a Single variable named **sngFine**.

5. Add the following code to set strFullName equal to the txtFirst and txtLast textboxes.

```
'Combine first and last name
strFullName = txtFirst.Text & " " & txtLast.Text
```

6. Add the following code to calculate the late fee.

```
'Calculate late fee
sngFine = Val(txtBooks.Text) * Val(txtWeeks.Text) * 0.05
```

7. Add the following code to display the results.

```
'Display Results
lblOutput.Caption = strFullName & " owes " & Format(sngFine, "$###.00")
lblOutput.Visible = True
```

8. Close the Code window and run the program.

9. Enter data into the textboxes to verify that the program works.

10. Change the data to verify that the text in the textboxes gets selected when you place the cursor in the textboxes.

11. End the program and save your changes, but leave Visual Basic open.

PROJECT 7C

1. Open **Transportation Needs** from your template files.

2. Set the **Enabled** property of the **Calculate** button to **False**.

3. Add code to the **txtPeople** and **txtPeoplePerBus** Change event procedure that will enable the Calculate button.

4. Add code to each textbox that will highlight the text when the textbox is selected.

5. Add code to the **Calculate** button that will disable the command button when it is clicked.

6. Run the program and verify that it works.

7. End the program and save your changes, but leave Visual Basic open.

CRITICAL THINKING ACTIVITY

Modify the Dog Years program you worked with in this lesson to include two new command buttons that convert human months to cow years and mouse years. (You may have to widen the form and reposition the controls. Don't forget to disable the new buttons.) Change the caption for the instructions so it applies to all three animals. The result of all calculations should be displayed in the label lblOutputAnimalYears. Use the following formulas to calculate the cow and mouse years.

Cow years = (5 * # of human months) / 12

Mouse years = (25 * # of human months) / 12

(Hint: Move the strYears and sngYears variables to the General Declarations section. You can then copy and paste from one section of code to another and change code as needed. Don't forget the code to enable and disable the buttons in the appropriate places.)

UNIT 2 REVIEW QUESTIONS

MATCHING

Write the letter of the description from Column 2 that best matches the term or phrase in Column 1.

Column 1	Column 2
_____ 1. alphanumeric	A. is declared within an event procedure and is accessible only within that procedure.
_____ 2. scope	B. the process of removing everything to the right of the decimal point.
_____ 3. variant	C. memory locations where temporary data is stored.
_____ 4. truncation	D. the process of interrupting the normal chain of events that occurs when an error is encountered and replacing that chain of events with your own code.
_____ 5. concatenation	E. text that can include letters or numbers.
_____ 6. comments	F. the rules related to the order in which operations are performed in mathematical calculations.
_____ 7. local variable	G. the reach of a variable.
_____ 8. order of operations	H. appending one string to the end of another.
_____ 9. variables	I. a data type that can hold data of any type.
_____ 10. error trapping	J. notes in the code that will be ignored by the compiler.

WRITTEN QUESTIONS

Write your answers to the following questions.

11. What property sets where the cursor will appear when a textbox is clicked?

12. What are symbols that perform specific operations in Visual Basic statements?

13. What are values entered directly into Visual Basic code?

14. What function converts data in a textbox to a number?

15. What are fields on a form that allow the user to enter a value?

16. What function can display custom error messages?

17. What code can force an event procedure to end regardless of whether or not there is more code?

18. What property can inactivate a command button?

19. What is evaluated first in the order of operations?

20. What kind of error occurs when a program is running?

UNIT 2 APPLICATIONS

Estimated Time: 1 hour

APPLICATION 2-1

Evaluate the following expressions.

Expression	Result
3 * 2 + 4	_____
3 + 3 * 2 − 1	_____
2 + 6 / 3 + 1 * 6 − 7	_____
(2 + 6) / (3 + 1) * 6 − 7	_____
(2 + 6) / (3 + 1) * (6 − 7)	_____

APPLICATION 2-2

1. Start Visual Basic and open **Stock** from your template files.

2. Add code to each of the four textboxes so that the text will be highlighted when the textbox is clicked.

3. Create two-form level variables, **strOutput** and **sngChange**. strOutput should be declared as a String data type, and sngChange should be declared as a Single data type.

4. Select **cmdGainLoss** from the Object list box.

5. Add the following code to create five local variables.

```
'Declare variables
Dim sngGainLoss As Single
Dim strGainLoss As String
Dim strChange As String
Dim strTotal As String
Dim sngTotal As Single
```

6. Add the following code to calculate the change per share.

```
'Calculate change per share
sngChange = Val(txtClose.Text) - Val(txtOpen.Text)
```

7. Add the following code to calculate the gain or loss.

```
'Calculate gain or loss
sngGainLoss = sngChange * Val(txtShares.Text)
```

8. Add the following code to calculate the total value of the stock.

```
'Calculate total worth
sngTotal = Val(txtClose.Text) * Val(txtShares.Text)
```

9. Add the following code to format each variable and set strOutput equal to the output.

```
'Copy data to output variable
strChange = Format(sngChange, "$##.00")
strGainLoss = Format(sngGainLoss, "$#,###,###.00")
strTotal = Format(sngTotal, "$###,###,###.00")
strOutput = "The total value of your " & txtName.Text & _
    " stock is " & strTotal & ". The " & txtName.Text & _
    " stock's change in price per share is " & strChange & _
    " for a total change of " & strGainLoss & "."
```

10. Add the following code to display the output and enable the Change button.

```
'Display output
MsgBox (strOutput)
cmdChange.Enabled = True
cmdGainLoss.Enabled = False
```

11. Select **cmdChange** from the Object list box.

12. Add the following code to create a string variable and single variable to store the percent change.

```
'Declare variables
Dim sngPercentChange As Single
Dim strPercentChange As String
```

13. Add the following code to calculate the percent change.

```
'Calculate percent change
sngPercentChange = (100 * (sngChange / Val(txtOpen.Text)))
```

14. Add the following code to display the percent change.

```
'Display Output
strPercentChange = Format(sngPercentChange, "####.0")
strOutput = "The percent change was " & strPercentChange & "%."
MsgBox (strOutput)
```

15. Add the following code to clear the strOutput string and enable the GainLoss button.

```
'Clear strOutput and enable GainLoss button
strOutput = " "
cmdGainLoss.Enabled = True
cmdChange.Enabled = False
```

16. Add code to the **Change** button that will check for errors and display a message before the percent change is calculated.

17. Add the following code after the ErrorHandler message box to enable the GainLoss button.

```
'Enable GainLoss button
cmdGainLoss.Enabled = True
cmdChange.Enabled = False
```

18. Run the program and verify that it works.

19. Save the changes to the project, then remove the project.

APPLICATION 2-3

Write code for the following scenarios as indicated below.

1. Simple interest is calculated based on the formula below.

```
Interest = Principal * Annual Interest Rate * Period in Years
```

Assuming you have a program that includes text boxes named txtPrincipal, txtInterest, and txtYears, write code in the space below to declare a variable of type Currency named curInterestEarned. Also write code to calculate simple interest based on the information and formula provided.

2. The amount of electrical current that flows through a resistor is calculated using the formula below.

```
Current in amps = Voltage / Resistance in ohms
```

Assuming you have a program that includes text boxes named txtVoltage and txtOhms, write code in the space below to declare a variable of type Single named sngAmps. Also write code to calculate the current in amps based on the information and formula provided.

3. Assume you have a program that includes a text box named txtMinutes. The program prompts the user to enter the length of a movie in minutes. In the space below, write code that will declare a variable of type Single named sngHours. Also write code to calculate the length of the movie in hours.

APPLICATION 2-4

Select one of the three scenarios in Application 2-3 and create a complete program based on the calculation performed in the scenario. Your program should include all of the following, if applicable.

1. A form with appropriately named and captioned labels and textboxes (include a label for the output).

2. Code with appropriate comments.

3. Meaningful variable names (including form-level variables if applicable) that use the appropriate naming prefixes.

4. The Val function for extracting values from text boxes.

5. Appropriate error trapping if implementing scenario 2 or 3.

6. Hiding of the output with the Visible property until appropriate to display or use of the MsgBox function (see step 14 of Application 2-2) to display output.

7. Use of SelStart and SelLength for textboxes.

8. Use of Format function to properly format output.

INTERNET ACTIVITY

In this activity, you will use the Internet to obtain real stock price data for the program you worked with in Application 2-2.

1. Open your Web browser.

2. Go to the Web address below.

   `http://www.programvb.com/basics`

3. On the home page, click the **Internet Activities** link.

4. Click the **Unit 2 Internet Activity** link. A list of Web sites that can be used to obtain up-to-date stock prices appears.

5. Go to one of the listed sites, select a stock, and obtain the information you need to run the program.

6. When you have the data you need, close the Web browser and run the **Stock** program from Application 2-2.

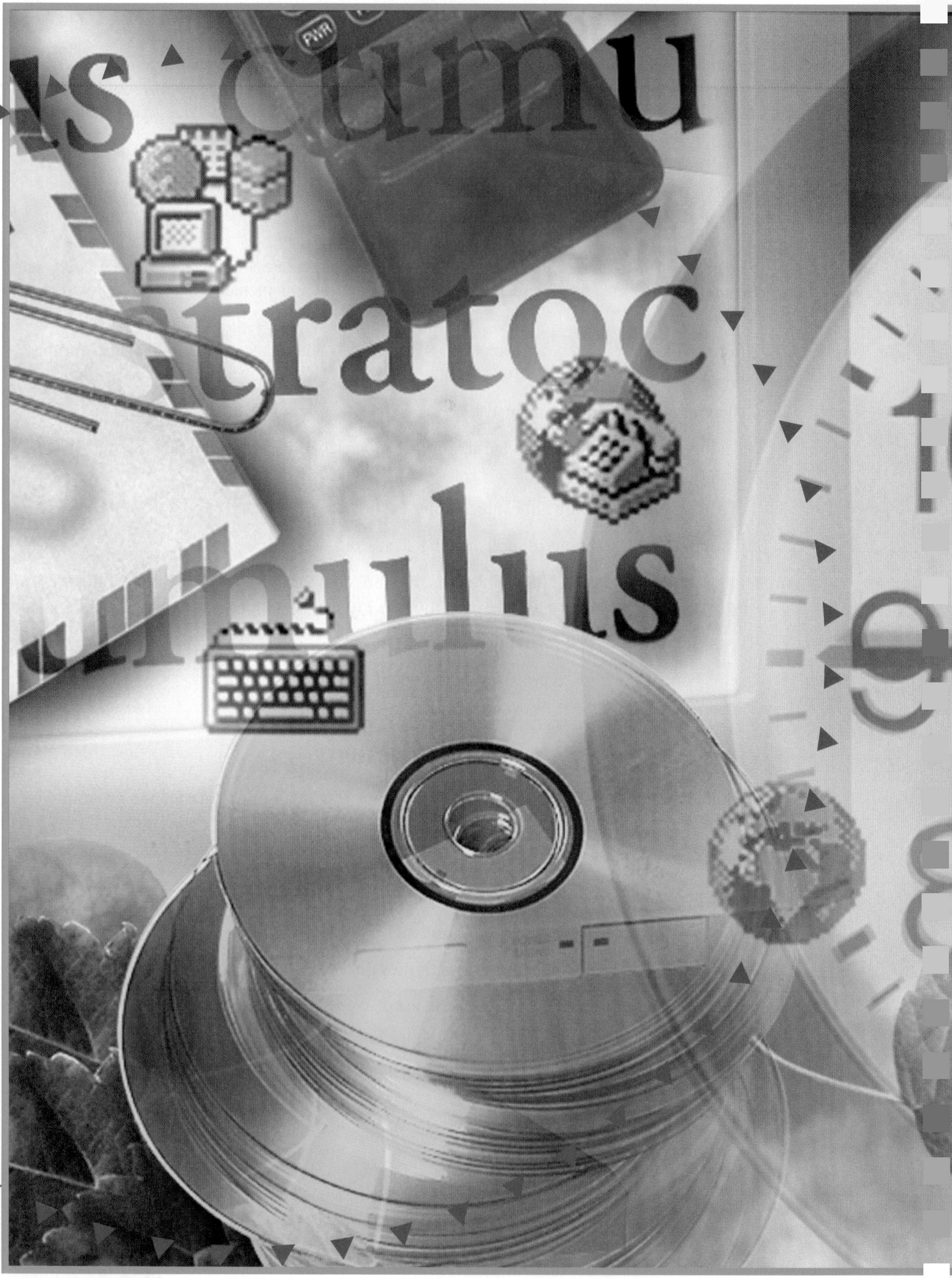

DECISION MAKING

UNIT 3

lesson 8   2 hrs.

If Statements

lesson 9   2 hrs.

**Nested If Statements
and Option Buttons**

Estimated Time for Unit 3: 4 hours

IF STATEMENTS

OBJECTIVES

When you complete this lesson, you will be able to:

■ Explain how decisions are made in a computer.

■ Use the conditional operators.

■ Use If statements to make decisions in programs.

■ Create and read basic flowcharts.

■ Use If...Else statements.

■ Use Check Box controls.

■ Use the logical operators.

⏱ **Estimated Time: 2 hours**

The Building Blocks of Decision Making

When you make a decision, your brain goes through a process of comparisons. For example, when you shop for clothes you compare the price with prices you have previously paid. You compare the quality to other clothes you have seen or owned. You probably compare the clothes to what other people are wearing or what is in style. You might even compare the purchase of clothes to other possible uses for your available money.

Although your brain's method of decision making is much more complex than what a computer is capable of, decision making in computers is also based on comparing data.

Programs are limited without the ability to make decisions. Although some programs, like the ones you have been writing up to this point, progress through a fairly straightforward path, most programs require some decision making along the way. When two or more possible paths of execution are available, the program must have a means to make a decision.

Suppose you have a dialog box that asks the user the weight of a package that he or she wants to ship (see Figure 8-1). You cannot control what keys the user will press. What you can do, however, is verify that what the user entered is valid. When the user clicks the OK button, you want to ensure that the value entered by the user is not less than zero. A package cannot weigh less than zero pounds.

Decision making in a computer is generally done in terms of a comparison that returns a True or False response. In the example above, the program asks "is the value entered by the user less than zero?" If the answer is Yes or True, the program can stop the operation and prompt the user again.

Using the Conditional Operators

The first step to making a decision in a program is to make a comparison. Comparisons are made using the *conditional operators*. They are similar to the symbols you have used in math when working with equations and inequalities. The conditional operators are shown in Table 8-1.

The conditional operators are used to compare two values. The result of the comparison is either True or False. Recall from Lesson 6 that Visual Basic has a *Boolean data type* that can hold the values True or False. A *Boolean variable* can be used to store the results of an expression that includes conditional operators. The following are some examples of conditional operators in use.

TABLE 8-1

CONDITIONAL OPERATORS

Operator	Description
=	Equal to
>	Greater than
<	Less than
>=	Greater than or equal to
<=	Less than or equal to
<>	Not equal to

```
blnTooBig = (Val(txtHeight.Text) > 72)
```

If the value keyed in the txtHeight text box is greater than 72, the variable blnTooBig is set to True.

```
lblOutput.Caption = (intLength >= 100)
```

If the value in intLength is greater than or equal to 100, the caption of the lblOutput label is set to True.

```
blnEqual = (sngA = sngB)
```

If the values in sngA and sngB are equal, the variable blnEqual is set to True.

NOTE:

When a caption of a label is set to a Boolean result, the label is set to either the word *True* or the word *False*.

1. Start Visual Basic and open **Compare** from your template files. If necessary, open the form in the Project Explorer.

2. Double-click the **Compare** button and add the code in CODE Step 2 to compare the values of each textbox.

3. Close the Code window and run the program.

4. Key **10** in both textboxes and click the **Compare** command button. The word *True* appears as the label caption, as shown in Figure 8-2.

5. Change the value in the textbox to the right of the equal sign to **15**.

6. Click the **Compare** button. The word *False* appears as the label caption.

FIGURE 8-2
The label caption is set to
the result of the expression.

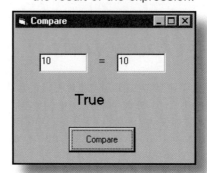

7. End the program and save the changes to the project.

8. Remove the project but leave Visual Basic open for Step-by-Step 8.2.

CODE Step 2

```
lblOutput.Caption = (Val(txtLeft.Text) = Val(txtRight.Text))
```

Using If Statements

In Visual Basic, the If statement is the most common way to make a decision. An *If statement* allows you to execute specified code when the result of a conditional expression is true. For example, an If statement can be used to present the user with a message box *if* the user enters a value that is out of the normal range of values.

Suppose you have a program that asks the user to enter the weight in pounds of a package that is to be shipped. The shipping method requires that you enter the weight to the nearest pound with a one pound minimum. You can use an If statement like the one below to ensure that the user does not enter zero or a negative number for the weight.

```
intPackageWeight = Val(txtWeight.Text)


If (intPackageWeight < 1) Then
    MsgBox("Package weight must be one or more pounds.")
End If
```

The code above converts the user's entry in the text box into an Integer variable. Then a conditional operator is used to test whether the value in the variable is less than one. The If statement is saying that *if* the result of the comparison is true, then present the message box. The End If statement marks the end of the If statement.

In many cases, there is more than one line of code between the If statement and the End If statement. All of the lines of code that appear between the If statement and End If statements are executed if the conditions specified in the If statement are true. Otherwise, the code between the If statement and the End If is skipped.

STEP-BY-STEP 8.2

1. Open the **Division** project you worked with in Lesson 5 and if necessary, open the form.

2. Double-click the **Calculate** button and add the code in CODE Step 2 to the beginning of the code to display a warning message if the divisor equals 0.

3. Add code so the text in the two textboxes will be highlighted when you click in them. (Hint: Use the SelStart and SelLength properties.)

4. Close the Code window and run the program.

5. Enter **9** for the divisor and **17** for the dividend and click the **Calculate** button.

The program displays the result (1 r 8).

6. Enter **0** for the divisor and **5** for the dividend and click the **Calculate** button. A message box appears warning you that the divisor cannot be zero, as shown in Figure 8-3.

7. Click the **OK** button in the message box. A second error message appears for the MsgBox code you added in Lesson 5.

8. Click the **OK** button to dismiss this message, then end the program.

9. Save the changes to the project and remove the project but leave Visual Basic open for Step-by-Step 8.3.

(continued on next page)

CODE Step 2

```
'If divisor is 0 display message
If Val(txtDivisor.Text) = 0 Then
    MsgBox ("The divisor cannot be zero.")
End If
```

FIGURE 8-3

The message box displayed is a result of the If statement you added to the program.

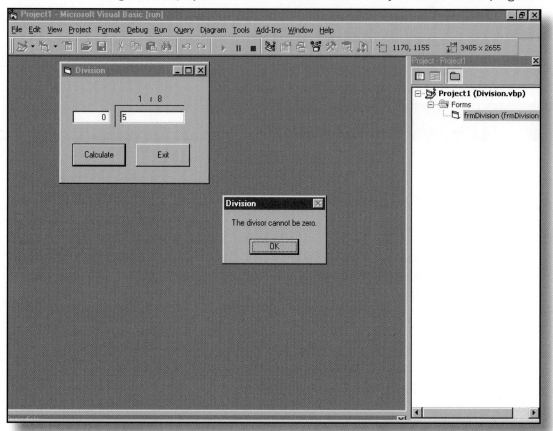

Creating and Reading Flowcharts

Now that you have used an If statement, you can see that programs often do more than just execute a list of instructions without variation. Input from a user, or other conditions, may require that a program's execution take a turn in a new direction or skip certain code. As the flow of execution in a program becomes more complex, it is often helpful to see the possible paths that a program might take in a visual form.

For many years, programmers have been using *flowcharts* to plan and to document program code. A flowchart uses symbols and shapes connected by lines to illustrate the steps of a program. Figure 8-4 shows a flowchart of the If statement discussed earlier.

There are many symbols used to create flowcharts. For our purposes, we will only be concerned with the three most basic flowchart symbols, shown in Figure 8-5. The rectangle represents processing data or taking action. Use the diamond for making decisions, such as an If statement. Use the parallelogram to represent input and output.

FIGURE 8-4

A flowchart gives a visual representation of the flow of execution in a program.

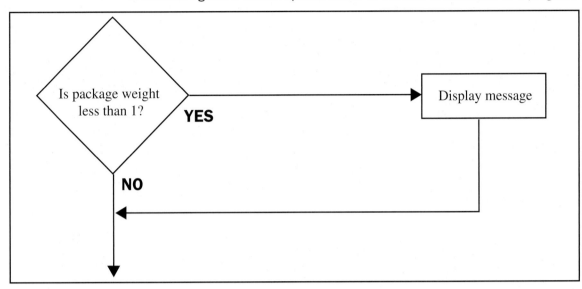

Because Visual Basic is an event-driven environment, flowcharts are not generally used to chart an entire program. However, flowcharts can be very useful for organizing the flow of execution within an event procedure.

FIGURE 8-5

Each shape in a flowchart has a special meaning.

Use the rectangle for processing data or for taking action.

Use the diamond for making decisions.

Use the parallelogram to show that something is input or output.

Using If...Else Statements

An If statement makes a decision to either perform some task or to do nothing. An If statement is called a one-way selection structure. A *one-way selection structure* is a program structure in which the decision is to go "one way" or just bypass the code in the If statement. But as you know from the everyday decisions you make, sometimes the decision involves more than Yes or No. Decisions are often a matter of choosing between two or more alternatives.

The If...Else statement allows you to choose between two paths. In an If...Else statement, one block of code is executed if the result of an expression is True and another block is executed if the result is False.

The code below displays one of two messages. If the value being tested is less than zero, a message is displayed announcing that the value is negative. If the value is not less than zero, a message is displayed saying that the value is either zero or positive.

```
If (intValue < 0) Then
    MsgBox("The value is negative.")
Else
    MsgBox("The value is zero or positive.")
End If
```

An If...Else statement is called a two-way selection structure. A *two-way selection structure* is a program structure in which one block of code is executed if the specified conditions are True or another block of code is executed if the specified conditions are False. The flowchart in Figure 8-6 charts the code shown above.

FIGURE 8-6

An If...Else statement is a two-way selection structure.

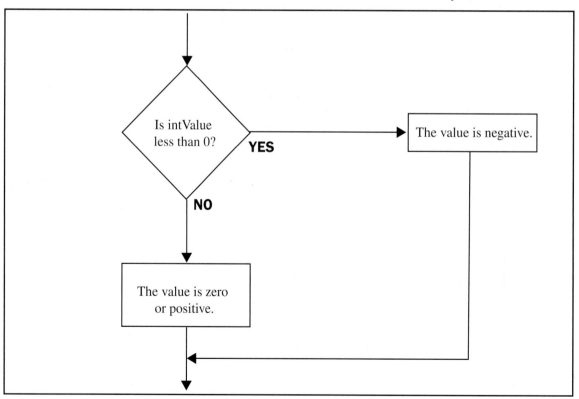

S TEP-BY-STEP ⟹ 8.3

1. Open **Numbers** from your template files and if necessary, open the form.

2. Double-click the **OK** button and add the code in CODE Step 2 to display Positive if the number is greater than or equal to 0.

3. Add the the code in CODE Step 3 to display Negative if the number is not greater than or equal to 0.

4. Close the Code window and run the program.

5. Key **38** in the textbox and click the **OK** button. The output below the textbox indicates that the number is positive, as shown in Figure 8-7.

6. Key **-7** in the textbox and click the **OK** button. The output indicates that the number is negative.

FIGURE 8-7
The If...Else statement determined that the number is positive.

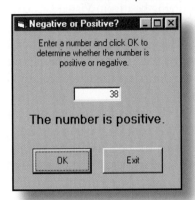

7. End the program and save the changes to the project.

8. Remove the project but leave Visual Basic open for Step-by-Step 8.4.

CODE Step 2

```
'Determine if number is positive or negative
If Val(txtNumber.Text) >= 0 Then
    lblResult.Caption = "The number is positive."
```

CODE Step 3

```
Else
    lblResult.Caption = "The number is negative."
End If
```

Using Checkboxes

Checkboxes are an important part of the Windows interface. *Checkboxes* allow the program to ask the user a Yes or No question or to turn an option on or off. For example, Figure 8-8 shows the Options dialog box from Visual Basic 6.0. The dialog box includes many options that are selected by clicking checkboxes. The options with a check in the box are on and the options without a check in the box are off.

Each checkbox has a Value property that is set to 1 (one) if the box is checked and 0 (zero) if the box is not checked. The label that appears beside the checkbox is part of the checkbox control. Therefore you do not have to create a label control next to the checkbox. The checkbox has a Caption property that specifies its label.

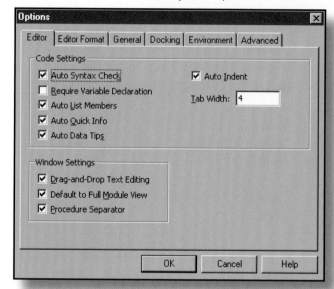

FIGURE 8-8
A checkbox allows the user to visually turn options on and off.

STEP-BY-STEP 8.4

1. Open **Coaster** from your template files and if necessary, open the form.

2. Double-click the **CheckBox** tool from the toolbar. A checkbox control is added to the form.

3. Move the checkbox control below the **Height in inches** label.

4. Create another checkbox control.

5. Resize and position the two checkbox controls so your screen appears similar to Figure 8-9.

6. Change the **Name** property of the first checkbox control to **chkBack**.

7. Change the **Caption** property of chkBack to **Back Trouble**. If necessary, resize the control so that the entire caption is displayed on one line.

8. Change the **Name** property of the second checkbox control to **chkHeart**.

9. Change the **Caption** property of chkHeart to **Heart Trouble**. If necessary, resize the control so that the entire caption is displayed on one line.

10. Save the changes to the project but leave the project open for Step-by-Step 8.5.

FIGURE 8-9
Checkbox controls are created in a way similar to other controls.

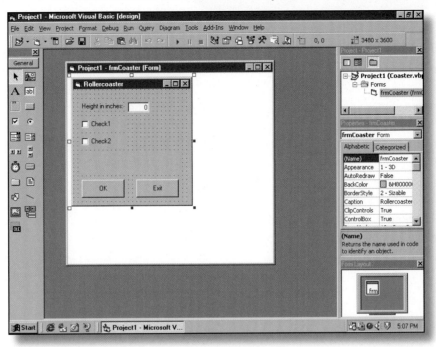

Checkboxes can be set to be either checked or unchecked by default, as shown in Figure 8-10. The option to make the checkbox have a grayed appearance is used in cases where the checkbox represents a more detailed set of options, some of which are on and some of which are off.

FIGURE 8-10
Checkboxes can default to a checked or unchecked state.

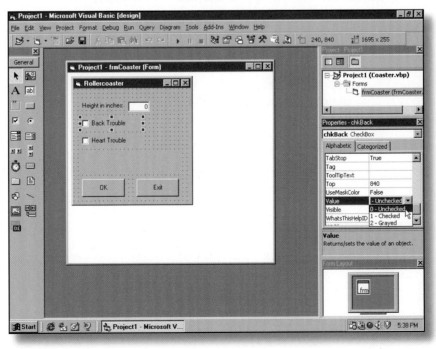

1. Run the program. Notice that each checkbox is empty.

2. End the program.

3. Select the **Heart Trouble** checkbox to select it.

4. Change the **Value** property from **0 - Unchecked** to **1 - Checked**. Notice that a checkmark appears in the checkbox on the form.

5. Run the program. The Heart Trouble checkbox is checked by default.

6. End the program.

7. Change the **Value** property of the Heart Trouble check box back to **0 - Unchecked**.

8. Leave the project open for Step-by-Step 8.6.

NOTE:

In Visual Basic, the equal sign (=) is used for two operations. It is used to assign values and to compare values to determine if they are equal.

The Value property can be set and/or read from code. For example, the code below assigns the value one (1) to a checkbox, causing it to appear checked.

```
chkHeart.Value = 1
```

Similar code can be used to test whether the checkbox is checked.

```
If (chkHeart.Value = 1) Then
    MsgBox("The checkbox is checked")
End If
```

S TEP-BY-STEP ⟹ 8.6

1. Double-click the **OK** button and add the code in CODE Step 1 to declare a variable named blnOKtoRide and set it equal to True. The blnOKtoRide variable will be used to track whether the rider passes the three tests for riding the roller coaster. The program will assume the rider is able to ride unless one of the pieces of information entered by the user disqualifies the rider.

CODE Step 1

```
Dim blnOKtoRide As Boolean
blnOKtoRide = True
```

2. Add the code in CODE Step 2 to determine if the rider is less than 45 inches tall. If the rider is less than 45 inches, the blnOKtoRide variable is set equal to False.

3. Add the code in CODE Step 3 to determine if the rider has back problems. If back problems are reported, the rider is not allowed to ride.

```
'Check for back problems
If chkBack.Value = 1 Then
```

CODE Step 3

```
    blnOKtoRide = False
End If
```

4. Add the code in CODE Step 4 to determine if the rider has heart problems. If heart problems are reported, the rider is not allowed to ride.

```
'Check for heart problems
```

CODE Step 4

```
If chkHeart.Value = 1 Then
    blnOKtoRide = False
End If
```

5. Add the code in CODE Step 5 to display whether the potential roller coaster rider can ride depending on the value of blnOKtoRide. After all the code is entered, your screen should appear similar to Figure 8-11.

(continued on next page)

CODE Step 2

```
'Check if rider is less than 45 inches tall
If Val(txtHeight.Text) < 45 Then
    blnOKtoRide = False
End If
```

CODE Step 5

```
'Display results
If blnOKtoRide = True Then
    lblResult.Caption = "OK to Ride."
Else
    lblResult.Caption = "Can't Ride!"
End If
```

FIGURE 8-11

The code assumes the rider is allowed to ride unless one of the checks causes the Boolean variable blnOKtoRide to change to False.

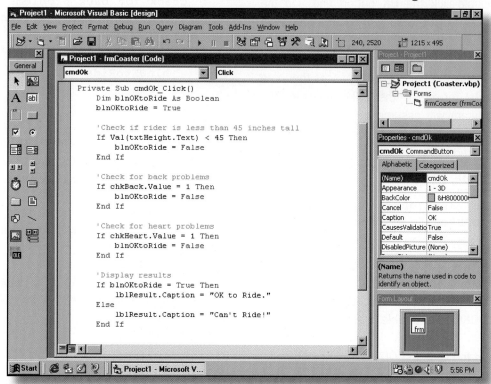

6. Close the Code window and run the program.

7. Key **30** in the textbox and click the **OK** button. The label *Can't Ride!* appears on the form.

8. Key **46** in the textbox, click the **Back Trouble** checkbox to add a checkmark, and click the **OK** button. Again the label *Can't Ride!* appears on the form.

9. Remove the checkmark from the **Back Trouble** checkbox, and click the **OK** button. The label *OK to Ride* appears on the form.

10. Check the **Heart Trouble** checkbox and click the **OK** button. The rider is refused.

11. End the program and save the changes to the program but leave the project open for Step-by-Step 8.7.

156

Using the Logical Operators

There is another important set of operators: the logical operators. *Logical operators* can be used to combine several comparisons into one statement. Table 8-2 shows the three most common logical operators. Logical operators are used with True and False values. For example, the Not operator reverses the value. In other words, True becomes False and False becomes True.

TABLE 8-2

LOGICAL OPERATORS

Operator	Description
Not	Reverses the value.
And	All expressions or values connected by the And operator must be True in order for the result to be True.
Or	Only one of the expressions or values connected by the Or operator must be True for the result to be True.

The And operator works like you might expect. The result of the And operator is True if both values connected by the And operator are True. For example, the code below sets the Boolean variable blnInRange to True if the variable intA is in the range of 0 to 100. It determines this by verifying that the value in intA is greater than or equal to 0 *and* less than or equal to 100.

```
blnInRange = (intA >= 0) And (intA <= 100)
```

The Or operator returns a True result if either of the values connected by the Or operator are True. For example, the code below sets the blnSellStock variable to True if the stock price moves higher than 92.5 per share *or* if the profits are less than one million.

```
blnSellStock = (sngStockPrice > 92.5) Or (curProfits < 1000000)
```

Order of Logical Operators

In the order of operations, logical operators are processed after the mathematical and conditional operators. Table 8-3 shows the order of operations, combining the mathematical, conditional, and logical operators. The table lists the operations from the first to the last. Items in parentheses are always evaluated first and will override the order here.

TABLE 8-3

ORDER OF OPERATIONS
Exponentiation
Unary plus and unary minus
Multiplication, division, integer division, and Mod
Addition and subtraction
The conditional operators
Not
And
Or

STEP-BY-STEP ⟹ 8.7

1. Double-click the **OK** button.

2. Delete the three segments of code that check for height and for back and heart problems.

3. Add the code in CODE Step 3 to replace the lines you just deleted to combine the three If statements into one.

4. Close the Code window and run the program.

5. Key **25** in the textbox and click the **OK** button. The label *Can't Ride!* appears on the form.

CODE Step 3

```
'Check if rider is legal to ride
If (Val(txtHeight.Text) < 45) Or (chkBack.Value = 1) Or _
    (chkHeart.Value = 1) Then
        blnOKtoRide = False
End If
```

6. Key **73** in the textbox, click the **Heart Trouble** checkbox to add a checkmark, and click the **OK** button. Again the label *Can't Ride!* appears on the form.

7. Remove the **checkmark** from the **Heart Trouble** checkbox, and click the **OK** button. The label *OK to Ride.* appears on the form.

8. Click the **Back Trouble** checkbox to add a checkmark and click the **OK** button. The label *Can't Ride!* appears on the form.

9. End the program, save the changes to the project, and exit Visual Basic.

Summary

■ Decisions are reached by making comparisons.

■ Comparisons in a computer generally return either a True or False value.

■ The conditional operators compare two values and return either True or False, depending on whether the expression is True or False.

■ A Boolean variable can be used to store the results of an expression that includes conditional operators.

■ The If statement is the most common way to make a decision in a program. An If statement is a one-way selection structure.

■ In an If statement, the code between the If and the End If is executed if the conditions in the If statement are met.

■ Flowcharts allow programmers to plan and document program code using symbols connected by lines.

■ An If…Else statement makes a decision between two paths. An If…Else statement is a two-way selection structure.

■ Checkboxes allow your program to ask the user Yes or No questions or to turn an option on or off.

■ The Value property of a checkbox is set to 1 (one) when the checkbox is checked and 0 (zero) when the box is not checked.

■ A checkbox can be set to be checked or unchecked by default.

■ Logical operators can be used to combine several comparisons into one statement.

■ Logical operators are used with True and False values.

■ The Not operator reverses the value of a Boolean variable or expression.

■ The And operator returns True if the values connected by the And operator are both True.

■ The Or operator returns True if either value connected by the Or operator is True.

■ The logical operators are last in the order of operations. Of the logical operators, Not comes first, then And, then Or.

TRUE/FALSE

Circle the T if the statement is true. Circle the F if it is false.

T F **1.** Decision making in computers is based on comparing data.

T F **2.** Boolean variables can be used to store the result of a comparison.

T F **3.** You cannot set the caption of a label to the result of a comparison.

T F **4.** Flowcharts are generally used to chart an entire Visual Basic program.

T F **5.** An If … Else statement is considered a one-way selection structure.

T F **6.** An End If statement does not need to be used in conjunction with the If … Else statement.

T F **7.** The CheckBox control includes a label that can be set with the Caption property.

T F **8.** Checkboxes are always set to be unchecked by default.

T F **9.** The same operator is used for assignment and equal comparison in Visual Basic.

T F **10.** Logical operators can be used to combine several comparisons into one statement.

WRITTEN QUESTIONS

Write your answers to the following questions.

11. What type of operator is used to compare two values?

12. What is the result of a comparison in Visual Basic?

13. What operator is used to represent "Not equal to?"

14. List two types of statements used to make decisions in a Visual Basic program.

15. What statement marks the end of an If statement?

16. Why are flowcharts important to programming?

17. What two possible values can be stored in the Value property of a checkbox control?

18. List the three logical operators.

19. Where do the logical operators fall in the order of operations?

20. What is the Not operator used for?

LESSON 8 PROJECTS

PROJECT 8A

1. Start Visual Basic and open the **Buses** program you worked with in Lesson 5.

2. Add the following code to the **Calculate** button to display a warning message if the number of people equals 0. (Substitute the name of the top textbox in your program for txtPeople.Text.)

```
'Check number of people
If Val(txtPeople.Text) = 0 Then
        MsgBox ("The number of people cannot be zero.")
End If
```

3. Add code so the text in the textboxes will be selected when you click in them.

4. Close the Code window and run the program.

5. Enter a **0** (zero) for number of people to verify that the changes made to the program work correctly.

6. Click the **OK** button to dismiss the message, then end the program.

7. Save the changes to the project and remove the project but leave Visual Basic open.

PROJECT 8B

Draw a flowchart of the roller coaster ride program created in this lesson.

PROJECT 8C

1. Open the **Numbers** program you worked with in this lesson.

2. Change the caption of the form to **Even or Odd**?.

3. Change the instructions at the top of the form to explain that the program will determine if the number is even or odd.

4. Edit the code for the **OK** button so it looks like the following code.

```
'Determine if number is even or odd
If Val(txtNumber.Text Mod 2) = 0 Then
    lblResult.Caption = "The number is even."
Else
    lblResult.Caption = "The number is odd."
End If
```

5. Run the program to verify that it can determine whether a number is even or odd, then end the program.

6. Save the changes to the project and remove the project but leave Visual Basic open.

PROJECT 8D

Your school is planning a trip for spring break. They have asked you to write a program that will calculate the total cost of the trip for each student. The basic price for the trip is $200.00. There are three additional options for the trip: rappelling, backpacking, and canoeing. Complete the steps below to finish the program.

1. Open **Trip** from your template files.

2. Add three checkboxes and change their captions so the form appears similar to Figure 8-12 (resize and reposition as necessary).

3. Change the name property of the checkboxes to **chkRappel**, **chkBackpack**, and **chkCanoe**.

4. Add the following code to the **Calculate** button to declare three variables and initialize curTotal to 200.

```
Dim curTotal As Currency
Dim strTotal As String
Dim strOutput As String
curTotal = 200
```

FIGURE 8-12
Add three checkboxes
as shown here.

5. Add the following code to add $30 to curTotal if the rappelling checkbox is checked.

```
'Check if Rappelling
If chkRappel.Value = 1 Then
     curTotal = curTotal + 30
End If
```

6. Add the following code to add $45 to curTotal if the backpacking checkbox is checked.

```
'Check if Backpacking
If chkBackpack = 1 Then
     curTotal = curTotal + 45
End If
```

7. Add the following code to add $25 to curTotal if the canoeing checkbox is checked.

```
'Check if Canoeing
If chkCanoe = 1 Then
      curTotal = curTotal + 25
End If
```

8. Add the following code to display the results.

```
'Display Output
strTotal = Format(curTotal, "$###.00")
strOutput = "The total price of your trip will be " & strTotal & "."
lblOutput.Caption = strOutput
```

9. Close the Code window and run the program to verify that all three checkboxes work correctly (you can check more than one checkbox at a time).

10. End the program, save the changes to the project and exit Visual Basic.

CRITICAL THINKING ACTIVITY

Extend the Roller Coaster program to do additional verification. The program should ask for the age of the rider. Regardless of height, if the rider is under 10 years old, the Child with Adult check box must be checked before the child can ride.

Make modifications to the user interface to match Figure 8-13 and add the required code to perform the checks. (Hint: Use And rather than Or in the code for the age requirement.)

FIGURE 8-13
Modify the Rollercoaster form to include a new label, textbox, and checkbox as shown here.

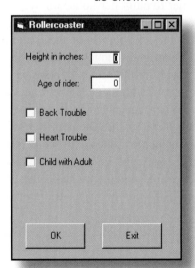

163

NESTED IF STATEMENTS AND OPTION BUTTONS

OBJECTIVES

When you complete this lesson, you will be able to:

■ Use Nested If statements.

■ Use Option buttons.

■ Use the Form Load event.

■ Use the Select Case statement.

⏱ **Estimated Time: 2 hours**

Using Nested If Statements

Decision-making is sometimes more complicated than selecting one of two paths. Often, once on a path, there are more decisions to be made. For example, suppose a homeowner is deciding whether to paint her house this year or next year. If she decides to do the job this year, she will have to make additional decisions, such as color. She won't have to decide what color to paint unless she makes the decision to go ahead and paint.

In programming, you regularly have decision-making similar to the example above. Recall that you can place multiple lines of code between an If statement and its End If statement. The lines of code within an If statement can be practically any kind of Visual Basic code, including more If statements.

When you place an If statement inside another If statement, the If statement inside is called a *nested If statement*. The code below reports the status of an automobile's fuel level to the driver. The first If statement checks to see if the fuel level is less than one quarter of a tank. If more than 1/4 of a tank exists, the Else clause reports that the Fuel level is fine. If less than 1/4 of a tank exists, an additional If statement checks the distance to the next gas station. Based on the distance to the next possible fill-up, the driver is either alerted to get fuel now or warned that fuel will be needed soon.

```
If sngFuelLevel < 0.25 Then
    If sngDistanceToNextGas > 30 Then
        MsgBox("Get fuel now.")
    Else
        MsgBox("Will need fuel soon.")
    End If
Else
    MsgBox("Fuel level OK.")
End If
```

When using nested If statements, it is important that you properly indent the code. As you can see, the code above is a little confusing at first. Just imagine how confusing it would be if there was no indentation to group the statements logically.

Other than careful attention to indentation, there is no new or special syntax to learn in order to use nested If statements. However, you will get errors if you fail to include the End If for every If statement.

In the exercise that follows, you will use nested If statements to recommend a type of checking account to a new bank customer. Banks normally have two or more types of checking accounts that are tailored for customers with different amounts of money to keep in the account. Often, banks have a low-cost account for people who plan to keep low balances and a free checking account for those who will maintain a slightly higher balance. They may also have an account that pays the customer interest if the customer will maintain a certain minimum balance.

The code in Figure 9-1 will recommend an account to the user. First, an If statement determines if the amount being deposited is less than $1000. If the deposit is less than $1000, further comparisons must be made. If the deposit is $1000 or greater, the Else clause recommends the interest-bearing account.

FIGURE 9-1

Nested If statements allow multi-level decisions.

```
'Determine checking account
If curDeposit < 1000 Then
  If curDeposit < 100 Then
    lblOutput.Caption = "Consider the EconoCheck account."
  Else
    lblOutput.Caption = "Consider the FreeCheck account."
  End If
Else
  lblOutput.Caption = "Consider an interest-bearing account."
End If
```

The nested If statement is only executed if the deposit is less than $1000. Its job is to choose between the two accounts that do not pay interest. If the deposit is less than $100, the EconoCheck account is recommended, otherwise (or else) the FreeCheck account is recommended.

STEP-BY-STEP ➤ 9.1

1. Start Visual Basic and open **Check** from your template files. If necessary, open **frmMain** from the **Forms** folder.

2. Double-click the **OK** button and add the code in CODE Step 2 to declare curDeposit as a Currency variable.

CODE Step 2

```
Dim curDeposit As Currency
```

(continued on next page)

3. Add code in CODE Step 3 to set curDeposit equal to the value in the textbox.

4. Add the code from Figure 9-1 into the event procedure. Your screen should appear similar to Figure 9-2.

5. Close the Code window and run the program.

6. Key **700** into the textbox and click the **OK** button. The output "Consider the FreeCheck account." appears on the form.

7. Key **50** into the textbox and click the **OK** button. The output "Consider the EconoCheck account." replaces the previous output.

8. Key **3500** into the textbox and click the **OK** button. The output "Consider an interest-bearing account." appears on the form.

9. End the program and save the changes to the project.

10. Remove the project but leave Visual Basic open for Step-by-Step 9.2.

CODE Step 3

```
curDeposit = Val(txtDeposit.Text)
```

FIGURE 9-2
Be sure to properly indent code that includes nested If statements.

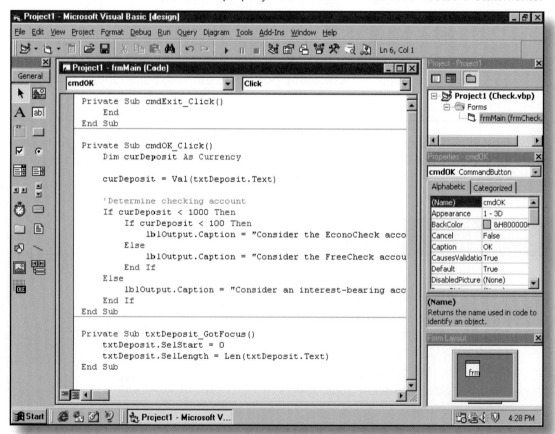

Using Option Buttons

*O*ption buttons are similar to checkboxes with one important difference. Option buttons always appear in groups and only one button in the group can be selected at a time. For example, the dialog box in Figure 9-3 is a typical Print Setup dialog box. When printing to most printers, you have the option of printing on the page across the top (portrait orientation) or down the side (landscape orientation). You can only select one of the two options. Therefore, option buttons are ideal for selecting the page orientation in the Print Setup dialog box.

FIGURE 9-3
Only one option button in a group can be selected.

 **NOTE:**

Option buttons are sometimes called *radio buttons*. They got the name from car radios. The buttons on a car radio that move the dial to a preset station are like option buttons. You can have only one station selected at a time.

Using option buttons in your programs is more complex than working with any of the other controls you have included in your programs up to this point. To successfully use option buttons, there are three steps involved.

1. Create a frame to group the option buttons.

2. Create the option buttons in the frame.

3. Write code to use the option buttons.

Creating a Frame Control

A *frame control* is a container for other controls. The controls that you place inside a frame are treated as one unit. If you move the frame, the controls in the frame move with it. If you delete the frame, the controls in the frame are deleted along with the frame. Figure 9-4 shows an example of a frame in a dialog box (the Choose a planet frame).

FIGURE 9-4
Frames are used to group controls into one unit.

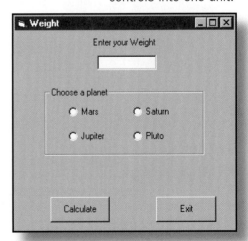

It is important to create the frame that will contain the option buttons before you create the option buttons themselves. When you draw the option buttons, you will draw them in the frame that they are to be associated with. Option buttons in a frame are sometimes referred to as an *option group*.

The two most important frame properties are Name and Caption. As in other controls, the Name property allows you to associate a name with the object in Visual Basic code. In a frame, the Caption property specifies the text that will appear at the top of the frame.

In Step-by-Step 9.2–9.8, you will create the program shown in Figure 9-4. The program will calculate your weight on other planets. You will select the planet for the calculation using option buttons.

STEP-BY-STEP ⟹ 9.2

1. Open **Planets** from your template files and if necessary, open **frmMain** from the **Forms** folder.

2. Double-click the **Frame** control from the toolbox. A frame appears in the center of the form.

3. Resize and move the frame so your screen appears similar to Figure 9-5.

4. Change the **Name** property of the frame to **fraPlanets** and change the **Caption** property to **Choose a planet**.

5. Save your changes but leave the project open for Step-by-Step 9.3.

FIGURE 9-5
Creating a frame is the first step to creating option buttons.

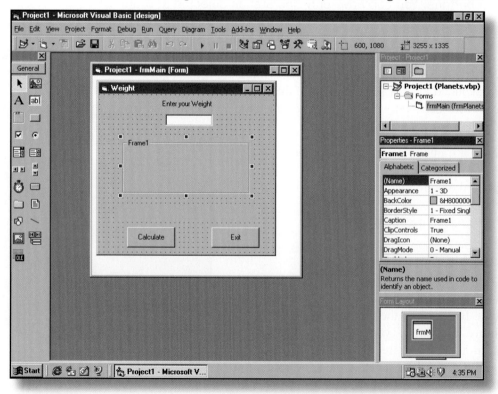

Creating Option Buttons in the Frame

Now that the frame is created, the next step is to add option buttons to the frame.

IMPORTANT:

When you create option buttons, click the OptionButton tool from the toolbox and drag within the frame to create the option button. If you double-click the OptionButton tool, the option button that is created will not be associated with the frame, even if it appears to be in the frame.

S TEP-BY-STEP ⇨ 9.3

1. Click the **OptionButton** control from the toolbox.

2. Position the mouse pointer inside the frame.

3. Drag to draw an option button inside the frame about 1/4 inch tall and 1 1/2 inches wide (1215 x 255).

4. Create three more identical option buttons inside the frame. Your screen should appear similar to Figure 9-6.

5. Save your changes but leave the project open for Step-by-Step 9.4.

FIGURE 9-6

Drawing option buttons in a frame will automatically associate them with the frame.

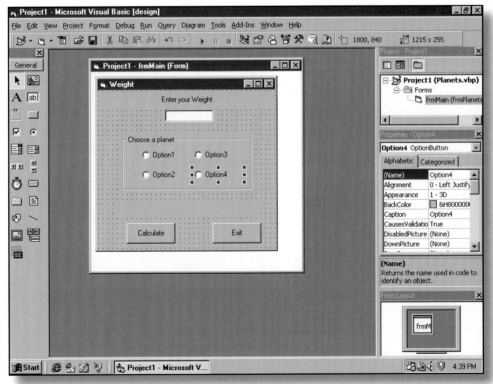

Like other controls, option buttons need to be named appropriately using the Name property. The Caption property of an option button is similar to the Caption property of a checkbox. The Caption property specifies the text for the attached label.

STEP-BY-STEP ⟹ 9.4

1. Select the first option button.

2. Change the Name property to **optMars** and change the Caption property to **Mars**.

3. Set the properties of the remaining option buttons as follows:

Name	Caption
optJupiter	Jupiter
optSaturn	Saturn
optPluto	Pluto

4. Run the program.

5. Click each of the option buttons to see that they are operating correctly.

6. End the program and save your changes but leave the project open for Step-by-Step 9.5.

Adding Code to the Option Buttons

Coding option buttons requires that you think in an event-driven way. Let's consider what happens when the user clicks an option button. The click on the option button generates a Click event. In addition, as you saw in the previous exercise, the option button is filled with the dot that indicates that it is selected. It is in the Click event procedure that you have the opportunity to specify what you want to happen if that option is selected.

It is not that simple, however. The user may click several option buttons before finally settling on a choice. This means you must keep track of the most recently clicked option button in the group and yet be prepared for another option button to be clicked instead. Here is how you do it.

Use form-level variables as the scope to keep track of the option that has been selected. For example, in this program that will calculate your weight on other planets, the Click event of each option button will set two variables. The first variable will store the name of the planet the user selected. The second variable will store the conversion factor necessary to calculate the user's weight on that particular planet. The code for the Mars option button Click event appears below.

```
Private Sub optMars_Click()
    sngPlanetWeight = 0.38
    strPlanetName = "Mars"
End Sub
```

Each of the option buttons will have a Click event procedure similar to the one above. So no matter how many option buttons the user clicks, the variables will reflect the values of the most recently clicked option button. Then when the user clicks the Calculate button, the values set in the option button's Click event procedure will be used in the calculation.

 **NOTE:**

Remember, the variables used in each of the option button event procedures must be declared at the form level.

STEP-BY-STEP ⟩ 9.5

1. Double-click the **Calculate** button and select **General** from the Object list box.

2. Add the code in CODE Step 2 to create two form-level variables.

CODE Step 2

```
Option Explicit
Dim sngPlanetWeight As Single
Dim strPlanetName As String
```

3. Select **optMars** from the Object list box and add the code in CODE Step 3 to assign the appropriate values to the two form-level variables when the Mars option button is clicked.

CODE Step 3

```
sngPlanetWeight = 0.38
strPlanetName = "Mars"
```

4. Select **optJupiter** from the Object list box and add the code in CODE Step 4 for the Jupiter Click event procedure.

CODE Step 4

```
sngPlanetWeight = 2.64
strPlanetName = "Jupiter"
```

5. Select **optSaturn** from the Object list box and add the code in CODE Step 5 for the Saturn Click event procedure.

CODE Step 5

```
sngPlanetWeight = 1.15
strPlanetName = "Saturn"
```

6. Select **optPluto** from the Object list box and add the code in CODE Step 6 to initialize the two form-level variables when the Pluto option button is selected. Your screen should appear similar to Figure 9-7.

CODE Step 6

```
sngPlanetWeight = 0.04
strPlanetName = "Pluto"
```

7. Close the Code window and save your changes but leave the project open for Step-by-Step 9.6.

FIGURE 9-7
Each option button must have a Click event procedure.

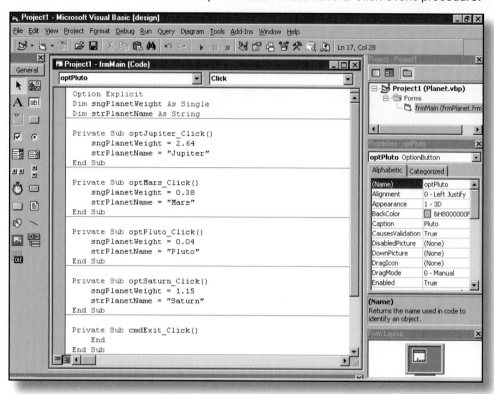

The final step is to calculate the result and create the output. To properly process the data, we will declare two variables in the Calculate command button's Click event procedure. We will use an integer to hold the result of the weight conversion and a string variable to hold the formatted result.

S TEP-BY-STEP ⟹ 9.6

1. Double-click the **Calculate** button and add the code in CODE Step 1 to declare the necessary local variables.

2. Add the code in CODE Step 2 to set intWeight equal to the value in the textbox multiplied by the variable sngPlanetWeight.

CODE Step 1

```
Dim intWeight As Integer
Dim strWeight As String
```

CODE Step 2

```
'Calculate Weight
intWeight = Fix(sngPlanetWeight * Val(txtWeight.Text))
strWeight = Format(intWeight, "####")
```

3. Add the code in CODE Step 3 to display the results in the caption of the lblOutput label.

4. Close the Code window and run the program.

5. Enter **150** into the textbox.

6. Click the **Jupiter** option button and click the **Calculate** button. The answer appears on the form.

7. Click each of the other option buttons and the **Calculate** button to test them. The answer should change each time.

8. End the program and save your changes but leave the project open for Step-by-Step 9.7.

CODE Step 3

```
'Display Output
lblOutput.Caption = "Your weight on " & strPlanetName _
          & " would be " & strWeight & " pounds."
```

Using a Form Load Event Procedure

Although our program works, there is still a problem. When the program runs, none of the option buttons are yet selected. So if the user fails to click any of the option buttons and clicks the Calculate button, the program will give no weight and will have no planet name to display.

STEP-BY-STEP ⟹ 9.7

1. Run the program.

2. Enter **150** into the textbox and click the **Calculate** command button. The output displays "Your weight on   would be   pounds." with no weight or planet name

because an option button was not selected.

3. End the program but leave the project open for Step-by-Step 9.8.

To correct this, we need to have one of the option buttons selected by default. Option buttons have a property that allows you to simulate a user's click from code. By setting the Value property of an option button to True, the option button is selected. In addition, the button's Click event is triggered. So the values are properly initialized as well. The code below, for example, will make the Mars option button the default button.

```
optMars.Value = True
```

But where can you place the code so that it is executed before the user has the opportunity to click the Calculate button? When a form is loaded and opened by the program, a special event called a *Load event* is triggered. Like other events, you can write an event procedure for the form's Load event.

1. Double-click the form (but not the title bar or one of the controls) displayed on the screen. The Code window opens, displaying the form's Load event procedure.

2. Add the code in CODE Step 2 to set the Mars option button as the default when the program is run.

CODE Step 2

```
optMars.Value = True
```

3. Close the Code window and run the program. Notice that the Mars option button is already selected.

4. Enter **123** into the textbox and click the **Calculate** button. The program calculates the weight on Mars.

5. End the program and save the changes to the project.

6. Remove the project but leave Visual Basic open for Step-by-Step 9.9.

Using Select Case

If statements allow you to program one-way decisions and If...Else statements allow you to program two-way decisions. By nesting If statements, you have seen that you can actually make decisions that branch in more than two paths. Visual Basic, however, provides a statement especially for multi-way decisions: the Select Case statement.

In a *Select Case statement*, you specify a variable to test and then list a number of cases that you want to test for. For example, the code below uses a Select Case statement to recommend a type of vehicle that should be rented, based on the number of passengers.

```
'Select type of vehicle to rent
Select Case intPassengers
  Case 1 To 2
    lblOutput.Caption = "You should rent a compact car."
  Case 3 To 4
    lblOutput.Caption = "You should rent a full size car."
  Case 5 To 7
    lblOutput.Caption = "You should rent a minivan."
  Case 8 To 15
    lblOutput.Caption = "You should rent a 15 passenger van."
  Case Is > 15
    lblOutput.Caption = "You should rent a bus."
  Case Else
    lblOutput.Caption = "Incorrect data"
End Select
```

The first line in the Select Case statement specifies the piece of data that is involved in the decision; in this case, the number of passengers (intPassengers). The Select Case statement ends with an End Select statement. Between the Select Case and End Select statements are a series of Case statements. In this code, most of the Case statements specify a range of values. For example, if the value of intPassengers is 6, the third Case statement will apply because 6 is in the range of 5 to 7.

You can use conditional operators in a Case statement as well. To use a conditional operator requires that you include the Is keyword. The fifth Case statement is an example of the use of a conditional operator. If the value in intPassengers is greater than 15, the recommendation is to rent a bus.

Finally, as a default, the code under the *Case Else statement* will be applied if no other Case statement catches it first. In this case, the Case Else will be triggered if the value is zero or less.

STEP-BY-STEP ➡ 9.9

1. Open **Transportation** from your template files and if necessary, open **frmMain** from the **Forms** folder.

2. Double-click the **OK** button and add the code in CODE Step 2 to declare an integer variable and set it equal to the value in the textbox.

3. Add the Select Case statement in CODE Step 3.

4. Close the Code window and run the program.

(continued on next page)

CODE Step 2

```
Dim intPassengers As Integer
intPassengers = Val(txtPassengers.Text)
```

CODE Step 3

```
'Select type of vehicle to rent
Select Case intPassengers
  Case 1 To 2
    lblOutput.Caption = "You should rent a compact car."
  Case 3 To 4
    lblOutput.Caption = "You should rent a full size car."
  Case 5 To 7
    lblOutput.Caption = "You should rent a minivan."
  Case 8 To 15
    lblOutput.Caption = "You should rent a 15 passenger van."
  Case Is > 15
    lblOutput.Caption = "You should rent a bus."
  Case Else
    lblOutput.Caption = "Incorrect data"
End Select
```

175

5. Key **14** as the number of passengers and click the **OK** button. The output shown in Figure 9-8 appears.

6. Enter other values and click the **OK** button to verify that each case works correctly.

7. Change the number of passengers to **0** and click the **OK** button. The output states that you entered incorrect data.

8. End the program and save the changes to the project, then exit Visual Basic.

FIGURE 9-8
The Select Case statement selects the output to display.

Summary

- If statements can be nested to make additional decisions within the code of the If statement.

- It is important to indent the code in a nested If statement to make the code readable.

- Each If statement within a nested If statement must end with the End If statement.

- Option buttons appear in groups. Only one option button in the group can be selected at a time.

- Option buttons are sometimes called radio buttons.

- The first step in creating a group of option buttons is to create a frame control to contain the option buttons. The controls within a frame are treated as one unit.

- The Caption property of a frame control specifies the text that appears at the top of the frame.

- To associate an option button with a frame, you must click the OptionButton tool only once and draw the option button in the frame. If you double-click to create an option button, it will not associate itself with the frame.

- The Caption property of an option button specifies the text that appears on the label attached to the option button.

- Coding option buttons involves using form-level variables that carry values that reflect the selected option.

- A form's Load event procedure is executed each time a form is loaded and opened by the program.

- The Select Case statement allows you to make multi-way selections.

- The Case statements in a Select Case can test a range or use conditional operators.

- Conditional operators in a Case statement must include the Is keyword.

- As a default, the Case Else statement is applied if no other Case is true.

LESSON 9 REVIEW QUESTIONS

TRUE/FALSE

Circle the T if the statement is true. Circle the F if it is false.

T   F   1. It is possible to write nested If statements in Visual Basic.

T   F   2. Only one option button in a group can be selected.

T   F   3. The first option button you place on a form automatically creates a frame in which you can place other option buttons.

T   F   4. The controls you place inside a frame are treated as one unit.

T   F   5. Drawing option buttons in a frame will automatically associate them with that frame.

T   F   6. The first option button you add to a form will be selected by default when you run the program.

T   F   7. Double-clicking on a form will display the General Declarations section of the code for that form.

T   F   8. To use a conditional operator in a Case statement, you must use the keyword Is.

T   F   9. The Select Case statement ends with an End Select statement.

T   F   10. Code under the Case Else statement is the default case in a Select Case statement.

WRITTEN QUESTIONS

Write your answers to the following questions.

11. Why is it important to properly indent your code when using multi-way selection structures?

12. What is the main difference between option buttons and checkboxes?

13. What is another name for option buttons?

14. What three steps are involved in creating a group of option buttons?

15. Which property specifies the text for the label attached to an option button?

16. What scope should the variables you use to keep track of a user' selection have?

17. How do you change the default selection in a group of option buttons?

177

18. What is a frame control?

19. What event procedure is triggered when a form is loaded?

20. Where is the piece of data involved in the decision located in a Select Case statement?

LESSON 9 PROJECTS

PROJECT 9A

1. Start Visual Basic and open **Final** from your template files.

2. Create a Boolean form-level variable named **blnExempt**.

3. In the **OK** Click event procedure, set **blnExempt** equal to **False**.

4. Add the following code to determine if the student needs to take the final exam.

```
'Determine if final needs to be taken
If Val(txtAverage.Text) >= 90 Then
    If Val(txtAbsences.Text) <= 3 Then
        blnExempt = True
    End If
Else
    If Val(txtAverage.Text) >= 80 Then
        If Val(txtAbsences.Text) <= 1 Then
            blnExempt = True
        End If
    End If
End If
```

5. Add the following code to display the results.

```
'Display Results
If blnExempt = True Then
    lblResult.Caption = "You DO NOT need to take the final exam."
Else
    lblResult.Caption = "You DO need to take the final exam."
End If

lblResult.Visible = True
```

6. Close the Code window and run the program with various scores and number of absences to verify that it works correctly.

7. Save the changes to the project and remove the project but leave Visual Basic open.

PROJECT 9B

1. Open **Animal Years9B** from your template files.

2. Add a frame with three option buttons to the form as shown in Figure 9-9.

3. Use Figure 9-9 to key the Caption properties of the frame and option buttons. Name the frame **fraAnimal** and name the option buttons **optDog**, **optCow**, and **optMouse**.

4. Add the following code in the General Declarations section to declare two new variables.

    ```
    Dim strYears As String
    Dim sngYears As Single
    ```

5. Add the following code into the Click event procedure of the Dog option button to calculate the number of Dog years.

    ```
    'Calculate Dog Years
    sngYears = (7 * intMonths) / 12
    ```

6. Add the following code into the Click event procedure of the Cow option button to calculate the number of Cow years.

    ```
    'Calculate Cow Years
    sngYears = (5 * intMonths) / 12
    ```

FIGURE 9-9
Add a frame with three option buttons as shown here.

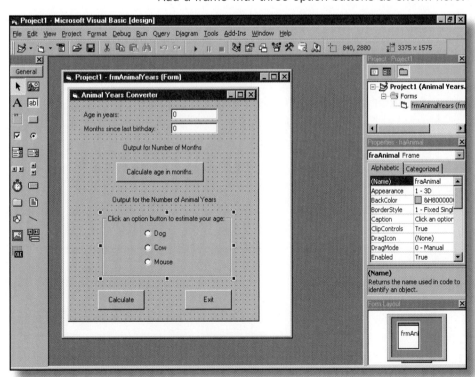

7. Add the following code into the Click event procedure of the Mouse option button to calculate the number of Mouse years.

```
'Calculate Mouse Years
sngYears = (25 * intMonths) / 12
```

8. Add the following code into the Click event procedure of the **Calculate** button to display the results.

```
'Display Results
strYears = Format(sngYears, "###.0")
lblOutputAnimalYears.Caption = "In animal years, you are " & _
      strYears & " years old."
lblOutputAnimalYears.Visible = True
```

9. Add the following code into the Click event procedure of the **Months** command button that will set the Dog option button to **True**.

```
'Set Dog option button as default
optDog.Value = True
```

10. Run the program and verify that everything works correctly.

11. Save the changes to the project and remove the project but leave Visual Basic open.

PROJECT 9C

Write a program that will determine the price per copy based on the following chart.

Number of Copies	Price Per Copy
1–200	0.10
201–500	0.08
501–1000	0.06
>1000	0.05

1. Open **Copies** from your template files.

2. Add the following code to the **OK** button to declare four different variables and set intNumber equal to the value in the textbox.

```
Dim intNumber As Integer
Dim strNumber As String
Dim curTotal As Currency
Dim strTotal As String

intNumber = Fix(Val(txtCopies.Text))
```

3. Add the case statement as follows to determine the total cost.

```
'Determine total cost
Select Case intNumber
    Case 1 To 200
        curTotal = intNumber * 0.1
    Case 201 To 500
        curTotal = intNumber * 0.08
    Case 501 To 1000
        curTotal = intNumber * 0.06
    Case Is > 1000
        curTotal = intNumber * 0.05
    Case Else
        lblOutput.Caption = "Incorrect data was entered."
End Select
```

4. Add the following code to display the results.

```
'Display results
If intNumber > 0 Then
    strNumber = intNumber
    strTotal = Format(curTotal, "$#,###.00")
    lblOutput.Caption = "The total cost for " & strNumber & _
        " copies is " & strTotal & "."
End If
```

5. Run the program and verify that everything works correctly with various numbers of copies, including entering a 0 (zero) to generate the incorrect data output.

6. End the program and save the changes to the project, then exit Visual Basic.

CRITICAL THINKING ACTIVITY

Modify the Planets program you created in this lesson so it calculates a person's weight on every planet in the solar system (resize your form and frame to include the new option buttons). Make Mercury the default option button. Use the following conversion factors for the new planets.

Planet	Multiply by
Mercury	0.37
Venus	0.88
Uranus	1.15
Neptune	1.12

UNIT 3 REVIEW QUESTIONS

MATCHING

Write the letter of the description from Column 2 that best matches the term or phrase in Column 1.

Column 1	Column 2
_____ 1. conditional operators	**A.** the event that is triggered when a form is loaded and opened.
_____ 2. option buttons	**B.** an If statement inside another If statement.
_____ 3. load event	**C.** a program structure in which the decision is whether to go "one way" or just bypass the code in the If statement.
_____ 4. two-way selection structure	**D.** symbols used in making comparisons.
_____ 5. frame control	**E.** option buttons in a frame.
_____ 6. nested If statement	**F.** a container for other controls.
_____ 7. flowcharts	**G.** allows you to execute specified code when the result of a conditional expression is True.
_____ 8. option group	**H.** a group of buttons that can only be selected one at a time.
_____ 9. one-way selection structure	**I.** used to plan and to document program code.
_____ 10. If statement	**J.** a program structure in which one block of code is executed if the specified conditions are True or another block of code is executed if the specified conditions are False.

WRITTEN QUESTIONS

Write your answers to the following questions.

11. What type of result does a comparison return?

12. How can you set a checkbox to be checked by default?

13. How do you label a checkbox?

14. Why might you use a logical operator?

15. How do you associate an option button with a frame?

16. How do you set the default selection for a group of option buttons?

17. Why might you write a nested If statement?

18. What statement ends the Select Case statement?

19. Which case in a Select Case statement is the default case?

20. How can you use a conditional operator in a Case statement?

UNIT 3 APPLICATIONS

Estimated Time: 1 hour

APPLICATION 3-1

Write the specified code in the space provided.

1. Write a statement that assigns the word True to the Caption property of the label named lblEqual if the value in sngA is equal to the value in sngB.

2. Write a statement that warns the user of a division by zero error if the value in intDivisor is equal to zero.

3. Write a statement that presents a message box that says "Value is too high" if curPrice is greater than $750 and a message box that says "Value is too low" if curPrice is less than $1.

APPLICATION 3-2

1. Start Visual Basic and open **Insurance** from your template files.

2. Add a frame with three option buttons to the form as shown in Figure U3-1.

3. Create a checkbox under the frame as shown in Figure U3-1.

4. Use Figure U3-1 to key the Caption properties of the frame, option buttons, and checkbox.
   Name the frame **fraMethod**, name the option buttons **optMonth**, **optQuarter**, and
   optAnnual and name the checkbox **chkGoodDriver**.

FIGURE U3-1

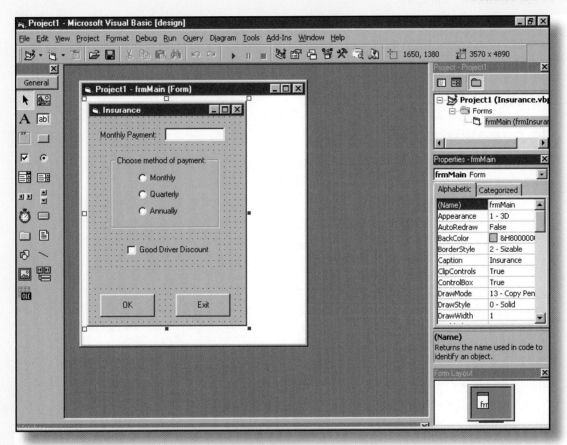

5. Add the following code in the General Declarations section to declare two new variables.

```
Option Explicit
Dim intMultiplier As Integer
Dim strPayment As String
```

6. Add the following code into the Click event procedure of the Monthly option button.

```
intMultiplier = 1
strPayment = "monthly"
```

7. Add the following code into the Click event procedure of the Quarterly option button.

```
intMultiplier = 4
strPayment = "quarterly"
```

8. Add the following code into the Click event procedure of the Annual option button.

```
intMultiplier = 12
strPayment = "annual"
```

9. Add the following code into the Click event procedure of the **OK** command button to declare and initialize three variables, decide whether a discount applies, and display the output.

```
Dim strTotalPayment As String
Dim curTotalPayment As Currency
Dim curMonthlyPayment As Currency

curMonthlyPayment = Val(txtPayment.Text)
curTotalPayment = curMonthlyPayment * intMultiplier

'Discount?
If chkGoodDriver.Value = 1 Then
    curTotalPayment = curTotalPayment * 0.95
End If

'Display Results
strTotalPayment = Format(curTotalPayment, "$#,###.00")
lblOutput.Caption = "Your " & strPayment & " payment will be " _
    & strTotalPayment & "."
```

10. Add the following code into the Form Load event procedure to set the monthly option button as the default.

```
optMonth.Value = True
```

11. Close the Code window and run the program to verify that it works correctly.

12. Save the changes to the project and remove the project.

APPLICATION 3-3

It is common for a computer to be connected to a device called an uninteruptable power supply (UPS). A UPS is a battery backup that immediately begins supplying power to the computer when a power outage or other power problem occurs. These UPSs come in many sizes, which are measured in volt-amps. When you purchase a UPS, you must decide how large a UPS is necessary for your system. For example, if you just need time to save your documents and shut down the computer in the event of an outage, you may only need 5 or 10 minutes of power to be provided by the UPS. Some computers, such as network servers, need much more time. In fact, you hope that the power will be restored to normal before the battery backup is exhausted.

In this project, you will design a program that recommends a UPS to a user based on the number of minutes of backup time required. The program should prompt the user for a number of minutes and use the Select Case statement below to decide which model UPS to recommend.

```
Select Case intMinutes
   Case 1 To 9
      strModel = "Power 300"
   Case 10 To 15
      strModel = "Power 450"
   Case 16 To 30
      strModel = "Power 650"
   Case 31 To 40
      strModel = "Power 750"
   Case 41 To 60
      strModel = "Power 1000"
   Case Is > 60
      strModel = "See sales representative"
   Case Else
      strModel = "Invalid or incomplete data"
End Select
```

Create the program using your own user interface design and save the project with an appropriate form and project name.

INTERNET ACTIVITY

Using the Internet, obtain the exchange rates for at least three foreign currencies. Links to currency exchange rates can be found at:

http://www.programvb.com/basics/unit3.htm

Write a program that prompts the user for an amount of money in your country's currency and use option buttons to allow the user to select the currency to which the money should be converted. Save the project with an appropriate form and project name.

LOOPS, MULTIPLE FORMS, MENUS, AND PRINTING

UNIT 4

lesson 10   2 hrs.

Do Loops

lesson 11   2 hrs.

For Next Loops and
Multiple Forms

lesson 12   2 hrs.

Menus and Printing

Estimated Time for Unit 4: 6 hours

189

LESSON

10

DO LOOPS

OBJECTIVES

When you complete this lesson, you will be able to:

■ Explain what a loop is.

■ Use the Do While and Do Until loops.

■ Use the InputBox function.

■ Use the DoEvents statement.

■ Use nested loops.

🕐 **Estimated Time: 2 hours**

What Are Loops?

You have probably noticed that much of the work a computer does is repeated many times. For example, when a computer prints a personalized form letter for each person in a database, the same operation is repeated for each person in the database. When a program repeats a group of statements a number of times, the repetition is accomplished using a *loop*. The code required to create a loop is sometimes called an *iteration structure*.

In Visual Basic, there are three kinds of loops. In this lesson, you will learn about two kinds of loops: the Do While and Do Until loop. Both types of Do loops repeat a block of code statements a number of times. The *Do While loop* repeats the statements *while* a certain condition is True. The *Do Until loop* repeats the statements *until* a certain condition is True.

Using The Do Loops

Knowing which of the Do loops to use is just a matter of experience. Often, the same result can be achieved with either a Do While or a Do Until. It may come down to a decision of which loop is best in a specific case.

Both types of Do loops rely on a condition to be either True or False. A loop's condition is similar to the condition used in an If statement. The condition applies some test to determine either a True or False result. Consider the Do While loop in the code below.

```
intValue = 1
Do While intValue < 10
   intValue = intValue + 1
Loop
```

In the code above, the variable intValue is assigned the value 1. The Do While loop will repeat the indented statement until intValue is no longer less than 10. The Loop keyword at the end of the code indicates the end of the block of code statements that are included in the loop.

 **NOTE:**

A loop can contain more than one statement. All of the statements between the Do While and the Loop keywords will be repeated.

Using Do While

A Do While loop is used when you want a block of code to repeat as long as a condition remains True. For example, suppose you want to write a program that calculates the number of times that a given number can be divided by two before the result of the division is less than 1. A Do While loop can be used in this case. The code below shows a Do While loop that will repeatedly divide a number in half as long as the result of the division is greater than or equal to 1.

```
Do While dblX >= 1
   dblX = dblX / 2
Loop
```

Suppose we want to write a program that counts the number of times the division must occur before the result is no longer greater than or equal to 1. The code below adds a counter to the loop to count the number of times the code in the loop is executed.

```
intCounter = 0

'Divide number
Do While dblX >= 1
   dblX = dblX / 2
   intCounter = intCounter + 1
Loop
```

1. Start Visual Basic and open **DoLoop** from your template files. If necessary, open the form.

2. Double-click the **Count** button and add the code in CODE Step 2 to count the number of times a number can be divided by two before the result is less than 1.

3. Close the Code window and run the program.

4. Key **8** and click the **Count** button. The program shows that the number 8 must be divided by 2 four times to obtain a result less than 1, as shown in Figure 10-1.

FIGURE 10-1
The program reports the value of intCounter.

5. End the program and save your changes but leave the project open for Step-by-Step 10.2.

```
CODE Step 2

Dim dblX As Double
Dim intCounter As Integer

'Initialize variables
dblX = Val(txtStart.Text)
intCounter = 0

'Divide number
Do While dblX >= 1
    dblX = dblX / 2
    intCounter = intCounter + 1
Loop

'Display Results
lblCounter.Caption = intCounter
lblCounter.Visible = True
```

Using Do Until

A Do Until loop is used when you want a block of code to repeat until a condition is no longer true. For example, the program from the previous exercise could easily be rewritten to use a Do Until loop instead of a Do While. Consider the following code.

```
intCounter = 0
Do
   dblX = dblX / 2
   intCounter = intCounter + 1
Loop Until dblX < 1
```

In the code above, the loop uses reversed logic. Instead of repeating as long as the number being divided is greater than or equal to 1, the code repeats until the number being divided becomes less than 1.

STEP-BY-STEP 10.2

1. Double-click the **Count** button and replace the loop under the comment **Divide number** with the code in CODE Step 1. Your screen should appear similar to Figure 10-2.

2. Close the Code window and run the program.

CODE Step 1

```
Do
    dblX = dblX / 2
    intCounter = intCounter + 1
Loop Until dblX < 1
```

(continued on next page)

FIGURE 10-2
The Do While loop is replaced with a Do Until loop.

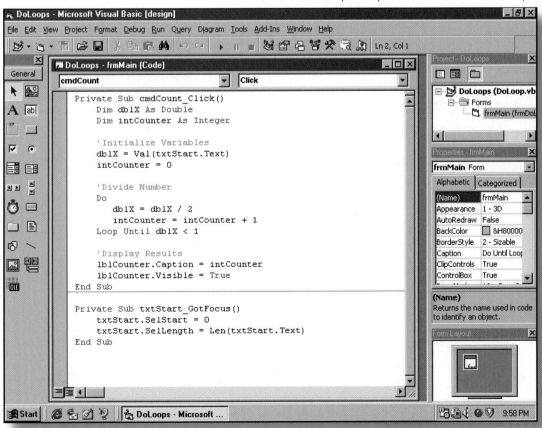

3. Key **156** and click the **Count** button. The number 156 can be divided eight times before the result is less than 1.

4. End the program. Do _not_ save your changes but leave the project open for Step-by-Step 10.3.

One of the primary differences between the two kinds of Do loops is where the condition is tested. A Do While loop tests the condition at the top of the loop. If the condition is False, the code inside the loop is never executed. The Do Until loop tests the condition at the bottom of the loop. Therefore, in a Do Until loop, the code in the loop is executed at least once.

The difference between the Do While and Do Until loops is important. For example, the program in Step-by-Step 10.2 actually provides an inaccurate answer in some cases because of the behavior of the Do Until loop. Let's run the Do Until loop again and identify the problem.

STEP-BY-STEP 10.3

1. Run the program.

2. Key **.75** and click the **Count** button. Notice that the program reports that the division occurred one time, as shown in Figure 10-3. Because the condition is tested at the end of the loop, the instructions in the loop are performed at least once, even though they did not need to be performed. The result is that the program produced an incorrect result.

3. End the program and remove the project. Do _not_ save your changes but leave Visual Basic open for Step-by-Step 10.4.

FIGURE 10-3
In this case, the Do Until loop did not generate the correct answer.

The program that uses the Do Until can be fixed by adding an If statement that causes the loop to be skipped if the value in dblX is already less than 1, as shown.

```
intCounter = 0
If dblX >= 1 Then
   Do
      dblX = dblX / 2
      intCounter = intCounter + 1
   Loop Until dblX < 1
End If
```

Rather than add the If statement to the code, however, most programmers would probably choose to use the Do While loop.

Using the InputBox Function

The InputBox function is kind of the opposite of the MsgBox function. Recall that the MsgBox function creates a window to display output. The *InputBox function* displays a window to ask the user for input. Figure 10-4 shows an example of an input box created with the InputBox function.

To use the InputBox function, you must supply two strings: the text that will prompt the user and the title for the window's title bar. It is optional to supply a third string: the text that you want to appear in the textbox by default. The InputBox function will return a string value. For example, the code below will create the InputBox shown in Figure 10-4.

FIGURE 10-4
The InputBox function displays a window to prompt the user for information.

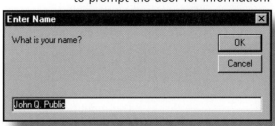

```
strName = InputBox("What is your name?", "Enter Name", _
                "John Q. Public")
```

In the code above, strName is the String variable that will hold the text entered by the user. Inside the parentheses that follow the InputBox keyword, separated by commas, you supply the prompt that the user will see, the title bar text, and the optional default entry.

STEP-BY-STEP 10.4

1. Open **InputBox** from your template files and if necessary, open the form.

2. Double-click the **Enter Name** button and add the code in CODE Step 2 to create an input box and display the text entered into it.

(continued on next page)

CODE Step 2

```
Dim strName As String

'Input name
strName = InputBox("What is your name?", "Enter Name", _
                "John Q. Public")

'Display name
lblName.Caption = strName
```

3. Close the Code window and run the program.

4. Click the **Enter Name** button. An input box appears on your screen, as shown in Figure 10-5.

5. Key your name and click the **OK** button. Your name appears on the form.

6. End the program, save your changes, and remove the project. Leave Visual Basic open for Step-by-Step 10.5.

FIGURE 10-5
The input box appears when the Enter Name button is clicked.

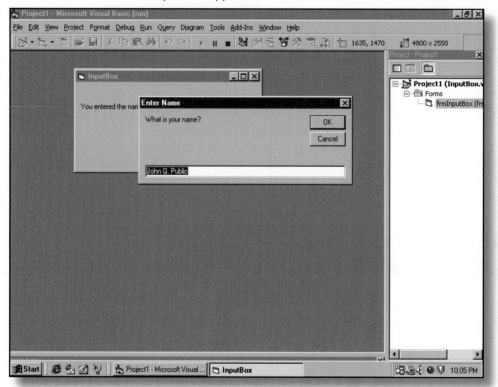

The InputBox function can be used inside a Do Until loop to repeatedly ask the user for data until a specified condition is met. For example, suppose you want to prompt the user for a list of numbers to be averaged. You do not know how many numbers the user will enter. All you know is that when the user enters a zero (0), the program should stop accepting numbers and calculate the average. This can be accomplished by placing a call to the InputBox function inside a Do Until loop.

STEP-BY-STEP ⇒ 10.5

1. Open **Numbers10** from your template files and if necessary, open the form.

2. Double-click the **Input Numbers** button and add the code in CODE Step 2 to declare and initialize the variables in the program.

3. Add the code in CODE Step 3 to input the numbers entered, perform the calculations and display the results.

(continued on next page)

CODE Step 2

```
Dim intNumber As Integer
Dim intAverage As Integer
Dim strAverage As String
Dim lngSum As Long
Dim strSum As String
Dim intCounter As Integer
Dim strCounter As String
Dim strDisplayTotal As String
Dim strDisplayAverage As String
Dim strDisplaySum As String


intCounter = 0
lngSum = 0
```

CODE Step 3

```
'Input Numbers
Do
   intNumber = Val(InputBox("Enter an Integer (0 to Quit):", _
            "Input Number"))

   If (intNumber > 0) Then
      lngSum = lngSum + intNumber
      intCounter = intCounter + 1
   End If

Loop Until (intNumber = 0)

intAverage = lngSum / intCounter

'Store Results
strAverage = Format(intAverage, "###")
strCounter = Format(intCounter, "#####")
strSum = Format(lngSum, "#####")

strDisplayTotal = "Numbers entered:    " & strCounter
strDisplaySum = "Sum of numbers:    " & strSum
strDisplayAverage = "Average of numbers:    " & strAverage

'Display Results
lblTotal.Caption = strDisplayTotal
lblSum.Caption = strDisplaySum
lblAverage.Caption = strDisplayAverage
lblTotal.Visible = True
lblSum.Visible = True
lblAverage.Visible = True
```

4. Close the Code window and run the program.

5. Click the **Input Numbers** button. An input box appears.

6. Key **10** and click the **OK** button. The input box reappears because a zero was not entered.

7. Key **20** and click the **OK** button.

8. Key **30** and click the **OK** button.

9. Key **0** and click the **OK** button. Because a zero was entered, the loop stops and the program displays the results on the form as shown in Figure 10-6.

FIGURE 10-6
Keying a zero stops **10.** the Do Until loop.

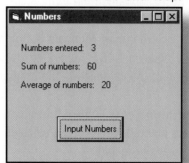

End the program, save your changes, and remove the project. Leave Visual Basic open for Step-by-Step 10.6.

Using the DoEvents Statement

As you already know, when an event is triggered, an event procedure is executed to handle the event. The event procedures you have created up to this point have been relatively short. The computer executes the code in the event procedure so quickly that you may not notice that it takes any time at all. When you begin using loops, however, an event procedure may occupy several seconds of the computer's time. There is also the potential that an endless loop may occur. Let's look at both of those possibilities.

Long Event Procedures

Suppose you have written a program that includes a loop that processes thousands of instructions. While the program is busy executing the loop, the program is unresponsive to other events because it is busy handling the current event.

STEP-BY-STEP 10.6

1. Open **LongLoop** from your template files and if necessary open the form.

2. Double-click the **Go** button and add the code in CODE Step 2 to create a loop that will count to five million.

3. Close the Code window and run the program.

CODE Step 2

```
Dim lngCounter As Long

lngCounter = 1
Do While lngCounter < 5000000
    lngCounter = lngCounter + 1
Loop
lblStatus.Caption = "Loop Ended"
```

4. Click the **Go** button. Notice that the program is unresponsive for a few seconds before the "Loop Ended" message appears.

5. Click the **Clear Label** button. The label becomes blank.

6. Click the **Go** button again. Again the program becomes unresponsive.

7. End the program and save your changes but leave the project open.

 **NOTE:**

Depending on the speed of your computer, you may want to adjust the value in the Do While loop's condition expression to more or less than five million.

Endless Loops

In an *endless loop*, the condition that is supposed to stop the loop from repeating never becomes True. This is usually a programming error. Inside every loop there should be code that causes a change that will eventually lead to the end of the looping. If no such code exists inside the loop, the loop may repeat endlessly.

1. Double-click the **Go** button.

2. Change the code inside the loop from lngCounter = lngCounter + 1 to **lngCounter = lngCounter + 0**.

   Your screen should appear similar to Figure 10-7. This will create an endless loop because the counter will never reach five million.

3. Close the Code window and run the program.

4. Click the **Go** button. Notice that the computer seems to freeze.

5. Allow a short time to confirm that the computer is not responding, then press **Ctrl+Break** to pause the program. The Code window opens and highlights the code where the program stopped.

6. Click the **End** button to end the program.

7. Change the code in the loop back to adding a one to lngCounter.

8. Close the Code window and save your changes but leave the project open.

FIGURE 10-7
Changing the code in the loop as shown will produce an endless loop.

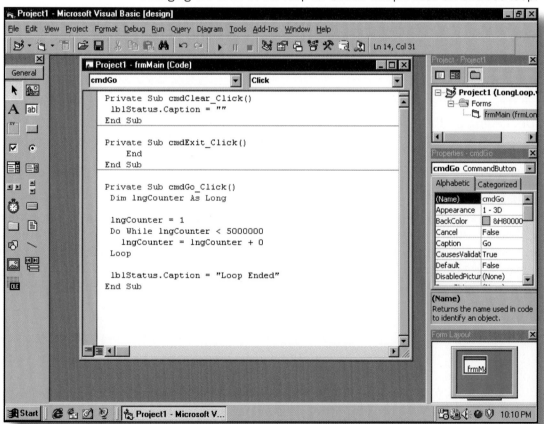

 **NOTE:**

Pressing Ctrl+Break while a program is in an endless loop does not end the program. It suspends the execution so that you can see the line of code being executed. It also gives you to opportunity to end the program with the End button.

The DoEvents Statement

The *DoEvents statement* allows the computer to process other events, even though the current event procedure is not yet complete. By adding the DoEvents statement inside the loop that may occupy a lot of the computer's time, you make it possible to handle other events while the loop is finishing its work. Let's look at the difference the DoEvents statement makes.

STEP-BY-STEP ⟹ 10.8

1. Double-click the **Go** button and add **DoEvents** as the first instruction of the loop as shown in Figure 10-8.

2. Close the Code window and run the program.

(continued on next page)

FIGURE 10-8
Adding the DoEvents code allows the computer to process other events while a loop is still taking place.

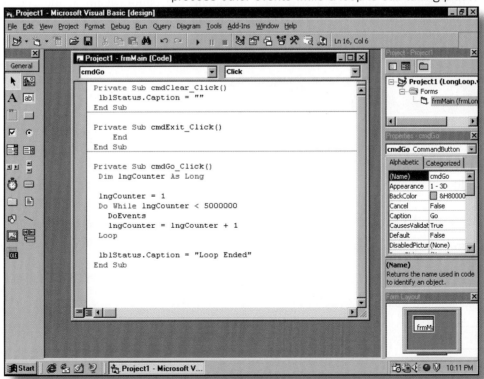

201

3. Click the **Go** button. The long loop starts again; however, by using DoEvents the computer allows other events to take place. The DoEvents statement actually slows down the loop, making it take a long time to reach five million.

NOTE:

The time required to complete the loop will vary between machines.

4. Click the **Exit** button. The loop ends and the program closes.

5. Change the value in the loop condition to 100000 and run the program again. The event procedure now completes in a shorter amount of time.

6. End the program and save your changes but leave the project open.

There is one more thing you should understand about using DoEvents. When the DoEvents statement is executed, the computer can process whatever other events are waiting to be processed, including the event that is not yet complete. For example, suppose you click a button to begin processing data. If the button's Click event procedure includes the DoEvents statement, you could actually click the same button again, starting the same process to begin again. This can have unpredictable and possibly disastrous results.

How do you prevent this from happening? It is a good idea to disable the button at the beginning of the event procedure to prevent the user from clicking the button again until the event is completely processed. Of course, you will want to enable the button again at the end of the procedure. Remember, the purpose of the DoEvents statement is to allow other events to be processed, not to allow the same event to be processed simultaneously.

STEP-BY-STEP ⟹ 10.9

1. Double-click the **Go** button and above the loop add the code in CODE Step 1 to disable the Go button.

CODE Step 1

```
cmdGo.Enabled = False
```

2. Below the loop add the code in CODE Step 2 to enable the Go button.

CODE Step 2

```
cmdGo.Enabled = True
```

3. Close the Code window and run the program.

4. Click the **Go** button. Notice that the Go button becomes disabled until the loop finishes counting, as shown in Figure 10-9.

5. When the Go button is enabled again, click the **Exit** button.

6. Save your changes and remove the project but leave Visual Basic open.

FIGURE 10-9

FIGURE 10-9
Disabling the Go button prevents
the same event procedure from being
restarted before it is complete.

Using Nested Loops

Like If statements, loops may be nested. It is not uncommon to need a loop within a loop. For example, suppose you have a program that counts from 1 to 1000 on the screen. The program is executing so fast that the first value that appears is 1000. Inside the loop that is doing the counting, you can place another loop that simply slows the computer down.

STEP-BY-STEP ▷ 10.10

1. Open **Counter** from your template files and if necessary open the form.

2. Run the program and click the **Go** button. Notice that the program counts to 1000 too quickly to see that it is counting.

3. End the program.

4. Add the code in CODE Step 4 between the line intDelay = 1 and the line Loop 'End of outer loop.

CODE Step 4

```
'Begin nested loop
Do While intDelay <= 100
   DoEvents
   intDelay = intDelay + 1
Loop 'End of nested loop
```

5. Run the program again. You will be able to watch the numbers increase toward 1000. The Go button is disabled while the event is handled. After the count reaches 1000, the Go button is enabled again.

6. End the program, save your changes, and exit Visual Basic.

Summary

- Much of the work a computer does is repeated many times.

- Repetition in programs is accomplished using loops.

- A Do While loop repeats a group of statements while a certain condition is True.

- A Do Until loop repeats a group of statements until a certain condition becomes True.

- A Do loop condition applies a test to determine either a True or False result.

- A Do While loop tests the condition at the top of the loop.

- A Do Until loop tests the condition at the bottom of the loop. The code in a Do Until loop is always executed at least once.

- The InputBox function creates a window that prompts the user for input.

- To use the InputBox function, you supply the text for the prompt, the title for the window's title bar, and the optional default text for the textbox.

- Sometimes long event procedures can make a program unresponsive to other events.

- An endless loop is a loop in which the condition which stops the loop is never met.

- Pressing Ctrl + Break will pause a program with an endless loop and will highlight the code where the program stopped.

- The DoEvents statement allows the program to process other events while an event procedure is executing.

- Loops can be nested in the same way If statements are nested.

LESSON 10 REVIEW QUESTIONS

TRUE/FALSE

Circle the T if the statement is true. Circle the F if it is false.

T   F   **1.** A loop will repeat a specified block of code a number of times.

T   F   **2.** Both types of Do loops rely on a condition to be either True or False.

T   F   **3.** A Do While loop tests the condition at the bottom of the loop.

T   F   **4.** In a Do Until loop, the code in the loop is executed at least once.

T   F   **5.** The MsgBox function displays a window to ask the user for input.

T   F   **6.** In an endless loop, the condition that will stop the loop from repeating never becomes true.

T   F   **7.** Unlike If statements, loops cannot be nested.

T   F   **8.** Using Do Events prevents the computer from running multiple programs.

T   F   **9.** You can use Ctrl+Break to pause a program that has entered an endless loop.

T   F   **10.** A loop can contain only one statement.

WRITTEN QUESTIONS

Write your answers to the following questions.

11. What is another name for the code required to create a loop?

12. What is the main difference between a Do While loop and a Do Until loop?

13. What keyword marks the end of the block of code contained within a loop?

14. Where is the condition of a Do Until loop tested?

15. What are the three parameters must you supply to the InputBox function?

16. What is the purpose of using the DoEvents statement?

17. How can you prevent the DoEvents statement from allowing a routine to be executed a second time before it is completely finished?

18. How many times will the following loop be executed?

```
intCount = 0
Do While intCount <= 5
        intCount = intCount + 1
Loop
```

19. How many times will the following loop be executed?

```
intCount = 7
Do While Count < 5
        intCount = intCount - 1
Loop
```

20. How many times will the following loop be executed?

```
intCount = 9
Do
        intCount = intCount - 1
Loop Until intCount <= 5
```

LESSON 10 PROJECTS

PROJECT 10A

1. Start Visual Basic and open **Multiply** from your template files. If necessary, open the form.

2. Add the following code to the **Enter Number** button to create two input boxes.

```
Dim intNumber As Integer
Dim intTimes As Integer
Dim intCounter As Integer
Dim lngTimeWaster As Long

intCounter = 1

intNumber = Val(InputBox("Enter a number:", "Enter Number"))
intTimes = Val(InputBox("Multiply number by 2 how many times?", _
                "Multiply"))
```

3. Add the following code to create a loop that will multiply intNumber by 2 intTimes number of times.

```
Do While intCounter < intTimes
    DoEvents
    intNumber = intNumber * 2
    lblAnswer.Caption = intNumber
    lngTimeWaster = 0
    'Slow program
    Do While lngTimeWaster < 500000
        lngTimeWaster = lngTimeWaster + 1
    Loop
    intCounter = intCounter + 1
Loop
```

4. Close the Code window and run the program to verify that it works correctly. (Remember that the maximum integer value is 32,767.)

5. Save your changes and remove the project but leave Visual Basic open.

PROJECT 10B

1. Open **Ball** from your template files and if necessary open the form.

2. Add the following code to the **Go** button to create an input box that will determine the number of times the ball will bounce.

```
Dim intBounces As Integer
Dim intCounter As Integer

intCounter = 0

'Input bounces
intBounces = Val(InputBox _
    ("How many times should the ball bounce back and forth?", _
    "Input Bounces"))
```

3. Add the following code below the code for the input box to move the ball on the form.

```
'Bounce ball
Do
    DoEvents

    'Move ball right
    Do While shpBall.Left < 4200
        DoEvents
        shpBall.Left = shpBall.Left + 10
    Loop

    'Move ball left
    Do While shpBall.Left > 0
        DoEvents
        shpBall.Left = shpBall.Left - 10
    Loop

    intCounter = intCounter + 1

Loop Until intCounter = intBounces
```

4. Close the Code window and run the program.

5. Click the **Go** button and enter data into the input box to verify that the ball will bounce back and forth across the screen.

6. End the program and save your changes but leave the project open.

PROJECT 10C

1. If necessary, open the **Ball** program you worked with in Project 10B and open the form.

2. Double-click the **Go** button and create an Integer variable named intTimeWaster.

3. Add the following code within each loop that moves the ball to slow down the speed of the ball.

```
'Slow the speed of the ball
intTimeWaster = 0
Do While intTimeWaster < 100
    DoEvents
    intTimeWaster = intTimeWaster + 1
Loop
```

4. Run the program and verify that the speed of the ball has decreased.

5. End the program and save your changes, then exit Visual Basic.

CRITICAL THINKING ACTIVITY

Extend the **Numbers10** program you worked with in Step-by-Step 10.5 to do additional calculations. The program should also find the largest and smallest numbers entered by the user. (Hint: Set the largest number variable equal to the smallest possible integer and set the smallest number variable equal to the largest possible integer.)

FOR NEXT LOOPS AND MULTIPLE FORMS

OBJECTIVES

When you complete this lesson, you will be able to:

- Use the Print statement to print text into a window.
- Use For Next loops.
- Nest For Next loops.
- Change label font settings.
- Use multiple forms in a project to add splash screens and About boxes.

Estimated Time: 2 hours

Using the Print Statement

Visual Basic includes a statement for printing to the screen that is a holdover from the original BASIC language. The Print statement will print text into the current window. There does not have to be a label control in the form. The Print statement prints directly into the window. For example, the statement below will print "Visual Basic" in the current window.

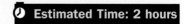

```
Print "Visual Basic"
```

The text produced by the Print statement is cleared using the Cls statement, which is short for *clear screen*. This is also a statement inherited from the original BASIC language.

Let's create a simple program that uses the Print and Cls statements.

STEP-BY-STEP ⟹ 11.1

1. Start Visual Basic and open a new Standard EXE project.

2. Create one command button near the bottom of the form. Name the button **cmdDisplay** and change the caption to **Display**.

3. Add the code in CODE Step 3 to the Click event procedure of the Display button.

4. Close the Code window and run the program.

5. Click the **Display** button. The text appears in the window as shown in Figure 11-1.

6. Click the **Display** button again. The text prints again, below the original text.

7. Click the **Display** button several more times. The text extends below the bottom of the window.

8. End the program.

9. Add the code in CODE Step 9 to the top of the **Display** button's Click event procedure.

10. Close the Code window and run the program again. Click the **Display** button several times to verify that the Cls statement is clearing the window each time the button is clicked.

11. End the program.

12. Save the form as **frmPrintCls** and save the project as **PrintCls**.

13. Remove the project but leave Visual Basic open for Step-by-Step 11.2.

FIGURE 11-1
The Print statement prints text in the active window.

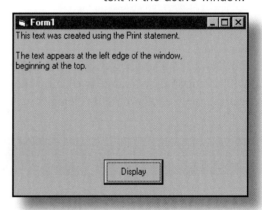

CODE Step 3

```
Print "This text was created using the Print statement."
Print " "   'This statement inserts a blank line.
Print "The text appears at the left edge of the window,"
Print "beginning at the top."
```

CODE Step 9

```
Cls 'Clear the window of any existing text
```

211

Using For Next Loops

The Do Loops that you used in Lesson 10 repeat while a certain condition is True or until a certain condition is True. Sometimes, however, you simply want to repeat a block of code a specific number of times. For example, you might have some code that you would like to repeat ten times. You can do this with a Do While loop, using code like the following.

```
intCounter = 1
Do While intCounter <= 10
    'code that you want to repeat ten times would go here
    intCounter = intCounter + 1
Loop
```

There is nothing wrong with using a Do While loop like the one above. However, Visual Basic provides another kind of loop, the *For Next loop*, that is specifically designed for repeating a block of code a specific number of times. Using a For Next loop, the same task provided by the Do While loop above can be achieved with code that is simpler and easier to read, like the example below.

```
For intCounter = 1 To 10
    'code that you want to repeat ten times would go here
Next
```

A For Next loop always begins with a For statement and ends with a Next statement. The statements between the For and Next statements are repeated the number of times specified in the For Next loop.

For Next loops always involve a Counter variable. This variable is usually an integer. If your loop will be counting in a range exceeding about 32,000, use a variable of type Long. While the loop is repeating, the Counter variable changes with each iteration of the loop.

STEP-BY-STEP ⟹ 11.2

1. Open **ForNext** from your template files and if necessary open the form.

2. Add the code in CODE Step 2 to the **Count by One** button's Click event procedure.

   ### CODE Step 2

   ```
   Dim intCounter As Integer

   Cls

   For intCounter = 1 To 10
       Print intCounter
   Next
   ```

3. Close the Code window and run the program.

4. Click the **Count by One** button. The For Next loop prints the numbers 1 through 10 in the window, as shown in Figure 11-2.

5. End the program and save your changes but leave the project open for Step-by-Step 11.3.

FIGURE 11-2
The For Next loop causes the numbers
1 to 10 to appear in the window.

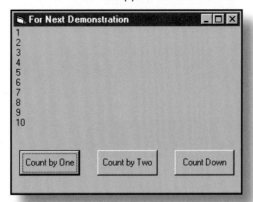

Using the Step Keyword

Another useful feature of the For Next loop is the ability to specify the way the For Next loop counts. The Step keyword is used to cause the loop counter to count by an increment other than one. For example, the For Next loop below will count from 2 to 10 by twos.

```
For intCounter = 2 To 10 Step 2
    Print intCounter
Next
```

STEP-BY-STEP 11.3

1. Add the code in CODE Step 1 to the **Count by Two** button's Click event procedure.

CODE Step 1

```
Dim intCounter As Integer

Cls

For intCounter = 2 To 10 Step 2
    Print intCounter
Next
```

2. Close the Code window and run the program.

3. Click the **Count by Two** button. The counter counts by two, as shown in Figure 11-3.

4. End the program and save your changes but leave the project open for Step-by-Step 11.4.

FIGURE 11-3
The Step keyword can be used to cause the loop to count by two.

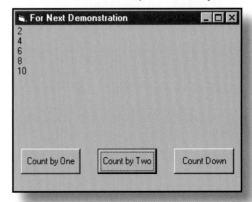

Would you like to count backwards? The Step keyword will allow you to do that too. Just use a negative value after the Step keyword. If you use a negative Step value, make sure that the value on the left of the to keyword is greater than the value to the right of the to keyword. For example, in the code below, the For Next loop counts from 10 to 0.

```
For intCounter = 10 To 0 Step -1
    Print intCounter
Next
```

STEP-BY-STEP 11.4

1. Add the code in CODE Step 1 to the **Count Down** button's Click event procedure.

2. Close the Code window and run the program.

3. Click the **Count Down** button. The counter counts backwards, as shown in Figure 11-4.

4. End the program and save your changes. Remove the project but leave Visual Basic open for Step-by-Step 11.5.

FIGURE 11-4
The Step keyword can be used to cause the loop to count backwards.

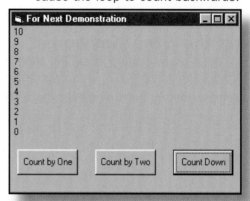

CODE Step 1

```
Dim intCounter As Integer

Cls

For intCounter = 10 To 0 Step -1
    Print intCounter
Next
```

Nesting For Next Loops

For Next loops can be nested within other For Next loops or within Do loops. When you nest For Next loops, each nested loop must be completely contained within the outer loop. For example, in the code below, two For Next loops are nested within an outer For Next loop.

```
For intOuter = 1 To 10
   For intInner1 = 1 To 2
      'Code goes here
   Next
   For intInner2 = 1 To 4
      'Code goes here
   Next
Next
```

The indentation of the code helps you to identify which Next statement is paired with each For statement. However, there is an optional feature that can be used to make code for nested loops clearer. Following the Next keyword, you can specify which loop the Next keyword is ending by including the counter variable name. For example, the nested loops shown above could be coded as shown below to increase readability.

```
For intOuter = 1 To 10
   For intInner1 = 1 To 2
      'Code goes here
   Next intInner1
   For intInner2 = 1 To 4
      'Code goes here
   Next intInner2
Next intOuter
```

In Step-by-Step 11.5, you will create a set of nested loops that will generate a pattern of the letters A, B, and C in a window. You may have noticed in your use of the Print statement that each time the Print statement is used, the cursor automatically moves to the next line, as if the Enter key were pressed. This automatic advance of the cursor to the next line is called a *carriage return*. In the code in Step-by-Step 11.5, you will use the semicolon (;) to cause the Print statement to leave the cursor on the current line. In other words, the semicolon prevents the automatic issue of a carriage return.

NOTE:

The term carriage return originated with the typewriter. The carriage was part of a mechanical typewriter. Even though there is no carriage involved in the electronic representation of text on your screen, the term is still used.

1. Open **NestedFor** from your template files and if necessary open the form. The Clear Window and Exit buttons have already been coded for you.

2. Add the code in CODE Step 2 to create the Click event procedure for the **Begin Loop** button. Don't forget to place the semicolons after the Print statements that appear in the loops.

3. Try to predict the pattern that will be created by the nested loops. Write your prediction on paper.

4. Close the Code window and run the program.

5. Click the **Begin Loop** button. The pattern appears at the top of the window. Was your prediction correct? (ABCCBCCBCC four times)

6. Click the **Begin Loop** button again. The pattern is repeated below the first pattern.

7. Click the **Clear Window** button. The window clears, as shown in Figure 11-5.

8. End the program and save your changes. Remove the project but leave Visual Basic open for Step-by-Step 11.6.

CODE Step 2

```
Private Sub cmdLoop_Click()
   'Declare loop counters
   Dim intA As Integer
   Dim intB As Integer
   Dim intC As Integer

   'Create a blank line in the window
   Print ""

   'Print the character pattern
   For intA = 1 To 4
     Print "A";
     For intB = 1 To 3
       Print "B";
       For intC = 1 To 2
         Print "C";
       Next intC
     Next intB
   Next intA
   Print " End" 'Print "End" to end the pattern
End Sub
```

FIGURE 11-5
The Clear Window button uses the
Cls statement to clear the window.

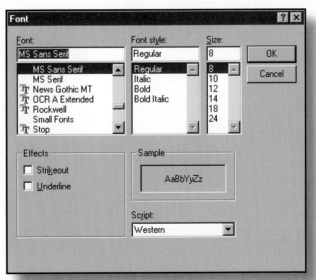

Changing Label Font Settings

When you create label controls on forms, you can control the font, style, and size using the Font property of the label control. You can make labels appear in any font installed on your computer.

To set the Font property of a label, select the label and click the ellipsis (…) in the Font property field in the Properties list. The Font dialog box appears, as shown in Figure 11-6.

FIGURE 11-6
The Font dialog box allows you to set
the font, style, and size of a label.

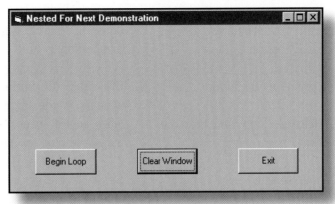

1. Choose **New Project** from the **File** menu to open a new Standard EXE project.

2. Create a new label control on the form.

3. Name the label **lblLarge** and set the caption to **Large Label**.

4. With the label control selected, click the **Font** property field in the Properties list. Then click the ellipsis that appears at the end of the field. The Font dialog box appears.

5. Select **Arial** as the font, **Bold Italic** as the style, and **18** for the size. If your computer does not have Arial installed, select another font.

6. Click the **OK** button. The label's text appears in the larger font. However, the label control needs to be expanded to make all of the text visible.

7. Set the label control's **AutoSize** property to True. The label is resized, as shown in Figure 11-7.

8. Save the form as **frmLabelFont**. Save the project as **LabelFont**, then exit Visual Basic.

FIGURE 11-7
The label appears in the new font.

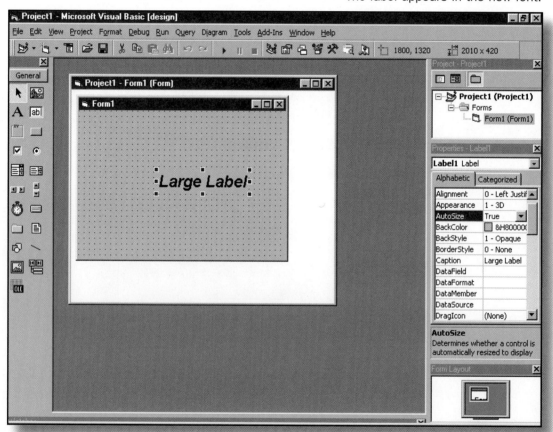

Using Multiple Forms

The programs you have been working with up to this point have involved only one form. Visual Basic, however, allows you to work with multiple forms. Common uses for additional forms include dialog boxes, splash screens, and About boxes.

You've seen examples of dialog boxes. Dialog boxes appear often in Windows programs. A *splash screen* is a window that appears briefly when a program is started. Programs like Microsoft Word have a splash screen that appears briefly while the program makes itself ready for use. An *About box* is a window that provides information about the program. An About box might include information like a registration number, version number, copyright, and information about the developer of the software.

S TEP-BY-STEP ⟹ 11.7

1. Start Visual Basic. Watch closely to see the splash screen that appears as Visual Basic loads, as shown in Figure 11-8.

2. The New Project dialog box that appears when you start Visual Basic is a good example of a dialog box. Click the **Cancel** button to remove the dialog box.

(continued on next page)

FIGURE 11-8
A splash screen is a window that appears briefly as a program loads.

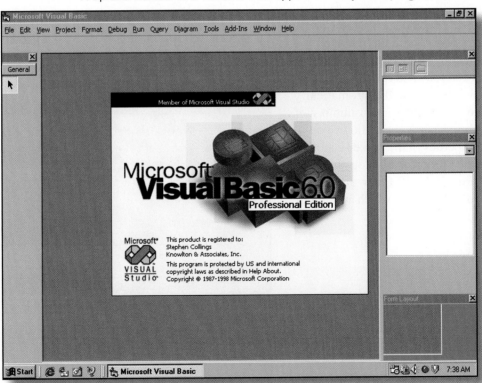

2 1 9

3. Choose **About Microsoft Visual Basic** from the **Help** menu. An About box opens, as shown in Figure 11-9.

4. Click the **OK** button. The About box closes.

5. Leave Visual Basic open for Step-by-Step 11.8.

FIGURE 11-9
An About box tells you something about the program itself.

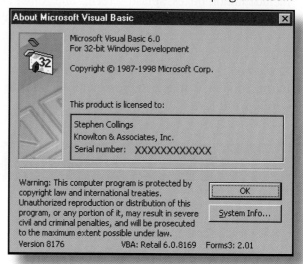

Visual Basic makes it easy to add additional forms to your programs. While there are many things that can be done with multiple forms, we are going to focus on two uses for multiple forms: splash screens and About boxes.

Setting Project Properties

Visual Basic will do most of the work of creating a splash screen and an About box for you. The splash screen and About box forms will automatically include the name and version number of your program. Visual Basic allows you to set these properties in the Make section of the Project Properties dialog box, as shown in Figure 11-10 (your dialog box may vary depending on which version of Visual Basic you are using).

FIGURE 11-10
The Project Properties dialog box allows you to set many options regarding the way your program is compiled and run.

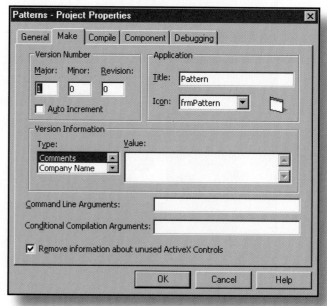

STEP-BY-STEP 11.8

1. Open **Patterns** from your template files and if necessary open the form. This program will create a pattern in the window, based on three nested loops, like the nested loop program you ran earlier in this lesson. This program allows you to specify the number of times each loop will repeat.

2. Run the program using various values in the three text fields and clicking the **Create Pattern** button. (Hint: The program runs best with values of 6 or less in the text boxes.) If the Create Pattern button becomes disabled, click the Clear Window button.

3. End the program.

4. Choose **Patterns Properties** (or choose Project 1 Properties) from the **Project** menu. The Project Properties dialog box appears.

5. Click the **Make** tab. The section of the dialog box that includes the application name and version number appears.

6. In the Version Number frame, change the zero (0) in the Minor text box to one (**1**). The version number is now 1.1.0.

7. In the application frame, change the Title to **Pattern Demonstrator**.

8. Click the **OK** button to close the dialog box.

9. Save your changes but leave the project open for Step-by-Step 11.9.

Adding a Splash Screen

When you want to give your programs a professional look, a splash screen is a good place to start. Like many other features, Visual Basic makes the process easy.

First, open the project to which you want to add the splash screen. Then choose Add Form from the Project menu. A dialog box will appear, allowing you to choose the kind of form you want to add, as shown in Figure 11-11 (options shown may vary).

FIGURE 11-11
There are several kinds of forms that can be added to a Visual Basic project.

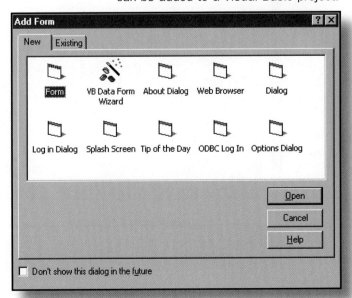

When you choose to add a splash screen, the form that appears already has a suggested layout. However, you can place any images and labels on the form that you like. The form also has labels that will be used to display the program name and version that you entered in the Project Properties dialog box. The code to insert the name and version number is generated automatically when the splash screen is created.

STEP-BY-STEP ➡ 11.9

1. Choose **Add Form** from the **Project** menu. The Add Form dialog box shown in Figure 11-11 appears.

2. Select the **Splash Screen** icon from the dialog box and click the **Open** button. A splash screen form appears, as shown in Figure 11-12 (options shown may vary).

3. There are several labels on the form to help create a suggested layout. For now, let's keep ours simple. Leave the image in place, but delete all of the labels except for the Product label and the Version label.

FIGURE 11-12
The splash screen form has a suggested layout for a splash screen already created.

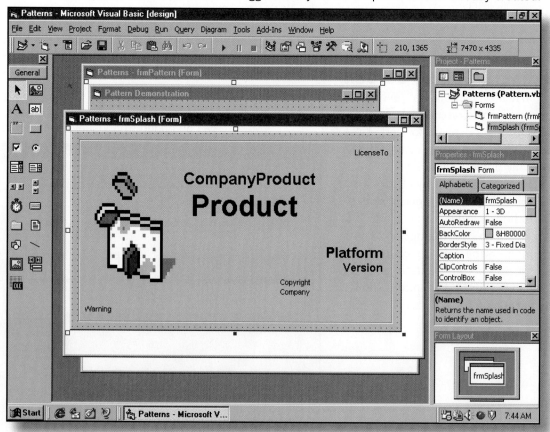

4. Change the font size of the Product label to **18** point. The splash screen form should appear similar to Figure 11-13.

5. Run the program. The splash screen does not appear. Why not?

6. End the program.

7. Save your changes (accept the proposed name for the splash screen file) but leave the project open for Step-by-Step 11.10.

FIGURE 11-13
The splash screen form is now ready.

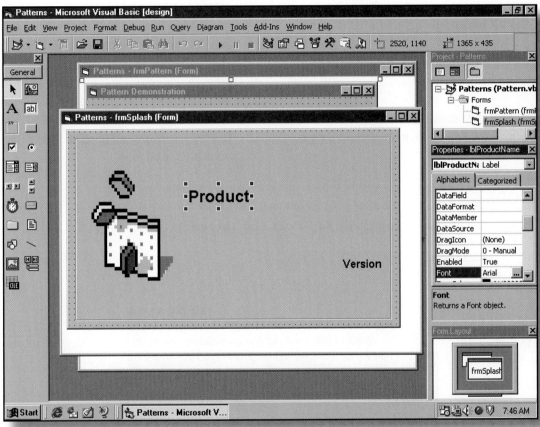

To get the splash screen you created to appear, you have to tell the project that you want to start with the splash screen form. But that's not all. You also have to code the splash screen to ensure that the correct form opens when the splash screen closes.

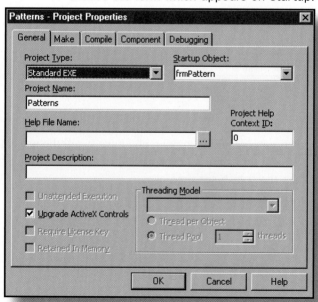

1. Choose **Patterns Properties** (or choose Project 1 Properties) from the **Project** menu. The Project Properties dialog box appears, as shown in Figure 11-14 (your dialog box may vary).

2. In the General section of the dialog box, choose **frmSplash** as the Startup Object.

3. Click the **OK** button. The Project Properties dialog box closes.

4. If necessary, double-click the splash screen form in the Project Explorer window to open the splash screen.

5. Double-click the center of the splash screen form. The frmSplash Code window appears.

6. Locate the event procedure named Form_KeyPress. After the Unload Me statement, add the statement **frmPattern.Show**. The procedure should appear similar to the code in CODE Step 6. This procedure is executed when the user presses any key while the splash screen is on the screen. The Unload Me statement closes the splash screen and the frmPattern.Show statement opens the program's main form.

CODE Step 6

```
Private Sub Form_KeyPress(KeyAscii As Integer)
     Unload Me
     frmPattern.Show
End Sub
```

FIGURE 11-14
The Project Properties dialog box allows you to choose the form which appears on startup.

7. We also want the splash screen to close when the splash screen is clicked. Locate the event procedure named Frame1_Click. Modify the procedure to appear as shown in CODE Step 7.

CODE Step 7

```
Private Sub Frame1_Click()
    Unload Me
    frmPattern.Show
End Sub
```

8. Close the Code window and run the program. The splash screen appears. Notice that the program name and version number that you entered in the Project Properties dialog box appears in the splash screen, as shown in Figure 11-15.

9. Press any key to activate the Form_KeyPress event procedure, which closes the splash screen and opens the program's main form.

10. End the program.

11. Run the program again. This time, click the splash screen to test the Frame1_Click event procedure.

12. End the program and save your changes but leave the project open for Step-by-Step 11.11.

FIGURE 11-15
The splash screen you created appears each time the program is run.

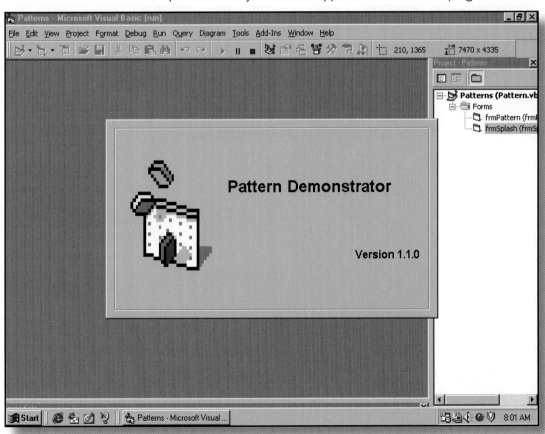

2 2 5

Adding an About Box

Adding an About Box is similar to adding a splash screen. Visual Basic will create a suggested About box for you. Rather than have the program start by displaying the About box, the About box is usually accessed by a command button or menu.

STEP-BY-STEP ⟹ 11.11

1. Choose **Add Form** from the **Project** menu. The Add Form dialog box appears.

2. Select the **About Dialog** icon from the dialog box and click **Open**. An About box form appears, as shown in Figure 11-16.

3. Delete the label that has the caption that begins with *Warning*.

4. Change the caption of **lblDescription** (the one that has the caption of App Description) to the sentence below.

    ```
    This program demonstrates how
    For Next loops can be used to
    create patterns of letters.
    ```

FIGURE 11-16
Visual Basic creates a suggested About box automatically.

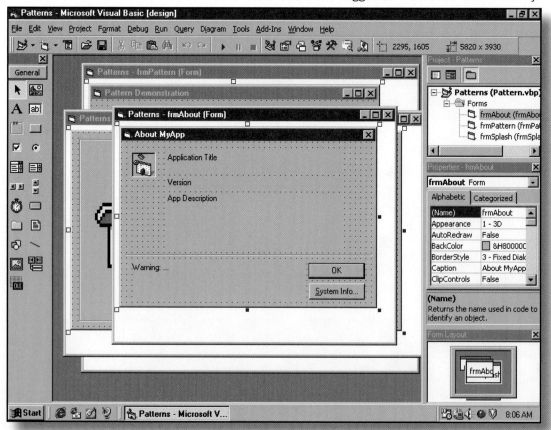

5. Close frmAbout. Make sure the main form (frmPattern) is open.

6. Double-click the **About** button. Add the code in CODE Step 6 to the button's Click event procedure.

    ┌─────────────┐
    │ CODE Step 6 │
    └─────────────┘

    `frmAbout.Show`

7. Close the Code window and run the program. The splash screen should appear.

8. Click the splash screen to remove it from the screen.

9. Click the **About** button to display the About box. Notice the program's name and version number appear in the About box.

10. Click the **OK** button to close the About box.

11. End the program.

12. Save your changes (accept the proposed name for the About file) and exit Visual Basic.

Summary

- Visual Basic includes a statement (the Print statement) for printing text in the current window.

- The Cls statement will clear the text from a window.

- A For Next loop is specifically designed for repeating a block of code a specific number of times.

- A For Next loop always begins with a For statement and ends with a Next statement. The statements between the For and Next statements are repeated the number of times specified in the For Next loop.

- For Next loops always involve a Counter variable.

- If you want a For Next loop to count by an increment other than one, you can use the Step keyword. The Step keyword can also be used to make a For Next loop count backwards.

- For Next loops can be nested.

- Indenting your code can help make nested For Next loops easier to read. You can also use Next statements that specify the counter variable of the loop.

- Using a semicolon in a Print statement will prevent the automatic carriage return at the end of the Print statement.

- You can use the Font property to change the font, style and size of a label.

- Visual Basic programs can include multiple forms. Splash screens and About boxes are two common uses for additional forms in a program.

TRUE/FALSE

Circle the T if the statement is true. Circle the F if it is false.

T F **1.** The Print statement will print text into the current window.

T F **2.** A Do While loop cannot be used to repeat a block of code a specific number of times.

T F **3.** A For Next loop always begins with a For statement and ends with a Next statement.

T F **4.** A For Next loop always involves a counter variable.

T F **5.** You cannot count backwards with a For Next loop.

T F **6.** When For Next loops are nested, each nested loop must be completely contained within the outer loop.

T F **7.** The term carriage return is no longer used since computers do not use a carriage to display characters on the screen.

T F **8.** A label's Font property can be used to control its appearance on a form.

T F **9.** An About box is a window that appears briefly when a program is started.

T F **10.** When you choose to add a splash screen to your program, Visual Basic already has a suggested layout for the form that you cannot change.

WRITTEN QUESTIONS

Write your answers to the following questions.

11. What language is the Print statement carried over from?

12. Where does text appear on a form when displayed using the Print statement?

13. What statement clears text produced by the Print statement?

14. For what purpose is the For Next loop specifically designed?

15. What keyword allows you to count by an increment other than one when used with a For Next loop?

16. Why might you include a counter variable name after the Next statement of a For Next loop?

17. Which character allows you to leave the cursor on the current line when using the Print statement?

18. Name three uses of multiple forms in a project.

19. What is a splash screen?

20. How do you choose which form will appear first when your program runs?

LESSON 11 PROJECTS

PROJECT 11A

1. Start Visual Basic and open **Name** from your template files. If necessary, open the form.

2. Add the following code to the **OK** button so a Print statement will display on the form using the name that is entered in the textbox.

```
Cls
Print "Hello " & txtName.Text; "!"
Print ""
Print "How are you today?"
```

3. Close the Code window and run the program.

4. Key your first name and click the **OK** button to verify that the program works.

5. End the program and save the changes. Remove the project but leave Visual Basic open.

PROJECT 11B

1. Open **ForNextLoops** from your template files and if necessary open the form.

2. Add the following code to the **Count by Three** button.

```
Dim intCounter As Integer

Cls

For intCounter = 3 To 21 Step 3
    Print intCounter
Next
```

3. Add the following code to the **Count Down by Four** button.

```
Dim intCounter As Integer

Cls

For intCounter = 24 To 0 Step -4
    Print intCounter
Next
```

4. Close the Code window and run the program.

5. Before clicking each button, try to determine what the output is going to be.

6. Click both buttons to verify if you were correct.

7. End the program and save your changes. Remove the project but leave Visual Basic open.

PROJECT 11C

1. Open the **InputBox** program you worked with in Lesson 10.

2. Change the font size of the **lblName** label to **12** and change the font style to **Bold**.

3. Run the program.

4. Enter data into the input box and notice how the name on the form has changed when you click the **OK** button.

5. End the program and save your changes. Remove the project but leave Visual Basic open.

PROJECT 11D

1. Open **ABC Pattern** from your template files and if necessary open the form.

2. Add the following code for the Begin Loop button to create a pattern using the letters A, B, and C.

```
'Declare loop counters
Dim intA As Integer
Dim intB As Integer
Dim intC As Integer

'Create a blank line in the window
Print ""
```

```
'Print the character pattern
For intA = 1 To 3
    Print "A";
    For intB = 1 To 4 Step 2
        Print "B";
    Next intB
    For intC = 3 To 9 Step 3
        Print "C";
    Next intC
Next intA

Print "    --- End ---"
```

3. Close the Code window and run the program.

4. Try to determine what the output is going to be, then click the Begin Loop button to verify if you are correct. (ABBCCC three times)

5. End the program, save your changes and exit Visual Basic.

CRITICAL THINKING ACTIVITY

Create a splash screen and an About box for the NestedFor project you worked with in Step-by-Step 11.5. You can decide whether you want to modify all the label control captions on the splash screen form or delete the labels that you don't need. Keep in mind the following items when completing this activity:

1. You will need to change the version number of the program.

2. You will need to create an About button on the form.

3. You will need to type a description of the program in the lblDescription label of the About form.

12 MENUS AND PRINTING

When you complete this lesson, you will be able to:

- Create menus using the Menu Editor.
- Write code for a menu command.
- Use check marks in menus.
- Create submenus.
- Insert separator lines in menus.
- Print from Visual Basic.

⏱ **Estimated Time: 2 hours**

Creating Menus Using the Menu Editor

In addition to buttons and other user interface elements, most Windows applications provide menus. In fact, in most programs, the menus provide the most complete set of options. Toolbars and other buttons are usually just shortcuts to what is available on menus.

Visual Basic allows you to create the standard menus that pull down from the menu bar. Like most other elements of the user interface, Visual Basic allows you to create menus without writing code. As with buttons, choosing a menu command triggers an event. The only coding required is writing the event procedure.

To make creating menus easy, Visual Basic includes a Menu Editor. The Menu Editor is a simple, yet powerful tool for quickly creating menus. It even allows you to create menus with submenus, like the one shown in Figure 12-1.

Because menus pull down from a menu bar, menus are always associated with a form. When you start the Menu Editor, it creates a menu for the currently open form.

The *Menu Editor*, shown in Figure 12-2, allows you to create menu items and set the properties of the menu controls. To access the Menu Editor, make sure the form you want to associate the menu with is open and choose Menu Editor from the Tools menu or click the Menu Editor button on the toolbar.

To learn about the Menu Editor and how to make menus for your programs, we are going to create a simple program that allows you to manipulate the properties of a form and an image using menus.

FIGURE 12-1
Menus created in Visual Basic can include all of the
features of Windows menus, including submenus.

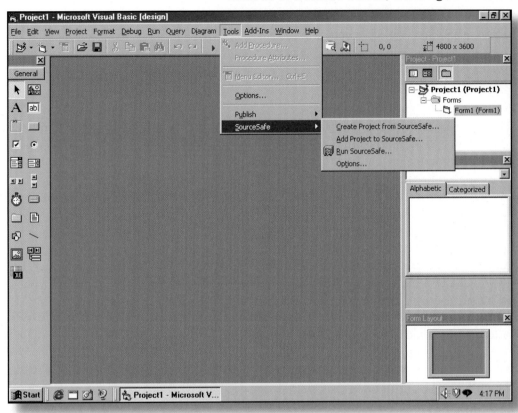

FIGURE 12-2
The Menu Editor allows you to
create menus for your programs.

1. Start Visual Basic and open **Amy** from your template files. The form includes an image.

2. With the form open and selected, choose **Menu Editor** from the **Tools** menu. Leave the Menu Editor open for Step-by-Step 12.2.

The top half of the Menu Editor allows you to build the menu items. The bottom half of the dialog box shows you the structure you have created. You can also make changes to menu items by selecting the item in the bottom portion of the Menu Editor.

Most applications that follow the standard Windows interface include a File menu. So the first menu we will create for our program is a File menu. The only command we are going to include on the File menu is the Exit command.

There are several controls available on the Menu Editor. Right now, we are only concerned with the Caption and Name fields, the arrow buttons, and the Next button.

As you might expect, the Caption field provides the text that will appear in the menu. The Name field gives a name to the menu item that will be used when referring to the item from code. When naming menu items, it is common to use the prefix *mnu*. It is also a good idea to name menu items after the caption of the menu item and the menu on which the item appears. For example, the Exit command on the File menu can be named mnuFileExit.

The left and right arrow buttons allow you to change the indentation of the selected menu item. By indenting the menu item, you indicate where the menu item will appear. For example, in Figure 12-3, the File menu item is not indented, indicating that it will appear on the menu bar. The Exit menu item, which is indented, will appear in the File menu. It is a sub-item of the File menu item. Indenting to a third level creates a submenu, like the one you saw in Figure 12-1.

The arrow buttons that point up and down allow you to change the order of the menu items by moving the selected item up or down in the list of menu items.

FIGURE 12-3
Indenting a menu item in the Menu Editor will cause it to become a sub-item.

STEP-BY-STEP 12.2

1. Key the word **File** in the Caption field of the Menu Editor.

2. Key **mnuFile** as the name of the menu item. The Menu Editor should look similar to Figure 12-4.

3. Click the **Next** button. The Menu Editor is ready for the next menu item to be created.

4. Create the Exit command by keying **Exit** in the Caption field.

5. Name the Exit command **mnuFileExit**.

6. Click the **right arrow button** to indent  the Exit command one level.

7. Click the **OK** button to close the Menu Editor. You can see that a menu bar now appears along the top of the form.

8. Run the program. Pull down the **File** menu to reveal the Exit command.

9. Choose the **Exit** command. As with command buttons, menu commands cannot carry out their commands until code is written.

10. Click the **End** button on the standard toolbar to end the program.

11. Save your changes but leave the project open.

FIGURE 12-4
To add a menu item, enter a caption and a name for the item.

Writing Code for a Menu Command

Writing code for a menu command is much like writing code for a command button. When the user selects a menu command, a Click event is triggered. When you code a menu command, you write an event procedure to handle the Click event.

To write a menu event procedure, choose the menu command from the menu bar that appears on the form as you design your program (not as you run your program). The event procedure will be set up for you.

1. While the program is stopped, pull down the **File** menu at the top of the form. The Exit command will appear.

2. Choose the **Exit** command by clicking it. The Code window opens. The Click event procedure is ready for your code.

3. Add the **End** code to the Click event procedure, as shown in Figure 12-5.

4. Close the Code window.

5. Run the program and test the Exit command in the File menu. The Exit command should now end the program.

6. Save your changes but leave the project open.

FIGURE 12-5

Event procedures for menu items are like those for command buttons.

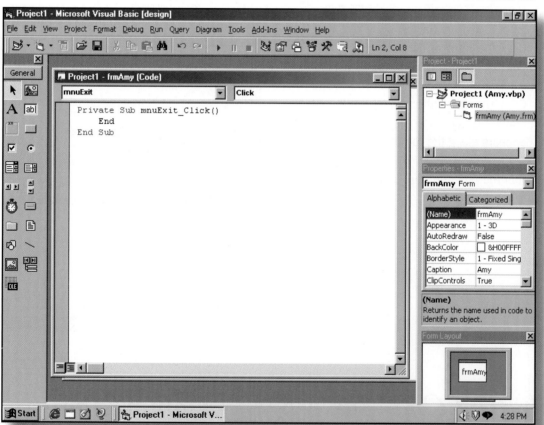

Using Check Marks in Menus

Often, a menu command is used to toggle an item on and off. For example, a menu command might be used to make a toolbar appear or disappear. To help the user determine when the item is active, a check mark can be made to appear in the menu, as shown in Figure 12-6.

You can add a check mark to a menu item at the time you create the item. You can also make the check mark appear and disappear by using Visual Basic code. The Checked check box in the Menu Editor allows you to control the presence of a check mark. From code, you can set the check mark by modifying the Checked property.

FIGURE 12-6

Check marks in menus can be used to determine when items are active.

STEP-BY-STEP ▷ 12.4

1. Click on the form to select it, then access the Menu Editor by clicking the **Menu Editor** button on the standard toolbar.

2. Click the first blank line below the indented Exit menu item. You can now add a new menu item.

(continued on next page)

3. Click in the Caption field and key **Image**.

4. Key **mnuImage** in the Name field.

5. Click the **Next** button.

6. Key **Visible** in the Caption field and key **mnuImageVisible** in the Name field.

7. Click the **right arrow button** to indent the menu item to the second level.

8. Click the Checked check box. The Menu Editor should appear similar to Figure 12-7.

9. Click the **OK** button to close the Menu Editor, then run the program.

10. Choose **Visible** from the **Image** menu.

11. Pull down the **Image** menu. Notice that Visible is checked. Because no code has been written, the check mark remained unchanged.

12. End the program and save your changes but leave the project open.

FIGURE 12-7
The Checked check box causes the menu item to be checked when the program is started.

The code for the Visible menu item will do two things: toggle the Visible property of the image and toggle the check mark. The Not operator can be used to reverse the current status of the properties. The Not operator will turn a True setting into False and a False setting into True.

STEP-BY-STEP ⟹ 12.5

1. Choose the **Visible** command from the **Image** menu to access the Code window.

2. Add the code in CODE Step 2 to the **Visible** menu item's Click event procedure. The first line of code uses the Not operator to set the

image's Visible property to the opposite of what it is currently. The second line of code uses the Not operator to set the menu item's Checked property to the opposite of what it is currently.

CODE Step 2

```
imgAmy.Visible = Not imgAmy.Visible
mnuImageVisible.Checked = Not mnuImageVisible.Checked
```

3. Close the Code window and run the program.

4. Pull down the **Image** menu. Notice that **Visible** is checked.

5. Click the **Visible** command. The image disappears.

6. Pull down the **Image** menu again. Notice that the check mark for **Visible** has also disappeared.

7. Click the **Visible** command again. The image reappears.

8. Pull down the **Image** menu and notice that the check mark also returned.

9. End the program and save your changes but leave the project open.

Creating a Submenu

*S*ubmenus (also called cascading menus) are often used to further organize the options in a menu. As mentioned earlier, indenting menu items in the Menu Editor to the third position creates submenus. In Step-by-Step 12.6, you will create a Size command in the Image menu and two submenus for the Size command.

STEP-BY-STEP ⟹ 12.6

1. Click on the form to select it, then access the Menu Editor.

2. Click the **Next** button four times to create another second-level indented menu item just below the Visible menu item, with the following properties.

Caption: **Size**
Name: **mnuImageSize**

3. Click the **Next** button and the **right arrow button** to create a third-level indented menu item just below the Size menu item, with the following properties.

Caption: **Small**
Name: **mnuImageSizeSmall**

4. Click the **Next** button to create another third-level indented item just below the Small menu item, with the following properties (see Figure 12-8).

Caption: **Large**
Name: **mnuImageSizeLarge**
Checked Checkbox Selected

5. Close the Menu Editor, then access the **Size** submenu in the **Image** menu and choose **Small.**

(continued on next page)

6. Add the code in CODE Step 6 to the **mnuImageSizeSmall** Click event procedure. This event procedure will adjust the Height and Width properties to change the size of the image. The code will also change the Checked property to ensure that the Large menu item loses its check mark and the Small menu item becomes checked.

7. Add the code in CODE Step 7 to the **mnuImageSizeLarge** Click event procedure. This event procedure is similar to the mnuImageSizeSmall event procedure. In this case, however, the image will be made large and the check mark will be moved to the Large menu item.

8. Close the Code window and run the program.

9. Pull down the **Image** menu, access the **Size** submenu, and choose the **Small** command. The image becomes small.

10. Pull down the **Image** menu and access the Size submenu. Notice the check mark is now on the Small menu item.

FIGURE 12-8
Submenus are created at the next level of indention.

11. Choose **Large**. The image becomes large again.

12. End the program and save your changes but leave the project open.

CODE Step 6

```
imgAmy.Height = 1700
imgAmy.Width = 2200
mnuImageSizeLarge.Checked = False
mnuImageSizeSmall.Checked = True
```

CODE Step 7

```
imgAmy.Height = 3400
imgAmy.Width = 4400
mnuImageSizeSmall.Checked = False
mnuImageSizeLarge.Checked = True
```

Inserting Separator Lines in Menus

Often, especially on large menus, separator lines between some menu items can improve readability. For example, Figure 12-9 shows how the Visual Basic Help menu is separated into three sections (items shown in your Help menu may vary). The *separator lines* group the items on the menu, making the menu more user-friendly. The separator lines cannot be selected by the user.

To create a separator line, create a menu item with a single hyphen (-) as the caption. Give each separator line a unique name in the Name property.

FIGURE 12-9

Separator lines can improve readability in menus.

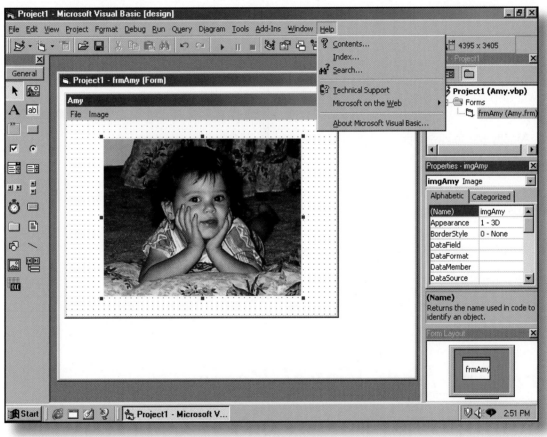

1. Click on the form to select it, then access the Menu Editor.

2. Select the **Size** menu item and click the **Insert** button. A new menu item appears above the Size menu item.

NOTE:

A menu separator should be indented to the same level as the menu items it will separate.

3. Modify the following properties of the new menu item (see Figure 12-10).

Caption: –
Name: **mnuImageSeparator**

4. Close the Menu Editor and run the program.

5. Pull down the **Image** menu. Notice the separator line that appears between the Visible and Size options.

FIGURE 12-10
Entering a hyphen as a caption for a menu item creates a separator line.

6. End the program and save your changes, then remove the project.

Printing from Visual Basic

Even with great user interfaces on the screen, you eventually need or want the information from a program on paper. Visual Basic actually provides a variety of ways to print to a printer. Most commercial software uses a set of Windows procedures that allow printing to any type of printer using many options. However, printing using this method is too complex to cover in this lesson. In this lesson, we'll look at two methods of printing to the default printer.

Printing a Form

Printing the current form is one way to send output to a printer. The *PrintForm command* will send the contents of the form to the printer. To improve the appearance of the printed output, you should hide the command buttons before you issue the PrintForm command and then show the buttons again after the PrintForm command is complete.

IMPORTANT:

The step-by-step exercises in this lesson assume that the computer running the programs has a printer attached, either directly or through a network. The step-by-step exercises that follow may not work on all printer and network configurations.

STEP-BY-STEP ⟹ 12.8

1. Open **Print Form** from your template files and if necessary open the form.

2. Double-click the **Print Form** button and add the code in CODE Step 2 to hide the command buttons, print the form, and then show the command buttons again.

   CODE Step 2

   ```
   'Hide Command Buttons
   cmdCalculate.Visible = False
   cmdPrint.Visible = False
   cmdExit.Visible = False


   'Print Form
   PrintForm


   'Show Command Buttons
   cmdCalculate.Visible = True
   cmdPrint.Visible = True
   cmdExit.Visible = True
   ```

3. Close the Code window and run the program.

4. Key your name in the employee textbox.

5. Key **817** as your total sales and click the **Calculate** button. The sales commission appears on the form.

6. Click the **Print Form** button. After a few seconds the form will begin to print on your default printer.

7. End the program and save your changes. Remove the project but leave Visual Basic open.

Printing Text to the Default Printer

Another way to send output to the printer is the *Printer object*. The Printer object is a collection of programming code that allows you to communicate with the printer. Although there are many options involved in using the printer object, it can be very simple to use. For example, the code below will send the sentence *The quick brown fox jumped over the lazy dog.* to the printer. The EndDoc method closes the connection to the printer. The EndDoc method also signals a laser printer to complete the current page and eject the page.

```
Printer.Print "The quick brown fox jumped over the lazy dog."
Printer.EndDoc
```

243

1. Choose **New Project** from the **File** menu and create a new **Standard EXE** project.

2 Set the form's **Name** property to **frmMain** and the **Caption** property to **Print**.

3. Create a command button.

4. Set the command button's **Name** property to **cmdPrint** and the **Caption** property to **Print**.

5. Double-click the **Print** button and add the code in CODE Step 5, which will print your name on the printer. Replace (Your Name) in the code with your name.

CODE Step 5

```
Printer.Print "(Your Name)"
Printer.EndDoc
```

6. Close the Code window and run the program.

7 Click the **Print** button. After a couple of seconds, your printer should begin printing your name.

8. Save the project with the form name **frmNamePrint** and the project name **NamePrint**, then exit Visual Basic.

Summary

■ Most Windows programs provide menus as part of the user interface.

■ Visual Basic allows you to create menus without writing code by using the Menu Editor.

■ A menu item's Caption property specifies the text that will appear on the menu.

■ Menu items also have a Name property which is used to identify the menu item in code.

■ The level of indention of the menu item in the Menu Editor determines where the menu item appears in the actual menus.

■ When the user selects a command from a menu, a Click event is triggered. Writing code for a menu item is like writing any other Click event procedure.

■ Check marks may be added to the items in a menu to indicate that an option is on or off.

■ Indenting the menu items to the third position creates submenus.

■ To better organize menus, you can insert separator lines by creating menu items with a hyphen as the caption. Separator lines cannot be selected by the user, but they can help group menu items.

■ You can print a form to the printer using the PrintForm command. It is a good idea to hide the command buttons on the form before performing the print operation.

■ You can also print text to the printer using the Printer object. The Printer object allows you to send lines of text to the default printer. The EndDoc method ejects the page from the printer and closes the connection.

LESSON 12 REVIEW QUESTIONS

TRUE/FALSE

Circle the T if the statement is true. Circle the F if it is false.

T F 1. In most programs menus provide the least complete set of options.

T F 2. The command performed by a toolbar button is usually also found on a menu.

T F 3. Visual Basic allows you to create the standard menus that pull down from the menu bar.

T F 4. A menu item you create will be fully functional without any additional code.

T F 5. Because menus pull down from a menu bar, they do not need to be associated with a form.

T F 6. It is common practice to name menu items after the caption of the menu on which they appear.

T F 7. You cannot modify the presence of a check mark next to a menu item from code.

T F 8. Separator lines are used to improve the readability of a menu.

T F 9. The PrintForm statement allows you to print the contents of a form to the default printer.

T F 10. When you create a separator line using the Menu Editor, you do not need to provide a name for the item.

WRITTEN QUESTIONS

Write your answers to the following questions.

11. What type of event is triggered when a user chooses a menu command?

12. What does Visual Basic provide to help you create menus?

13. Where can you include code for the menu item?

14. Which field provides the text that will appear in the menu?

15. What prefix is commonly used when naming menu items?

16. How do you create a sub-menu using the Menu Editor?

17. How do you create a "checked" menu using the Menu Editor?

18. What is another name for a submenu?

19. How do you add a separator line to a menu?

20. Why might the PrintForm statement not work with some computer configurations?

LESSON 12 PROJECTS

PROJECT 12A

1. Start Visual Basic and create a new Visual Basic project.

2. Name your form **frmMain** and give it the caption **Menu.**

3. Create a File menu.

4. Create an Exit menu item indented under the File menu.

5. Add code to the Exit menu item that will end the program.

6. Run the program to verify that it works.

7. Save the project with the form named **frmMenu** and the project named **Menu.**

8. Remove the project but leave Visual Basic open.

PROJECT 12B

1. Open **Print Name** from your template files and if necessary open the form.

2. Add the following code to the Click event procedure of the **Print Name to Printer** button.

```
Dim strName As String

strName = txtName.Text

Printer.Print strName
Printer.EndDoc
```

3. Add code to the textbox that will highlight the text when it is clicked.

4. Create a new menu item that is not indented with the following properties.

   Caption: **File**
   Name: **mnuFile**

5. Create a menu item just below the File menu item, indented to the second level, with the following properties.

   Caption: **Print Name**
   Name: **mnuFilePrintName**

6. Create a menu item just below the Print Name menu item, also indented to the second level, with the following properties.

   Caption: **Exit**
   Name: **mnuFileExit**

7. Create a separator line between the Print Name and Exit menu items.

8. Copy the code for the cmdPrint Click event procedure to the Click event procedure for mnuFilePrintName.

9. Add code to mnuFileExit, which will end the program.

10. Run the program to test the code for the command button and the two menu items.

11. End the program and save your changes. Remove the project but leave Visual Basic open.

PROJECT 12C

1. Open the project **Amy** you worked with earlier in this lesson.

2. Click on the blank line below the last menu item and create a new menu item that is not indented with the following properties.

   Caption: **Color**
   Name: **mnuColor**

3. Create a menu item just below the Color menu item, indented to the second level, with the following properties.

   Caption: **White**
   Name: **mnuColorWhite**
   Checked Checkbox Selected

4. Create a menu item just below the White menu item, also indented to the second level, with the following properties.

   Caption: **Red**
   Name: **mnuColorRed**

5. Create a menu item just below the Red menu item, also indented to the second level, with the following properties.

   Caption: **Blue**
   Name: **mnuColorBlue**

6. Add the following code to the mnuColorWhite Click event procedure. This event procedure will change the background color of the form to white.

   frmAmy.BackColor = vbWhite
   mnuColorWhite.Checked = True
   mnuColorRed.Checked = False
   mnuColorBlue.Checked = False

7. Add the following code to the mnuColorRed Click event procedure. This event procedure will change the background color of the form to Red.

   frmAmy.BackColor = vbRed
   mnuColorWhite.Checked = False
   mnuColorRed.Checked = True
   mnuColorBlue.Checked = False

7. Add the following code to the mnuColorBlue Click event procedure. This event procedure will change the background color of the form to Blue.

   frmAmy.BackColor = vbBlue
   mnuColorWhite.Checked = False
   mnuColorRed.Checked = False
   mnuColorBlue.Checked = True

9. Run the program and verify that the form's background color changes.

10. End the program and save your changes. Remove the project but leave Visual Basic open.

PROJECT 12D

1. Open the **Print Form** project you worked with earlier in this lesson.

2. Create a new menu item that is not indented with the following properties.

   Caption: **File**
   Name: **mnuFile**

3. Create a menu item just below the File menu item, indented to the second level, with the following properties.

   Caption: **Print**
   Name: **mnuFilePrint**

4. Create a menu item just below the Print menu item, also indented to the second level, with the following properties.

   Caption: **Exit**
   Name: **mnuFileExit**

5. Create a separator line between the Print and Exit menu items.

6. Copy the code for the Print command button into the mnuFilePrint Click event procedure.

7. Add code for the mnuFileExit Click event procedure to end the program.

8. Run the program and verify that the options in the File menu work correctly.

9. End the program, save your changes, and exit Visual Basic.

CRITICAL THINKING ACTIVITY

Modify the Profit and Loss program you worked with in Lesson 4. Your program should include all of the following.

1. Menu items that perform the events in each command button.

2. A Print menu item that will print the form.

3. Separator lines in the menus where appropriate.

4. Code with appropriate comments.

5. The use of SelStart and SelLength in each text box.

UNIT 4 REVIEW QUESTIONS ▽

TRUE/FALSE

Circle the T if the statement is true. Circle the F if it is false.

T F   1. As a rule, a Do Loop cannot be nested within a For Next Loop.

T F   2. The Loop keyword marks the end of a block of code contained within a For loop.

T F   3. The For Next loop allows you to count by an increment other than one.

T F   4. The Print statement allows you to print the current form on the default printer.

T F   5. A Click event is triggered when a user chooses a menu command.

MATCHING

Write the letter of the description from Column 2 that best matches the term or phrase in Column 1.

Column 1

_____   6. splash screen

_____   7. iteration structure

_____   8. carriage return

_____   9. separator line

_____   10. submenu

Column 2

A. the automatic advance of the cursor to the next line.

B. a window that appears briefly when a program is started.

C. a cascading menu used to further organize the items in a menu.

D. a line that groups items on a menu.

E. the code required to create a loop.

WRITTEN QUESTIONS

Write your answers to the following questions.

11. Which type of Do loop should you use if you want the code within the loop to be executed at least once?

12. Why is a Counter variable necessary in a For Next loop?

13. How could you use a For Next loop to count backwards?

14. What is an endless loop?

15. Why might it be dangerous to use the DoEvents statement in an event procedure?

16. What function displays a window to prompt the user for input?

17. How do you access the Menu Editor in Visual Basic?

18. How do you associate a menu with a particular form?

19. What value should you enter for the Caption property if you want to create a separator line on a menu?

20. What is the Printer object used for?

UNIT 4 APPLICATIONS

Estimated Time: 1 hour

APPLICATION 4-1

There is a problem in each of the following code segments. State what the problem is, then correct the code.

1.
```
Dim I As Integer
I = 1
Do While I <= 10
        Print "Iteration Number: " & I
Loop
```

2.
```
Dim I As Integer
I = 10
Do
        Print "Iteration Number: " & I
        I = I + 1
Loop Until I = 10
```

3.
```
Dim intCounter As Integer
For intCounter = 1 To 10
        Sum = Sum + 1
Next Sum
```

251

APPLICATION 4-2

Open the **Planets** program you worked with in the Critical Thinking Activity in Lesson 9. Create a Print command button and add code to its Click event procedure to print the form. Include code that will make the command buttons cmdCalc, cmdPrint, and cmdExit invisible on the printed hard copy. Make sure to include code to make them reappear so that the end user can use them. Also include any necessary comments in the code.

APPLICATION 4-3

The *factorial* of a number is the product of all the positive whole numbers from 1 to *n*. The symbol for factorial is !. In the following steps you will add code to a program so it will calculate the factorial of a number entered by the user.

1. Open **Factorial** from your template files.

2. Add the following code to the **Calculate** event procedure.

```
Dim strMessage As String
Dim dblNumber As Double
Dim dblResult As Double
dblNumber = Val(txtNumber.Text)

If dblNumber > 17 Then
    MsgBox "The value is too big.  Please enter another number."
Else
    Dim I As Integer
    dblResult = dblNumber
    For I = dblNumber - 1 To 1 Step -1
        dblResult = dblResult * I
    Next I
    strMessage = dblNumber & "! = " & dblResult
    MsgBox strMessage
End If
```

3. Add code for the textbox that will highlight the text when the textbox is clicked.

4. Test the program by running it, then entering a value and clicking the **Calculate** button.

5. Stop the program by choosing **Exit** from the **File** menu.

6. Add a splash screen to the program. The splash screen should contain at least the name of the program. Save this form as **frmSplash.frm**.

7. Add code to the project, and make the necessary changes to the project settings so that the splash screen is displayed when the program is run.

8. Create an About box that contains your name and the name of the program.

9. Use the Menu Editor to add a **Help** menu to the main form.

10. Add an "About" submenu to the Help menu and add the necessary code to display the About box.

11. Run the program to verify that it works correctly.

12. End the program, save the changes, then remove the project.

APPLICATION 4-4

Find an image that represents your school. The image can be found in a yearbook or magazine and scanned to your computer or you can find an appropriate image on the Internet. Add the image to a form and create menu items (including the Checked property and separator lines where appropriate). The menu items should:

■ Change the size of the image.

■ Show and hide the image.

■ Change the position of the image.

■ Change the BackColor of the form.

■ Print the form.

■ End the program.

INTERNET ACTIVITY

In this activity, you will use the Internet to learn more about earthquakes and write a program that gives information about earthquakes based on an earthquake's measurement on the Richter scale.

1. Open your Web browser.

2. Go to the Web address below.

   `http://www.programvb.com/basics`

3. On the home page, click the **Internet Activities** link.

4. Click the **Unit 4 Internet Activity** link. A list of Web sites that can be used to obtain information about earthquakes appears.

5. Click the links that lead to information about the Richter and Mercalli methods of measuring earthquakes.

6. Click the links to charts that compare the two measurement scales.

7. Write a program that prompts the user for an earthquake measurement using the Richter scale. The program should provide the user with the equivalent (or range) in the Mercalli scale and give the user a description of the effects felt by an earthquake of that magnitude. Include a splash screen and an About box that tells what the program will do.

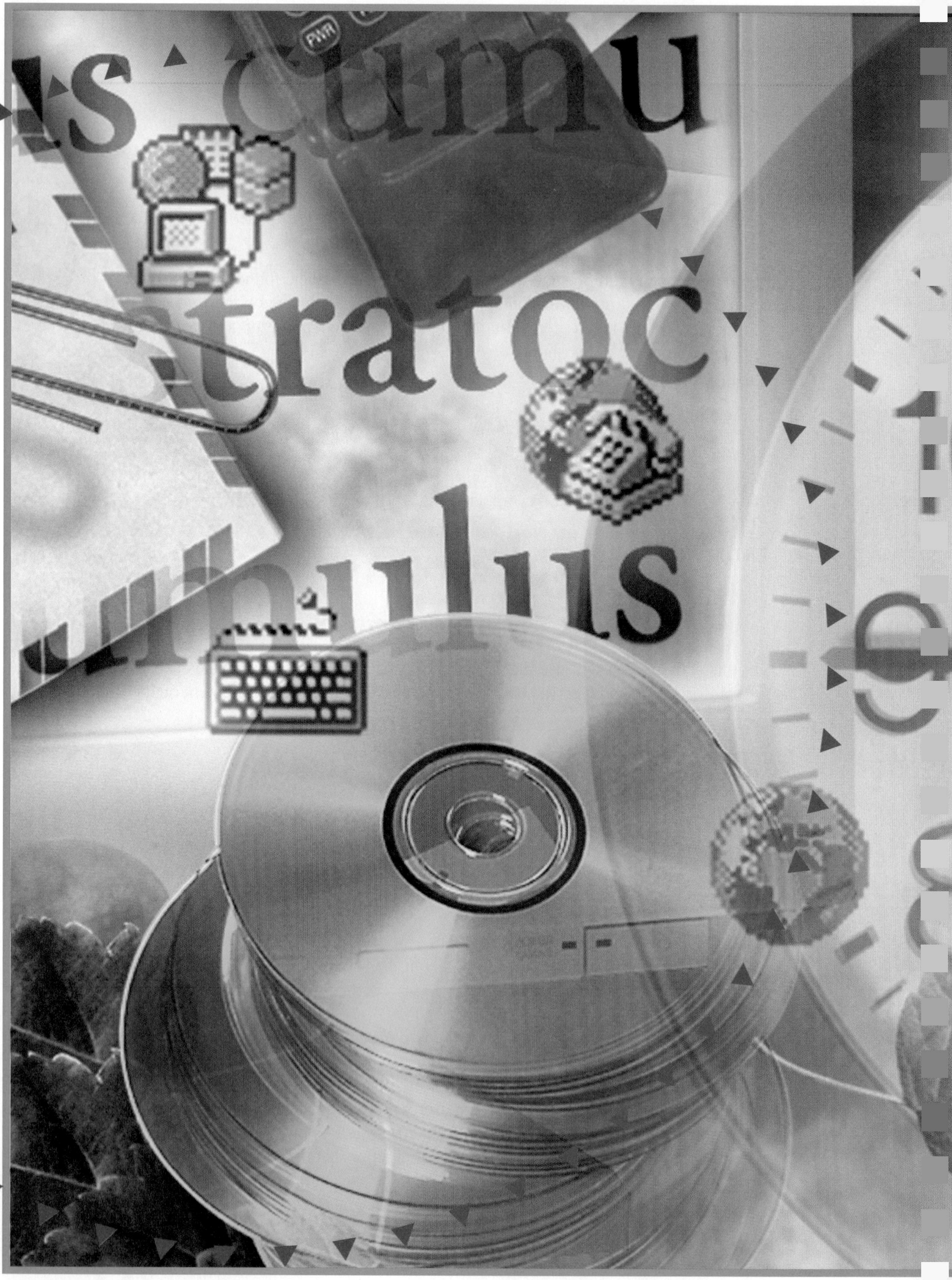
cumu
tratoc
ulus
PWR

GRAPHICS
AND DRAWING

UNIT 5

lesson 13 2 hrs.

Lines and Shapes

lesson 14 1.5 hrs.

Case Study—
Snake Game

Estimated Time for Unit 5: 3.5 hours

LESSON

13

LINES AND SHAPES

OBJECTIVES

When you complete this lesson, you will be able to:

■ Create Line controls.

■ Create Shape controls.

■ Change properties of Line and Shape controls.

■ Manipulate Line and Shape control properties from code.

■ Draw lines from code.

■ Change the ScaleMode property.

■ Draw boxes from code.

🕐 **Estimated Time: 2 hours**

Creating Line Controls

There are two ways to create lines on forms. You can create an object called a Line control or you can use Visual Basic code to draw lines on forms (the Line method). You will learn how to do both in this lesson. First, however, let's look at how to create a Line control.

To create a Line control, use the Line tool, as shown in Figure 13-1. As with other controls, you can click the tool once and draw the line manually, or you can double-click the tool to have a default line drawn for you.

A Line control is like other controls. It has properties and can be manipulated as an object on the form. When naming a Line control, use the lin naming prefix.

Line
Tool

FIGURE 13-1
The Line tool allows you to create Line controls on forms.

STEP-BY-STEP 13.1

1. Start Visual Basic and create a new project.

2. Set the **Name** property of the form to **frmMain** and set the **Caption** property to **Lines & Shapes**.

3. Click the **Line** tool in the toolbox. Move the pointer over the form. Notice that the pointer changes to a cross.

4. Near the top of the form, drag the cross pointer to draw a horizontal line about 3255 twips long. Your screen should appear similar to Figure 13-2.

5. Set the **Name** property of the line to **linLine1**.

6. Near the bottom left of the form, draw a diagonal line that is about 2055 twips long.

7. Set the **Name** property of the diagonal line to **linLine2**.

8. Save the form as **frmLines&Shapes** and the project as **Lines&Shapes**. Leave the project open for Step-by-Step 13.2.

FIGURE 13-2

Line controls exist as objects on a form and have their own set of properties.

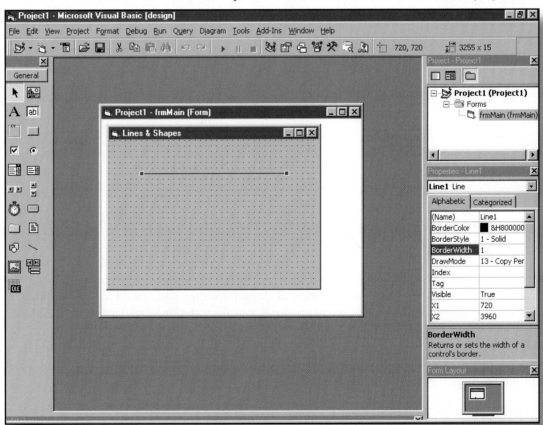

257

Creating Shape Controls

Shape controls are similar to Line controls. A Shape control has additional properties beyond that of a Line control. One of the most important properties of a Shape control is the Shape property. The Shape property specifies the actual shape of the object. A Shape control can be in the form of a rectangle, square, circle, oval, rounded rectangle, or rounded square.

The Shape tool, shown in Figure 13-3, is located to the left of the Line tool. When naming shapes, use the shp naming prefix.

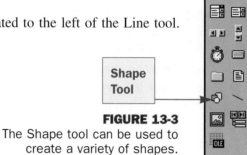

Shape Tool

FIGURE 13-3
The Shape tool can be used to create a variety of shapes.

STEP-BY-STEP ▷ 13.2

1. Click the **Shape** tool in the toolbox. Move the pointer to the bottom right of the form. Notice that the pointer changes to a cross.

2. Drag the cross pointer diagonally towards the middle of the form to create a rectangle (about 2055 X 1095 twips). Your screen should appear similar to Figure 13-4.

3. Set the **Name** property to **shpOval.**

4. Select the **Shape** property.

5. Click the **down arrow** and select **Oval** from the drop-down list. The rectangle changes to an oval.

6. Save the changes but leave the project open for Step-by-Step 13.3.

Changing Properties of Line and Shape Controls

Line and Shape controls have the typical properties that you would expect to find. The BorderColor property specifies the color of the lines that form the line or shape. The BorderWidth property specifies the width of those same lines.

In addition to the BorderColor and BorderWidth properties, Shape controls have a FillStyle and FillColor property. The FillStyle property allows you to fill the shape with a pattern or a solid color. The FillColor property specifies the color of the pattern in the shape.

FIGURE 13-4
Shapes appear as rectangles by default.

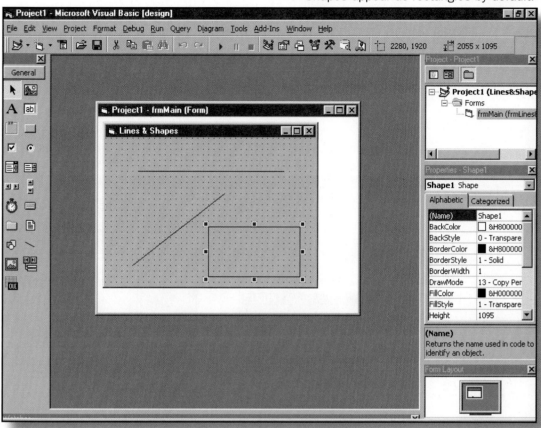

S TEP-BY-STEP ⟩ 13.3

1. Select **linLine1** and click the **BorderColor** property. A down arrow will appear.

2. Click the **down arrow** and click the **Palette** tab. A list of colors appears.

3. Click a blue square. Notice that the line changes to the color blue.

4. Change the **BorderWidth** property to **4**. The width of the border line for the square becomes wider.

5. Select the oval.

6. Select the **BorderColor** property.

7. Click the **down arrow** and click the **Palette** tab. A list of colors appears.

8. Click a red square. Notice that the border of the oval changes to the color red.

9. Click the **FillStyle** property.

10. Click the **down arrow** and select **Solid** from the drop-down list. The color of the oval becomes black with a red border, as shown in Figure 13-5.

(continued on next page)

11. Click the **FillColor** property.

12. Select **Red** from the color palette. The oval changes to red.

13. Save the changes to the project and remove the project.

FIGURE 13-5
The BorderColor, BorderWidth, FillStyle, and FillColor properties allow you to change the appearance and color of lines and shapes.

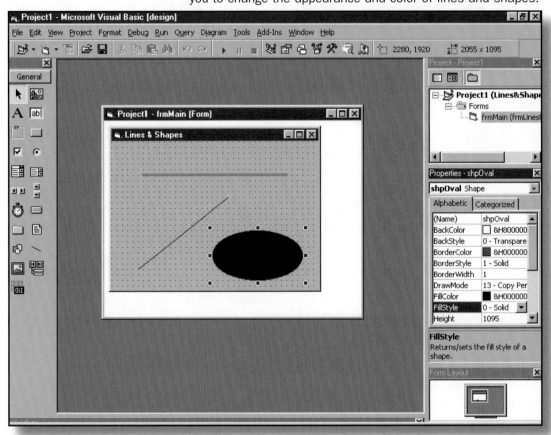

Manipulating Line and Shape Control Properties from Code

Like other properties, the properties of lines and shapes can be changed from Visual Basic code. For example, the shape of a Shape control can be changed as a program runs.

STEP-BY-STEP 13.4

1. Open **ShapeDraw** from your template files and if necessary, open **frmMain**. Your screen should appear similar to Figure 13-6.

2. Double-click the **Draw** button. The Code window appears. Before entering the code for the Draw button's event procedure, we need a form-level variable to store the current shape of the Shape control.

3. Add the code in CODE Step 3 to the General Declarations section to make sngShape a Single variable.

CODE Step 3

```
Option Explicit
Dim sngShape As Single
```

4. If necessary, select **cmdDraw** from the Object drop-down box, and add the code in CODE Step 4 to make shpMyShape become visible and set its shape equal to sngShape.

CODE Step 4

```
shpMyShape.Visible = True
shpMyShape.Shape = sngShape
```

5. Close the Code window but leave the project open for Step-by-Step 13.5.

FIGURE 13-6
This program allows the user to select the shape of the Shape control.

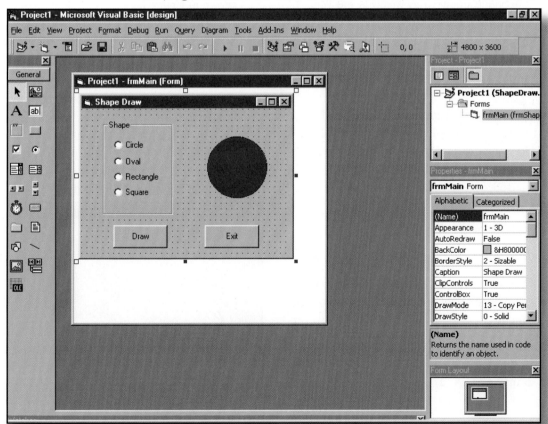

Recall that when using option buttons in a program, you write an event procedure for each option button that takes the appropriate action for that button. In this case, each time an option button is clicked, the sngShape variable will be set to the value of the shape that corresponds to that button. When the Draw button is clicked, the actual Shape property will be set to the value of the most recently clicked option button.

STEP-BY-STEP ⇒ 13.5

1. Double-click the **Circle** option button. The Code window opens.

2. Add the code in CODE Step 2 to set sngShape equal to 3, which is the value of a circle.

   CODE Step 2

   ```
   sngShape = 3
   ```

3. Select **optOval** from the Object drop-down box, and add the code in CODE Step 3 to set sngShape equal to 2, which is the value of an oval.

   CODE Step 3

   ```
   sngShape = 2
   ```

4. Select **optRectangle** from the Object drop-down box, and add the code in CODE Step 4 to set sngShape equal to 0, which is the value of a rectangle.

   CODE Step 4

   ```
   sngShape = 0
   ```

5. Select **optSquare** from the Object drop-down box, and add the code in CODE Step 5 to set sngShape equal to 1, which is the value of a square.

   CODE Step 5

   ```
   sngShape = 1
   ```

6. Select **Form** from the Object drop-down box, and add the code in CODE Step 6 to make the Circle the default option button by setting the value of optCircle equal to True.

   CODE Step 6

   ```
   optCircle.Value = True
   ```

7. Close the Code window and run the program.

8. Select the **Square** option button and click the **Draw** button. A blue square appears as shown in Figure 13-7.

9. Test the other option buttons, then end the program.

10. Save the changes to the project and remove the project.

FIGURE 13-7
The shape changes when the code changes the Shape property.

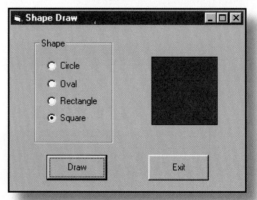

Drawing Lines from Code

Visual Basic provides a method for drawing lines from code called the *Line method*. The lines drawn from code, however, are not Line controls. The lines drawn from code are drawn on the form but are not treated as a separate object. This is similar to the way the text created by the Print command appears in a form but is not a Label control.

IMPORTANT:

Once you have drawn a line using the Line method, you cannot manipulate its properties.

The Line method is easy to use. But to understand how to use the Line method, you must first understand the coordinate system on a form.

Understanding Coordinates

You have used the coordinate system of a form in earlier lessons. The properties like Top and Left that you used to position buttons and images were using the coordinate system. The top left point on a form has an X coordinate of zero and a Y coordinate of zero. The Top and Left properties measure the distance from the top and the distance from the left, respectively.

To use the Line method, you need to think in terms of X and Y rather than Top and Left. For example, a horizontal line might extend from point (500, 500) to point (2500, 500), as shown in Figure 13-8. The main difference between the coordinates on a form and the coordinates you have used in geometry is that the origin (0, 0) appears at the top left corner rather than in the center of the form. If you understand geometry well, you might want to think of the form as the fourth quadrant of the coordinate plane. There are no negative values of X or Y. As you move toward the bottom of the form the X-coordinate value increases. As you move toward the right side of a form, the Y-coordinate value increases.

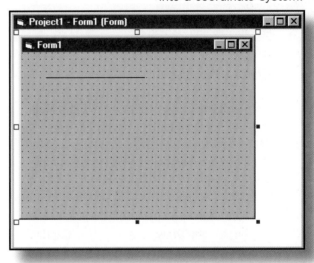

FIGURE 13-8
A Visual Basic form is mapped into a coordinate system.

Using the Line Method

To use the Line method, you must specify the endpoints of the line you want to draw and the color in which you want the line to appear. You can specify color using a numeric value or you can use one of the predefined names shown in Table 13-1.

For example, the code below will draw a blue line from coordinate (20, 20) to coordinate (20, 100).

```
Line (20, 20)-(20, 100), vbBlue
```

By default, the coordinate system is measured in twips. You used twips when positioning controls with the Top and Left properties. Twips are so tiny (1440 per inch) that a line that is 100 twips long appears very small on the screen.

TABLE 13-1

COLOR VALUES

Name	Color
vbBlack	Black
vbRed	Red
vbGreen	Green
vbYellow	Yellow
vbBlue	Blue
vbMagenta	Magenta
vbCyan	Cyan
vbWhite	White

STEP-BY-STEP 13.6

1. Create a new project.

2. Set the **Name** property of the form to **frmMain** and set the **Caption** property to **Triangle**.

3. Create a command button and place it in the bottom right corner of the form.

4. Set the **Name** property of the command button to **cmdDraw** and set the **Caption** property to **Draw**.

5. Double-click the **Draw** button.

6. Add the code in CODE Step 6 to draw a blue vertical line in the upper left corner of the form.

CODE Step 6

```
Line (20, 20)-(20, 100), vbBlue
```

7. Close the Code window. Run the program and click the **Draw** button. Notice that a small blue line appears as shown in Figure 13-9.

8. End the program.

9. Save the form as **frmTriangle** and save the project as **Triangle**. Leave the project open for Step-by-Step 13.7.

FIGURE 13-9
The Line method draws a tiny line on the form.

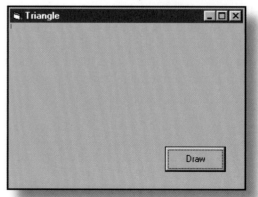

1. Double-click the **Draw** button. Just below the previous code, add the code in CODE Step 1 to draw a blue horizontal line that begins at the base of the vertical line.

2. Close the Code window and run the program. Verify that a small blue L shape appears at the top of the form when the **Draw** button is clicked.

3. End the program. Double-click the **Draw** button and add the code in CODE Step 3 to draw a blue diagonal line that connects the two other lines.

4. Close the Code window and run the program again.

5. Click the **Draw** button. A small blue triangle appears in the top right corner of the screen as shown in Figure 13-10.

6. End the program and save your changes but leave the project open for Step-by-Step 13.8.

FIGURE 13-10
The three Line methods combined draw a triangle.

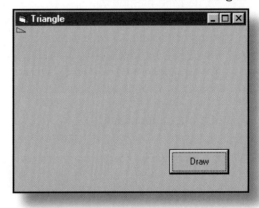

CODE Step 1

```
Line (20, 100)-(200, 100), vbBlue
```

CODE Step 3

```
Line (200, 100)-(20, 20), vbBlue
```

Changing the ScaleMode Property

Using twips as the unit of measure is not always the most practical. While Visual Basic defaults to the measurement in twips, you can use other scales, such as pixels and points. The *ScaleMode property* allows you to adjust the coordinate system on a form to be measured (from largest to smallest) in points, pixels, or twips.

 NOTE:

There are 72 points in an inch.

For example, to change the unit of measure to pixels, use a line of code as follows:

```
ScaleMode = vbPixels
```

To set other scales, replace vbPixels with vbTwips or vbPoints.

1. Double-click the **Draw** button.

2. Above the code that draws the triangle, add the code in CODE Step 2 to set the scale mode to pixels instead of twips.

   CODE Step 2

   ```
   ScaleMode = vbPixels
   ```

3. Close the Code window and run the program.

4. Click the **Draw** button. Notice that changing the scale mode to pixels increased the size of the triangle.

5. End the program, save the changes, and remove the project.

Drawing Boxes from Code

The Line method can also be used to draw a box on a form. The code below will draw a box with its top left corner at (40, 40) and its bottom right corner at (200, 100). The addition of the "B" at the end of the line of code directs the method to create a box rather than a diagonal line.

```
Line (40, 40)-(200, 100), vbBlue, B
```

What would be the endpoints of a line become the corners of a box when the B is added to the end of the Line method.

1. Create a new project.

2. Set the **Name** property of the form to **frmMain** and set the **Caption** property to **Box**.

3. Create a command button and place it in the bottom right corner of the form.

4. Set the **Name** property of the command button to **cmdDraw** and set the **Caption** property to **Draw**.

5. Double-click the **Draw** button.

6. Add the code in CODE Step 6 to draw a blue diagonal line.

   CODE Step 6

   ```
   ScaleMode = vbPixels
   Line (40, 40)-(200, 100), vbBlue
   ```

7. Run the program and click the **Draw** button. Notice that a blue line appears as shown in Figure 13-11.

8. End the program and double-click the **Draw** button.

9. Position the cursor at the end of the line of code entered in CODE Step 6 and key **, B** as shown in CODE Step 9.

10. Close the Code window and run the program.

11. Click the **Draw** button. Notice that instead of drawing a diagonal line, the Draw button now draws a box.

12. End the program. Save the form as **frmBox** and the project as **Box**. Leave the project open for Step-by-Step 13.10.

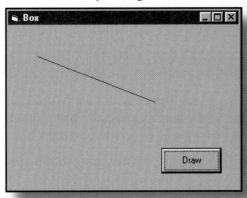

FIGURE 13-11
This blue line can become a box
by adding a B to the code.

CODE Step 9

```
Line (40, 40)-(200, 100), vbBlue, B
```

There is one more option you can use when creating boxes. By adding an "F" to the end of the code, as shown below, you can create a box filled with color, rather than just bordered by color.

```
Line (40, 40)-(200, 100), vbBlue, BF
```

STEP-BY-STEP ⟹ 13.10

1. Double-click the **Draw** button.

2. Position the cursor at the end of the line of code that draws the box and add **F** as shown in CODE Step 2.

3. Close the Code window and run the program.

4. Click the **Draw** button. Notice that the box is now solid blue, as shown in Figure 13-12.

5. End the program and save the changes, then exit Visual Basic.

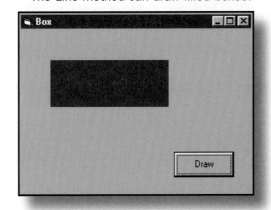

FIGURE 13-12
The Line method can draw filled boxes.

CODE Step 2

```
Line (40, 40)-(200, 100), vbBlue, BF
```

Summary

- There are two ways to create lines on forms. You can create a Line control, or you can use the Line method to draw a line on a form using Visual Basic code.

- A Shape control is similar to a Line control except that the Shape control contains several additional properties, which allow you to change the shape and shading of the control.

- The BorderColor and BorderWidth properties specify the color and width of ordinary lines and the color and width of border lines for a shape. The FillColor and FillStyle properties specify how a shape will be filled.

- The properties of both Line controls and Shape controls can be manipulated from Visual Basic code much like any other control you might create.

- Once you have drawn a line with the Line method, you cannot manipulate it. Like the Print statement, the Line method draws directly on a form.

- Distance and position on a form is measured using coordinates. The top left corner of a form has the coordinates (0, 0).

- All coordinates are positive. As you move toward the bottom of a form, the X-coordinate value increases. As you move toward the right of a form, the Y-coordinate value increases.

- You specify where the Line method should draw a line by using specific coordinates. You can also specify the color of the line in the parameters.

- The ScaleMode property allows you to adjust the coordinate system of a form to be measured in twips, pixels, or points.

- The Line method can also create boxes, either filled or unfilled.

LESSON 13 REVIEW QUESTIONS

TRUE/FALSE

Circle the T if the statement is true. Circle the F if it is false.

T F   1. There are two ways to create lines on forms.

T F   2. The lin naming prefix is used for Line controls.

T F   3. A Line control cannot be manipulated from code.

T F   4. A Line control does not have a FillColor property.

T F 5. The Line method for creating Line controls does not have the ability to set the line's color.

T F 6. The Shape tool is located on the standard toolbar.

T F 7. The BorderWidth property has no effect on a Shape control.

T F 8. You can use the Line method to draw a box.

T F 9. You cannot adjust the properties of a line drawn with the Line method.

T F 10. By default the coordinate system is measured in pixels.

WRITTEN QUESTIONS

Write your answers to the following questions.

11. What naming prefix is used to name a Shape control?

12. How do you change the shape of a Shape control?

13. Which property allows you to change the color of a Line control?

14. How many twips are in an inch?

15. Name the six possible forms for a Shape control.

16. What coordinates are assigned to the top left corner of a form?

17. Which property allows you to adjust the scale of measurements on a form?

18. Rank the three coordinate system scales in order from largest to smallest.

19. Why are coordinates (25, -10) not valid when positioning an object on a form?

20. What does the addition of **BF** to the end of the code using the Line method indicate?

PROJECT 13A

Start Visual Basic. Using the Line and Shape tools, draw a wagon similar to the one in Figure 13-13.

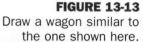

FIGURE 13-13
Draw a wagon similar to the one shown here.

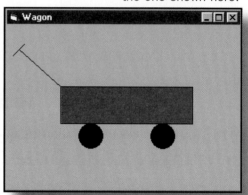

PROJECT 13B

1. Open **GrowingCircle** from your template files.

2. Add the following code for the **Grow** button to make the width of the circle increase by 5 until it reaches 3000.

```
Dim intWidth As Integer

For intWidth = 100 To 3000 Step 5
   shpCircle.Width = intWidth
Next intWidth

cmdGrow.Enabled = False
cmdShrink.Enabled = True
```

3. Add the following code for the **Shrink** button to make the width of the circle decrease by 5 until it reaches 100.

```
Dim intWidth As Integer

For intWidth = 3000 To 100 Step -5
   shpCircle.Width = intWidth
Next intWidth

cmdShrink.Enabled = False
cmdGrow.Enabled = True
```

4. Run the program to verify that the circle increases and decreases in size.

5. Save the changes to the project but leave the project open.

PROJECT 13C

1. If necessary, open the **GrowingCircle** project you modified in Project 13B.

2. Create a command button beneath the Shrink command button.

3. Set the **Name** property of the new button to **cmdChangeShape** and set the **Caption** property to **Change Shape**.

4. Add the following code for the **Change Shape** button to cycle between the different shapes.

```
If shpCircle.Shape < 5 Then
    shpCircle.Shape = shpCircle.Shape + 1
Else
    shpCircle.Shape = 0
End If
```

5. Run the program to verify that the circle changes shape.

6. Save the changes to the project, then remove the project.

CRITICAL THINKING ACTIVITY

Draw a stick figure similar to the one in Figure 13-14 using Visual Basic code. The program should use four different option buttons to change the color of the stick figure. (HINT: Use strcolor as the declared variable.)

FIGURE 13-14
Using code, draw a stick figure
similar to the one shown here.

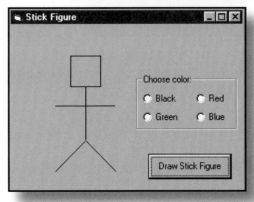

CASE STUDY— SNAKE GAME

OBJECTIVES

When you complete this lesson, you will be able to:

■ Run the Snake Game.

■ Draw with individual pixels and use AutoRedraw.

■ Describe how the Snake Game draws and controls the direction of the snake.

■ Describe how the code of the Snake Game functions.

⏱ Estimated Time: 1.5 hours

Running the Snake Game

The Snake Game that you ran in Lesson 1 is an example of how a simple game can be created in Visual Basic with very little code. Let's run the program again as a reminder of how the game is played.

STEP-BY-STEP ⟹ 14.1

1. Start Visual Basic and open **SnakeGame** from your Lesson 1 template files.

2. Run the program and play the game at least once to re-familiarize yourself with the game's operation.

3. End the program and remove the project.

The Snake Game is based on a very simple principle. A blue line (the snake) grows within a blue box. The user can change the direction in which the snake grows. As long as the user steers the line in a direction that keeps a clear path ahead of the line, the game continues. But if the line crosses itself or hits the blue box, the game ends.

Writing a program like the Snake Game is not difficult. Visual Basic includes a method that allows a single pixel to be changed to a particular color. To draw the growing snake, a loop must repeat until the snake crosses its own tail or hits the blue box. With each iteration of the loop, another pixel is turned blue.

Drawing with Pixels and Using AutoRedraw

There are only three Visual Basic features that the Snake Game uses that you have not yet used in the lessons of this book. The first is the method that allows you to draw on a form one pixel at a time. The second is a feature that allows you to retrieve the color of a specific pixel. Finally, there is a feature that prevents the graphics you draw from being erased if another windows covers the graphics you have drawn.

Using PSet to Draw

The *PSet method* is an easy-to-use feature that allows you to change the color of individual pixels on a form. PSet uses the same coordinate system you learned about in Lesson 13. To use PSet, you identify the pixel using X,Y coordinates and specify a color for the pixel. The example below turns the pixel at point (120, 200) red.

```
PSet (120, 200), vbRed
```

NOTE:

The PSet method is best used when the ScaleMode property is set to pixel measurement.

Even though you might think of PSet as turning on individual pixels, in reality the method just changes the color of the pixel. It is best for you to think of all of the pixels as on at all times. Many of the pixels are set to the background color, which makes them appear to be "off". The PSet method can be used to change a pixel to a color that is different from the background or return the pixel to the background color.

1. Create a new Visual Basic project.

2. Set the **Name** property of the form to **frmMain** and set the **Caption** property to **Draw Line**.

3. Create a command button.

4. Set the **Name** property to **cmdLine** and set the **Caption** property to **Draw Line**.

5. Double-click the **Draw Line** button to open the Code window.

6. Add the code in CODE Step 6 to draw a red line one pixel at a time.

CODE Step 6

```
ScaleMode = vbPixels
Dim Counter As Integer

For Counter = 40 To 200
    PSet (Counter, 50), vbRed
Next Counter
```

7. Close the Code window and run the program.

8. Click the **Draw Line** button. A red line is drawn as shown in Figure 14-1.

9. End the program. Save your form as **frmDrawLine** and save your project as **DrawLine**. Remove the project but leave Visual Basic open.

FIGURE 14-1
Clicking the Draw Line command button draws a red line on the form one pixel at a time.

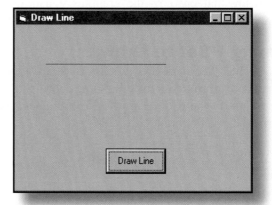

Using the Point Method

The *Point method* retrieves the Visual Basic color constant of the specified pixel. The method works hand-in-hand with the PSet method. Use PSet to change the color of a pixel and use Point to determine the current color of a pixel. For example, the code below stores the color of the pixel at Point (120, 200) to the variable lngPixelColor.

```
lngPixelColor = Point(120, 200)
```

You will see the Point method in action when you analyze the Snake Game code.

Using AutoRedraw

The *AutoRedraw property* allows you to choose whether you want to draw temporary graphics or persistent graphics. A *temporary graphic* is one that is not redrawn once another window or object hides the graphic. A *persistent graphic* is one that will automatically redraw itself and be redisplayed after being hidden by another window or object.

For example, suppose you have a program that uses PSet to plot a mathematical function on the screen. While the program is drawing the graphic, a dialog box pops up to alert you to some condition involving another program or the network. If the dialog box covers all or part of the graphic, the drawing will be lost if it has been created as a temporary graphic. A persistent graphic, however, will be automatically redrawn as soon as the dialog box covering it is removed.

To make the graphics created with the Line and PSet methods persistent, use the line of code below.

```
AutoRedraw = True
```

You will see an example of the difference AutoRedraw makes as we analyze the code of the Snake Game.

How the Snake Game Draws the Snake

The snake that appears on the Snake Game is drawn one pixel at a time using PSet. When the user clicks one of the direction buttons, the path of the snake changes to reflect the direction the user selected.

There are four variables that are key to drawing and controlling the snake. The first two variables, sngX and sngY, specify the point on the form where the next pixel will appear. When the pixel at point (sngX, sngY) is turned blue, the values of sngX and sngY are changed to the position of the next pixel. These adjustments to sngX and sngY are accomplished using two other variables: sngXFactor and sngYFactor.

The variable sngXFactor specifies the number of pixels that are to be added to sngX to advance the head of the snake in the X direction. The variable sngYFactor specifies the number of pixels that are to be added to sngY to advance the head of the snake in the Y direction.

For example, suppose the head of the snake is moving down, as shown in Figure 14-2. When the head is moving down, sngXFactor is zero because there is no change to the X coordinate as the snake moves down. The variable sngYFactor is one because with each iteration of the loop the Y coordinate must increase by one pixel.

FIGURE 14-2
When moving down, the Y coordinate must increase by one. The X coordinate, however, must stay constant.

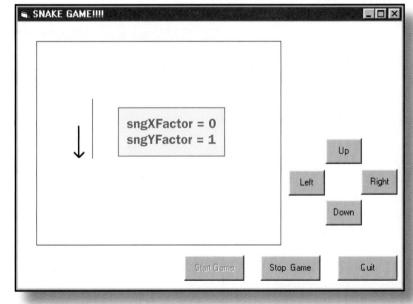

In Figure 14-3, the head of the snake is moving to the right. In this case, sngXFactor is one because the X coordinate must increase by one pixel with each iteration of the loop. The Y coordinate, however, does not change because the movement is horizontal. Therefore, sngYFactor is zero.

FIGURE 14-3
When moving to the right, the X coordinate must increase
by one. The Y coordinate, however, must stay constant.

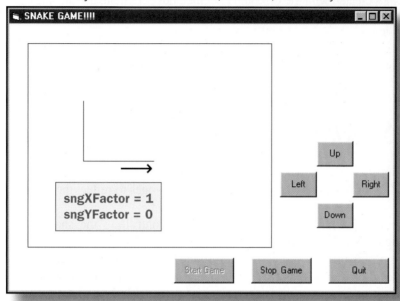

FIGURE 14-4
When moving up, the Y coordinate must be decreased by adding -1.

Moving the snake up and left requires negative values because the snake is moving toward either the top or the left. To move the head of the snake up, the sngYFactor must be –1. Adding the negative value to sngY moves the XY coordinate nearer to the top of the form. In Figure 14-4, you can see how when sngXFactor is zero and sngYFactor is negative one, the snake moves up.

Finally, to move the head of the snake to the left, sngXFactor must be –1. Figure 14-5 shows the coordinate factors necessary to move left.

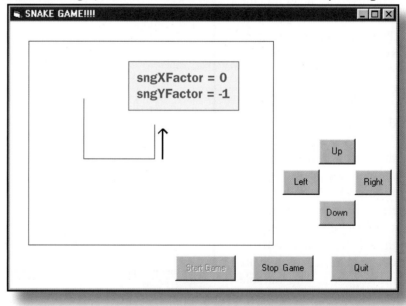

As we analyze the code, you will see how the sngXFactor and sngYFactor are set to the appropriate values and how the snake is actually drawn.

FIGURE 14-5
Moving to the left is similar to moving right,
except the sngXFactor becomes -1.

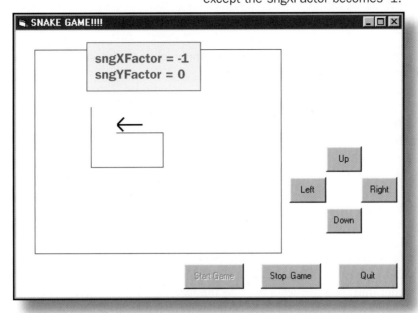

Analyzing the Snake Game Code

Before we analyze the details of the Snake Game code, let's get an overview of how the program flow is controlled and what each button actually does.

STEP-BY-STEP ⟹ 14.3

1. Open the **Snake Game** project again and if necessary, open **frmMainForm**.

2. If necessary, resize the project window to see all seven command buttons.

3. Double-click the **Start Game** button to open the Code window.

4. Scroll to the top of the Code window.

5. Leave the Code window open as a reference as you read the paragraphs that follow.

The primary work of the game is done in the Start Game button's Click event procedure. When the user clicks the Start Game button, the box that contains the snake is drawn and a loop begins that starts drawing the snake a pixel at a time. This loop continues until one of three things happens:

1. The user runs the snake into a wall or into its tail
2. The user clicks the Stop Game button
3. The user clicks the Quit button

As you will see when we look at the code, the DoEvents function allows other events to be processed as the Start Game button's Click event procedure is being executed. For example, even though the Start Game button's Click event procedure is still being executed, the user can click the Stop Game button to end the game. The Do Events function also allows the user to click the direction buttons.

The Up, Down, Left, and Right buttons simply change the sngXFactor and sngYFactor variables to change the direction of the snake.

Let's look at the code in detail.

Form-Level Variables

There are three form-level variables necessary. First, we need a way to stop the program if the user clicks the Stop Game button. We can declare a Boolean variable named blnStop to signal that the user wishes to stop the game. The declaration of the blnStop variable is shown below.

```
Dim blnStop As Boolean    'Flag to stop game when user clicks the
Stop Game button
```

You'll see later in the code how the blnStop variable is used to stop the game.

Two more form-level variables are necessary. The sngXFactor and sngYFactor variables you learned about earlier must be form-level because the factors will be changed by the direction buttons and used by the Start Game button. By making them form-level variables, the values set by the code for the direction buttons will be available in the Start Game button's Click event procedure. The two declarations appear below.

```
Dim sngYFactor As Single
Dim sngXFactor As Single
```

The Start Game Button

As you learned earlier, the primary code for the game is in the Start Game button's Click event procedure. At the heart of the event procedure is a loop. The loop repeats until the snake runs into itself or the wall. The loop will also stop if the user clicks the Stop Game button or quits the program.

S TEP-BY-STEP ⇒ 14.4

1. If necessary, select **cmdStart** from the object drop-down box in the Code window. The Start Game button's Click event procedure is visible in the Code window.

2. Leave the Code window open as a reference as you complete Lesson 14.

Before we look at the details of the loop, let's see what the procedure does before the loop begins.

First, six local variables are declared to be used within this procedure.

```
Dim sngX As Single
Dim sngY As Single
Dim lngSnakeColor As Long
Dim lngWasteTime As Long
Dim lngMySpeed As Long
Dim intI As Integer
```

The variables sngX and sngY are used to keep track of the next pixel that will be turned blue as the snake grows. The variable lngSnakeColor will store the color used to draw the box and the snake. We will set this to blue later. The lngWasteTime variable will be used as a counter in a loop that simply delays the loop so that the snake does not move too fast. The lngMySpeed variable will allow you to adjust the length of the delay created by the lngWasteTime loop. Finally, the intI integer is just a variable required for using the MsgBox function.

The next two lines of code (shown below) take care of some housekeeping before the loop begins. First, the Start Game button is disabled. This is important because we do not want the user to start more than one instance of the game simultaneously. The second line sets the blnStop variable to False. This Boolean variable is set to True if the user clicks the Stop Game button.

```
cmdStart.Enabled = False 'Disable Start Game button
blnStop = False 'Set Stop flag to false
```

The next lines of code initialize the key variables to prepare for the start of the game. As shown in the line of code below, the snake color is set to vbBlue. The color saved in lngSnakeColor is used to draw the box and the snake. Therefore, you can change the color here to vbRed or some other selection and that color will be used by the code that follows.

```
lngSnakeColor = vbBlue
```

The lngMySpeed variable is initialized to 200000. Depending on the speed of your computer, this value may need to be adjusted to achieve the playing speed you desire. The sngX and sngY variables are set to 100. This places the starting point for the snake at point (100, 100). By setting sngXFactor to 0 and sngYFactor to 1, the snake will initially be heading down the form.

```
lngMySpeed = 200000
sngX = 100
sngY = 100
sngXFactor = 0
sngYFactor = 1
```

The next lines (shown below) turn AutoRedraw on, set the ScaleMode to measure in pixels, and make the Snake Game logo invisible to prepare for the drawing of the box.

```
AutoRedraw = True
ScaleMode = vbPixels
imgSnakeLogo.Visible = False 'Make Snake Game logo invisible
```

1. With the Code window still open, run the **Snake Game** program.

2. Click the **Start Game** button to begin the game.

3. Click the **Stop Game** button. A message box appears notifying you that the game has been stopped.

4. Drag the title bar of the message box to move the message box around the screen. Notice that because AutoRedraw is set to True the lines created as you played the Snake Game remain on the screen when the dialog box is moved.

5. Click the **OK** button to dismiss the message box, then end the program. The Code window should still be open with the cursor in the **cmdStart** Click event procedure.

6. Change the code for **AutoRedraw** to **False**.

7. Run the program and click the **Start Game** button.

8. Click the **Stop Game** button.

9. Drag the dialog box to the top left corner of the Snake Game form.

10. Drag the dialog box to the bottom right corner of the Snake Game form. Notice that any of the blue lines that were beneath the dialog box disappeared as shown in Figure 14-6.

11. Click the **OK** button to dismiss the message box, then end the Snake Game program.

12. Set **AutoRedraw** back to **True**.

13. Leave the Code window open and follow along with the paragraphs below that analyze the code. Scroll the Code window as needed.

Now that all of the initial work is done and the variables are initialized, the next step is to draw the box. Two lines of code (shown below) draw the box and erase anything that might be in the box. The first Line method draws the box using the color specified by lngSnakeColor. The second Line method draws a white box that is filled with white inside the first box. The result is that any lines left over from the last time the game was played are painted white to clear the playing area.

```
'Draw box
Line (25, 25)-Step(330, 265), lngSnakeColor, B
Line (27, 27)-Step(326, 260), vbWhite, BF
```

There is a slight difference between the code above and the way you have used the Line method. The Step keyword causes the second point to be defined in relation to the first one. In other words, the lower right corner of the box is 330 pixels to the right and 265 pixels down from the upper left corner. Therefore, if you change the position of the upper left corner, the lower right will adjust to retain the same size box.

FIGURE 14-6
When AutoRedraw is set to False, the lines drawn
by the Snake Game are only temporary graphics.

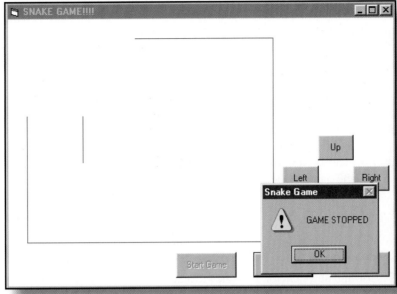

The Start Game Button's Loop

We are finally ready to analyze the loop. The loop adds one pixel to the snake with each iteration. The sngXFactor and sngYFactor determine where the next pixel is added. Look at the code below. With each iteration of the loop, the PSet method draws a pixel in the color of the snake. Then the code immediately increases sngX by the value in sngXFactor. The code also increases sngY by the value in sngYFactor.

```
'Event loop
Do
    DoEvents 'Allows other programs to run
    For lngWasteTime = 0 To lngMySpeed
    Next lngWasteTime
    PSet (sngX, sngY), lngSnakeColor
    sngX = sngX + sngXFactor
    sngY = sngY + sngYFactor
Loop Until ((Point(sngX, sngY) = lngSnakeColor) Or blnStop = True)
```

The loop continues drawing pixels until the snake hits a wall or its tail or until blnStop becomes True. To determine if the snake has hit a wall or its tail, the Point method is used to test the color of the pixel that the loop will set in the next iteration. If that pixel is already the color of the snake and wall, the loop ends.

The loop also includes the DoEvents statement to allow other buttons and events to be processed while the game runs. Because the snake will grow too quickly on most computers, a For Next loop is used to delay the loop for an instant during each iteration of the loop. Adjusting lngMySpeed to a number other than 200000 will change the speed of the snake.

Game Over

When the loop finally ends, we want to inform the user of the reason the game has ended. If the variable blnStop is still False, then the game ended because the snake hit the wall or its tail. If blnStop is True, then we know the user stopped the game with the Stop Game button. The code below uses an If statement to decide which message should be displayed.

```
If blnStop = False Then
  intI = MsgBox("GAME OVER!", vbExclamation, "Snake Game")
Else
  intI = MsgBox("GAME STOPPED", vbExclamation, "Snake Game")
End If
```

After the user has closed the message box presented by the code above, the Start Game button is re-enabled to allow the game to be played again—even without quarters.

```
cmdStart.Enabled = True
```

Changing the Coordinate Factors

The sngXFactor and sngYFactor variables are adjusted through the Click event procedures of the four direction buttons. For example, when the user clicks the Right command button, the coordinate factors are set as shown in the code below.

```
Private Sub cmdRight_Click()
    sngXFactor = 1
    sngYFactor = 0
End Sub
```

Because sngXFactor and sngYFactor are form-level variables, the new values for these factors will remain as set here until one of the other direction buttons changes the values. For the Left command button, the X factor is –1 and the Y factor is 0. For the Down command button, the Y factor is 1 and the X factor is 0. For the Up command button, the Y factor is –1 and the X factor is 0.

Remember, the event loop in the Start Game button's event procedure will not end when the user clicks one of the direction buttons. The direction button just changes the coordinate factors, thereby changing the direction the snake is headed. Once the event procedure above is executed, the Start Game button's event procedure continues looping.

The Stop Game Button

The code for the Stop Game button simply changes the value of blnStop to True. If the Stop Game button is pressed while the game is in play, the form-level variable blnStop will be changed to True, which will stop the loop.

```
Private Sub cmdStop_Click()
    blnStop = True
End Sub
```

The Quit Button

The Quit button differs from the Stop Game button. The Quit button does more than stop the current game. It ends the program.

```
Private Sub cmdQuit_Click()
    End
End Sub
```

STEP-BY-STEP ⟹ 14.6

1. Run the program.

2. Play the Snake Game one more time.

3. When the game ends, make a list of possible enhancements to the game.

4. Exit **Visual Basic** without saving any changes.

Summary

- The Snake Game is an example of a simple game created in Visual Basic.

- The PSet method allows you to change the color of individual pixels on a form.

- The Point method retrieves the color of the specified pixel.

- The AutoRedraw property allows you to choose whether you want the graphics drawn from code to be temporary or persistent graphics.

- A temporary graphic is one that is not redrawn after another window or object hides the graphic. A persistent graphic is one that will automatically redraw itself and be redisplayed after being hidden by another window or object.

- The Snake Game keeps track of a point on the form where the next pixel will appear as the snake grows.

- The snake is controlled by two factors. One factor specifies the change in the X coordinate and the other factor specifies the change in the Y coordinate.

- Once in play, the Snake Game continues until the user runs the snake into a wall or the snake's tail. The Stop Game and Quit buttons also end the game.

- The direction buttons change the factors that control the direction of the snake. The variables that store the factors are form-level so that multiple buttons can change the value of the factors.

- The color of the wall and snake are controlled by changing the value of lngSnakeColor.

- The speed of the snake is controlled by adjusting the value of lngMySpeed.

- When the game ends, an If statement determines whether the game ended because the snake hit the wall or its tail or if the user stopped the game with the Stop Game button.

TRUE/FALSE

Circle the T if the statement is true. Circle the F if it is false.

T F 1. The PSet method turns a specific pixel on or off.

T F 2. PSet can be used to change the color of a specific pixel

T F 3. The Point method returns a VB color constant.

T F 4. Setting the AutoRedraw property to True allows you to create persistent graphics.

T F 5. If sngXFactor is set to 0, and sngYFactor is set to1, the snake will move up.

T F 6. If sngXFactor and sngYFactor are both set to 0, the snake will continue to move in its current direction.

T F 7. Changing the value stored in lngMySpeed will change the speed of the moving snake.

T F 8. If the DoEvents statement were removed from the cmdStart_Click event procedure, the direction buttons would not change the movement of the snake.

T F 9. The final value of blnStop tells us whether the user stopped the game, or the game ended because the snake ran into itself or the wall.

T F 10. The Quit button allows the user to end the current game without ending the program.

WRITTEN QUESTIONS

Write your answers to the following questions.

11. What coordinate system does PSet use?

12. What method retrieves the current color of a specific pixel?

13. Explain the difference between temporary graphics and persistent graphics.

14. What are the variables sngX and sngY used for?

15. If sngXFactor is set to -1 and sngYFactor is set to 0, which direction will the snake move?

16. What effect will a negative X or Y factor value have on the movement of the snake?

17. Why is it necessary to declare the sngXFactor and sngYFactor variables at the form level?

18. Why is the Step keyword used in the Line method?

19. Why is the Start Game button disabled at the beginning of the cmdStart_Click event procedure?

20. What purpose does the variable lngWasteTime serve?

LESSON 14 PROJECTS

PROJECT 14A

1. Open the **DrawLine** program that you created in Step-by-Step 14.2.

2. Change the caption of the command button to **Draw Lines**.

3. Change the caption of the form to **Draw Lines**.

4. Modify the code so it matches the following.

```
ScaleMode = vbPixels
Dim Counter As Integer

For Counter = 40 To 200
   PSet (Counter, 50), vbRed
   PSet (Counter, 75), vbBlack
   PSet (Counter, 100), vbBlue
   PSet (Counter, 125), vbGreen
Next Counter
```

5. Close the Code window and run the program.

6. Click the **Draw Lines** button. Four different colored lines appear on the form.

7. Save the changes to the project, then remove the project.

PROJECT 14B

1. Open the **Snake Game** program.

2. Change the value of **lngSnakeColor** to **vbRed**.

3. Run the program and start the game. Notice that the border and the color of the snake have changed to red.

4. Save the changes to the project when the game ends but leave the project open.

PROJECT 14C

1. Open the **Snake Game** program if it is not already opened.

2. Create a command button above the Up command button.

3. Set the **Name** property to **cmdSpeed** and the **Caption** property to **Faster**.

4. Add the following code to toggle the speed at which the snake moves and to change the caption of the command button.

```
If cmdSpeed.Caption = "Faster" Then
    lngMySpeed = 10000
    cmdSpeed.Caption = "Slower"
Else
    lngMySpeed = 200000
    cmdSpeed.Caption = "Faster"
End If
```

5. Move the code **Dim lngMySpeed** from the **cmdStart** section to the General Declarations section.

6. Run the program and start the game.

7. Click the **Faster** button. Notice that the snake moves faster, and the caption of the command button changes to Slower.

8. Click the **Slower** button to slow the snake down.

9. Save the changes to the project when the game ends but leave the project open.

PROJECT 14D

1. Open the **Snake Game** program if it is not already opened.

2. Create a label at the top right corner of the form named **lblScore** and set the **Caption** property equal to **0**. Change the **BackColor** property to white.

3. Create another label to the left of lblScore named **lblScore2** and set the **Caption** property equal to **Score:** (change the **Alignment** property to **Right Justify** for this caption). Change the **BackColor** property to white. Your screen should appear similar to Figure 14-7.

FIGURE 14-7
Add two labels as shown here.

FIGURE 14-7
Add two labels as shown here.

4. Create a variable named **lngScore** in the cmdStart event procedure.

5. Initialize **lngScore** to **0**.

6. Add the following code to the DoEvents code (just below the PSet code) to increment lngScore by 1 and set lblScore equal to lngScore.

```
lngScore = lngScore + 1
lblScore.Caption = Val(lngScore)
```

7. Run the program and start the game. Notice that the more the snake grows the higher your score becomes.

8. Save the changes to the project when the game ends but leave the project open.

PROJECT 14E

Look at the list of possible enhancements to the game that you created in Step-by-Step 14.6. Choose one of the enhancements and implement the enhancement or at least describe how the enhancement might be implemented.

Create four additional direction buttons that will make the snake move diagonally. You should create a new event procedure for each button that uses the appropriate x and y coordinates. The form layout should look similar to Figure 14-8.

 NOTE:

When the snake moves diagonally, the snake can occasionally cross another diagonal line without ending the game. Try it and see. You may have to try several times before successfully crossing a diagonal line. Can you describe why this is possible?

FIGURE 14-8
Add four small diagonal direction buttons as shown here.

UNIT 5 REVIEW QUESTIONS

TRUE/FALSE

Circle the T if the statement is true. Circle the F if it is false.

T   F   **1.** There are two ways to create a line on a form.

T   F   **2.** The shape of a Shape control cannot be changed as a program runs.

T   F   **3.** The Line method allows you to manipulate an existing Line control from code.

T   F   **4.** A Shape control can appear in one of six different shapes.

T   F   **5.** The coordinates (0, 0) are assigned to the top right corner of a form.

T   F   **6.** The Pset method retrieves the color of the specified pixel.

T   F   **7.** A persistent graphic is one that will automatically redraw itself.

T   F   **8.** Pset works best with the ScaleMode property set to points.

WRITTEN QUESTIONS

Write your answers to the following questions.

  9. What naming prefix is used to name a Line object?

10. Name two different techniques you can use to draw a box on a form.

11. How can you access the Shape tool from within Visual Basic?

12. What must you adjust to change the unit of measurement used in the coordinate system of a form?

13. What property must you adjust to create a solid shape with the Shape control?

14. How do you specify where the Line method should draw?

15. What property of a Shape control holds the value that specifies the actual shape of the object?

16. What does the BorderColor property do for a line? for a shape?

17. How do you adjust the properties of a line drawn with the Line method?

18. How do you set a line's color using the Line method?

19. What is the method that allows you to change the color of individual pixels on a form?

20. Which property allows you to choose whether to draw temporary graphics or persistent graphics?

UNIT 5 APPLICATIONS

⏱ Estimated Time: 1 hour

APPLICATION 5-1

Write the code necessary to perform the following tasks.

1. Draw a red line from Point (0, 0) to Point (40, 30).

2. Draw a yellow line from Point (0, 40) to Point (0, 10).

3. Draw a green box with its top left corner at Point (20, 20) and its bottom right corner at Point (100, 80).

4. Change the scale mode to pixels, then draw a black box with its top left corner at Point (10, 10) and its bottom right corner at Point (50, 50).

5. Draw a blue box filled with blue color with its top left corner at Point (50, 30) and its bottom right corner at Point (120, 100).

APPLICATION 5-2

Create a program that will ask the user to input the height and width of a box, convert the values to points and draw the box on the form.

1. Open **SizeBox** from your template files.

2. Add code to the **Draw** event procedure to:

   a. Declare two integers named intHeight and intWidth.

   b. Clear the form using the Cls command.

 **NOTE:**

The Cls command can be used to clear lines drawn on a form from code.

c. Set the ScaleMode to points.

d. Set intHeight equal to the value in the txtHeight textbox multiplied by 72 which is the number of points in an inch.

e. Set intWidth equal to the value in the txtWidth textbox multiplied by 72.

f. Draw a blue box starting at Point (25, 75) and ending with (intWidth, intHeight).

3. Add code to the two textboxes to highlight their values when they have the focus.

4. Run the program to verify that it works correctly.

5. Save the changes to the program, then remove the program.

APPLICATION 5-3

Create a program that will change the Shape, Size, and Fill Color properties of a Shape control using menus.

1. Open **Shapes** from your template files.

2. Create the following menu items.

Caption	Name	Position	Additional Properties
File	mnuFile	1	
Exit	mnuFileExit	2	
Shape	mnuShape	1	
Circle	mnuShapeCircle	2	Checked
Rectangle	mnuShapeRectangle	2	
Square	mnuShapeSquare	2	
Oval	mnuShapeOval	2	
Appearance	mnuAppearance	1	
Size	mnuAppearanceSize	2	
Small	mnuAppearanceSizeSmall	3	
Large	mnuAppearanceSizeLarge	3	
Fill Color	mnuAppearanceColor	2	
Red	mnuAppearanceColorRed	3	
Green	mnuAppearanceColorGreen	3	
Blue	mnuAppearanceColorBlue	3	

3. Add code to each of the Shape menu items to change **shpShape.Shape** to the number for the appropriate shape and change the code for the **Checked** property to **True** for that shape.

4. Add the following code to the **mnuAppearanceSizeSmall** event procedure to center the shape and make it smaller.

```
shpShape.Height = 600
shpShape.Left = 2000
shpShape.Top = 1000
shpShape.Width = 1000
```

5. Add the following code to the **mnuAppearanceSizeLarge** event procedure to center the shape and make it larger.

```
shpShape.Height = 2000
shpShape.Left = 900
shpShape.Top = 600
shpShape.Width = 3000
```

6. Add code to each of the Fill Color menu items to change **shpShape.FillColor** to the appropriate color.

7. Add code to the Exit menu item to end the program.

8. Run the program to verify that it works correctly.

9. Save the changes to the program, then remove the project.

APPLICATION 5-4

Create a program that will prompt the user for the name and stock symbol of a stock and the high and low of the stock for three consecutive days. The program should graph the information using lines to connect the highs and dots to draw the lows. The name should appear at the top of the graph followed by its stock symbol in parentheses.

1. Open **Stock Watch** from your template files.

2. Double-click the **Graph** button to open the Code window.

3. Scroll through the code for the Graph button. Notice that the code consists of a series of nested If statements that verify that valid data has been entered in each of the textboxes.

4. Locate the comment that reads 'Center the title on the graph and display it. Below the comment add the following code to place the stock name and symbol at the center of the graph.

```
lblTitle.Caption = txtName.Text & " (" & txtSymbol.Text & ")"
lblTitle.Left = (frmMain.Width / 2) - (Len(lblTitle.Caption) * 45)
lblTitle.Visible = True
```

5. Locate the comment that reads 'Get coordinates for Day1 High. Below the comment add the following code to get the X and Y values of the stock's high for each day.

```
lngXCoordinate1 = lblDay1Graph.Left + (lblDay1Graph.Width / 2)
lngYCoordinate1 = linYAxis.Y1 - (Val(txtDay1High) * 23) — 60

'Get coordinates for Day2 High
lngXCoordinate2 = lblDay2Graph.Left + (lblDay2Graph.Width / 2)
lngYCoordinate2 = linYAxis.Y1 - (Val(txtDay2High) * 23) - 60

'Get coordinates for Day3 High
lngXCoordinate3 = lblDay3Graph.Left + (lblDay3Graph.Width / 2)
lngYCoordinate3 = linYAxis.Y1 - (Val(txtDay3High) * 23) - 60
```

6. Locate the comment that reads 'Draw line connecting Highs. Below the comment add the following code to draw a red line connecting each day's stock high.

```
Line (lngXCoordinate1, lngYCoordinate1)- _
     (lngXCoordinate2, lngYCoordinate2), vbRed
Line (lngXCoordinate2, lngYCoordinate2)- _
     (lngXCoordinate3, lngYCoordinate3), vbRed
```

7. Locate the comment that reads 'Graph Day1 low. Below the comment add the following code to get the X and Y values of the stock's low for each day and draw a blue dot at each point.

```
lngXCoordinate1 = lblDay1Graph.Left + (lblDay1Graph.Width / 2)
lngYCoordinate1 = linYAxis.Y1 - (Val(txtDay1Low) * 23) - 60
PSet (lngXCoordinate1, lngYCoordinate1), vbBlue

'Graph Day2 low
lngXCoordinate2 = lblDay2Graph.Left + (lblDay2Graph.Width / 2)
lngYCoordinate2 = linYAxis.Y1 - (Val(txtDay2Low) * 23) - 60
PSet (lngXCoordinate2, lngYCoordinate2), vbBlue

'Graph Day3 low
lngXCoordinate3 = lblDay3Graph.Left + (lblDay3Graph.Width / 2)
lngYCoordinate3 = linYAxis.Y1 - (Val(txtDay3Low) * 23) - 60
PSet (lngXCoordinate3, lngYCoordinate3), vbBlue
```

8. Add code to the Exit menu item to end the program.

9. Run the program to verify that it works correctly. (If your instructor wishes, go to the Web links from Internet Activity 2 on page 141 and gather stock data to enter into the program. All values must be less than $100.)

10. Save the program, then exit Visual Basic.

INTERNET ACTIVITY

In this activity, you will use the Internet to obtain information about the size of the planets of our solar system and write a program that graphically represents the difference in the size of planets.

1. Open your Web browser.

2. Go to the Web address below.

   http://www.programvb.com/basics

3. On the home page, click the **Internet Activities** link.

4. Click the **Unit 5 Internet Activity** link. A list of Web sites that can be used to obtain information about planets appears.

5. Find the diameters of each of the following planets: Mercury, Venus, Earth, Mars, Saturn, Neptune Uranus, Jupiter, and Pluto.

6. Write a program that adjusts the size of two circle objects to represent the relative size of two planets. The user interface should appear similar to Figure U5-1. Your program should incorporate the following features:

   ■ A File menu that contains an Exit command.

   ■ A menu named 'Planet A' that contains a menu command for each of the nine planets.

   ■ Planet A should be represented by an appropriately sized circle object on the left half of the form.

   ■ A menu named 'Planet B' that contains a menu command for each of the nine planets.

   ■ Planet B should be represented by an appropriately sized circle object on the right half of the form.

   ■ Each of the planet menus should have a check mark by the currently displayed planet.

   ■ The largest planet (Jupiter) should be used as the guide for scaling your drawings. Make sure that Jupiter fits comfortably and that the smaller planets are represented to scale.

FIGURE U5-1

   ■ A label should appear below each of the two planets, indicating the currently displayed planet.

   ■ When the program starts, the default should display Earth as Planet A and Jupiter as Planet B. (Hint: Copy the captions for the default checked items to the Form Load section.)

   ■ The planet size and label should change immediately upon selecting a planet from one of the menus.

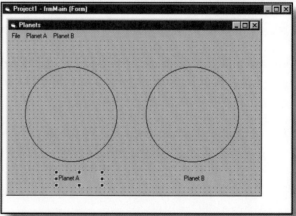

GLOSSARY

A

About box a window that provides information about the program (p. 219)

ActiveX a type of control for Web pages that can be added to your programs (p. 18)

alphanumeric text that can include letters or numbers (p. 118)

Application Wizard a feature of Visual Basic that allows you to create a complete program with standard Windows features already included (p.18)

assignment operator (=) assigns the value to the right of the operator to the item to the left of the operator (p.64)

AutoRedraw property allows you to choose whether you want to draw temporary graphics or persistent graphics (p.274)

AutoSize property adjusts the size of a control to fit its contents (p.102)

B

Boolean data type a data type that can hold the values True or False (p.145)

Boolean variable a variable that can store the results of an expression that includes conditional operators (p.145)

C

Cancel property the property that when set to True activates a certain command button when the Esc key is pressed (p.48)

carriage return automatic advance of the cursor to the next line (p.215)

Case Else statement the default code applied if the code for no other Case statement is executed (p.175)

case-sensitive a system where an uppercase letter is distinguished from its lowercase counterpart (p.40)

checkboxes allow a program to ask the user a Yes or No question or to turn an option on or off (p.152)

clear screen (Cls) a statement for clearing the text produced by a Print statement (p.210)

code label a name that appears in code (p.90)

command button a standard pushbutton control (p.27)

comments notes in the code that will be ignored by the compiler (p.68)

concatenation appending one string to the end of another (p.121)

conditional operators symbols used in making comparisons (p.145)

controls the command buttons, text boxes, scroll bars, and other objects that make up the user interface (p.26)

Currency data type used for dollars and cents calculations (p.125)

D

declaring the process of letting the compiler know that you want to set up a memory location as a variable, what you want to call the variable, and what data type you want the variable to have (p. 104)

Default property the property that when set to True activates a certain command button when the Enter key is pressed (p.48)

Do Until loop repeats statements *until* a certain condition is True (p.190)

Do While loop repeats statements *while* a certain condition is True (p.190)

DoEvents statement allows the computer to process other events, even though the current event procedure is not yet complete (p.201)

Double data type used for general decimal types exceeding six or seven digits (p.125)

E

ellipsis three small dots appearing in a row, representing the opportunity to browse the hard drive (p.42)

Enabled property can make a control take on a grayed appearance, making it inactive but still visible (p.128)

endless loop a loop in which the condition that is supposed to stop the loop from repeating never becomes True (p.199)

error handler (error-handling routine) the code that will be executed if an error occurs (p.89)

error trapping the process of interrupting the normal chain of events that occurs when an error is encountered and replacing that chain of events with your own code (p.89)

event procedure the code written to handle a specific event (p.39)

event an action taken by the user or generated by some process that causes an event-driven program to respond (p.38)

event-driven a system where user-triggered events direct the operation of the program (p.38)

exception an unexpected error condition (p.88)

Exit Sub statement forces the event procedure to end, regardless of whether there is more code in the procedure (p.93)

exponentiation the process of raising a number to a power (p.82)

F

factorial the product of all the positive whole numbers from 1 to n (p.252)

Fix function returns a truncated whole number after a calculation is performed (p.72)

flowcharts charts used to plan and to document program code (p.148)

focus the object that is currently active (p.30)

For Next loop a loop specifically designed for repeating a block of code a specific number of times (p.212)

Form Layout window the window that shows the position the form will take when the program is run (p.13)

Format function allows you to apply custom formatting to a number before displaying the value (p.126)

form-level variable declared in the General Declarations section of a form's Code window and is accessible to all objects on the form (p.108)

forms objects that become the windows and dialog boxes when the application runs (p.20)

frame control a container for other controls (p.167)

G

global variable declared in a code module's General Declarations section and is accessible to all forms in the program (p.108)

H

hard-coded refers to information that is entered directly into the source code and cannot change while the program runs (p.64)

I

If statement allows you to execute specified code when the result of a conditional expression is True (p.146)

image control an object that provides a framework for displaying an image on a form (p.42)

InputBox function displays a window to ask the user for input (p.195)

integer division returns only the whole number portion of division of integers (p.74)

integers whole numbers (p.74)

Intellisense® the technology used in Visual Basic that will anticipate what you are about to key and will complete your statements for you (p.40)

internal documentation comments added to programs (p.87)

iteration structure the code required to create a loop (p.190)

L

label control used to place text on a form (p.63)

Len function determines the length of the text in a textbox (p.130)

Line method a method for drawing lines and boxes on a form from code (p.263)

line-continuation character tells the compiler to skip to the next line and treat the text there as if it were a part of the same line (p.66)

literals values that are keyed directly into source code (p.64)

Load event the event that is triggered when a form is loaded and opened (p.173)

local variable declared within an event procedure and is accessible only within that procedure (p.108)

logical operators operators that can be used to combine several comparisons into one statement (p.157)

loop a method to repeat a group of statements a number of times (p.190)

M

Menu Editor a feature that allows you to create menu items and set the properties of the menu controls (p.232)

message the order sent to an object to trigger a method to be performed (p.47)

method a command that directs an object to make a change to its state (p.46)

modulus returns the remainder of integer division (p.74)

MsgBox function causes a dialog box to pop up, displaying a message that you specify (p.91)

N

nested If statement an If statement inside another If statement (p.164)

O

objects the items that make up a Visual Basic program (p.10)

one-way selection structure a program structure in which the decision is whether to go "one way" or just bypass the code in the If statement (p.150)

operators symbols that perform specific operations in Visual Basic statements (p.62)

option buttons a group of buttons that can only be selected one at a time (p.167)

Option Explicit a statement that causes Visual Basic to generate an error message if you attempt to use a variable that has not been declared (p.110)

option group option buttons in a frame (p.168)

order of operations the rules related to the order in which operations are performed in mathematical calculations (p.82)

P

persistent graphic a graphic that will automatically redraw itself and be redisplayed after being hidden by another window or object (p.274)

Point method retrieves the Visual Basic color constant of the specified pixel (p.274)

Printer object a collection of programming code that allows you to communicate with the printer (p.243)

PrintForm command a command that sends the contents of the form to the printer (p.242)

project a group of files comprising a program (p.4)

Project Explorer the window that allows you to see the forms and files that make up your program (p.7)

Properties window the window that allows you to see and change characteristics of a selected object (p.10)

properties the characteristics of an object (p.10)

PSet method a feature that allows you to change the color of individual pixels on a form (p.273)

R

radio buttons option buttons (p.167)

run-time error any error that occurs when the program is running (p.88)

S

ScaleMode property allows you to adjust the coordinate system on a form to be measured in points, pixels, or twips (p.265)

scope the reach of a variable (p.107)

Select Case statement a statement in which you specify a variable to test and then list a number of cases that you want to test for (p.174)

SelLength property specifies how many characters should be selected to the right of the cursor (p.130)

SelStart property specifies the location where the cursor will be inserted when the textbox gets the focus (p.130)

separator lines lines used to group items on a menu (p.241)

Single data type used for general decimal types not exceeding six or seven digits (p.125)

software development tool a tool that allows you to create computer programs (p.2)

splash screen a window that appears briefly when a program is started (p.219)

standalone program a program that will run in a Windows environment whether or not the system has Visual Basic installed (p.49)

standard toolbar the toolbar that appears by default (p.6)

Stretch property the property that allows the image to be resized to fit the size of the image control (p.44)

string literal coded text (p.119)

strings data types that hold text (p.118)

submenus (cascading menus) used to further organize options in a menu (p.239)

subroutine a section of code set up for you when you open the Code window. The subroutine performs a specific task (p.40)

T

tab order the sequence in which the objects in a window get focus as the Tab key is pressed (p.30)

temporary graphic a graphic that is not redrawn once another window or object hides the graphic (p.274)

text boxes the fields placed on dialog boxes and in other windows that allow the user to enter a value (p.65)

tool tip a name that appears when you position the mouse pointer on a toolbar button (p.6)

toolbox the collection of tools that allows you to add objects to the forms you create in Visual Basic (p.11)

truncation the process of removing everything to the right of the decimal point (p.72)

twips a unit of measurement used to position objects on forms. There are 1440 twips in one inch (p.33)

two-way selection structure a program structure in which one block of code is executed if the specified conditions are True or another block of code is executed if the specified conditions are False (p.150)

U

unary minus using the subtraction operator to perform negation (making a positive value negative or making a negative value positive) (p.71)

V

Val function takes numbers that are in a text format and returns a numeric value that can be used in calculations (p.66)

variables memory locations where temporary data is stored (p.101)

variant a data type that can hold data of any type (p.110)

INDEX

A

About box
    adding an, 226-227
    described, 219, 295
ActiveX, 18, 295
addition operator (+), 64
alphanumeric data, 118, 295
And operator, 157
apostrophe, use of, 68
Application Wizard, 18, 295
assignment operator (=), 64, 295
asterisk, use of, 72
AutoRedraw property, 274, 295
Autosize property, 102, 295

B

BackColor property, 32
Basic language, 210
bln prefix, 105
Boolean data type, 101, 145, 295
Boolean variable, 145, 295
BorderColor property, 258
BorderWidth property, 258
boxes
    adding fill color, 267
    drawing from code, 266-267
byt prefix, 105
byte data type, 101

C

Calculate button, 69
calculating a future value, 84
Cancel property, 48, 295
Caption property, 25, 63

carriage return, 215, 295
cascading menus (See submenus)
Case Else statement, 175, 295
case-sensitive, 40, 295
Case statements, 175
check marks in menus, 237-238
checkboxes, 152-153, 295
clear screen (Cls), 210, 295
click events, 38
cmd prefix, 25
code label, 90, 295
code statements
    splitting among lines, 66-69
    use of apostrophe in, 68
Code window, 39-41
    General Declarations section
      of, 108
Code window editor, 40
color values, 264
command button
    adding code to, 40-41
    described, 27, 295
    setting properties of, 28
    using the Enabled property,
      128
CommandButton tool, 27
comments
    described, 68, 295
    using, 87-88
compiler
    components of, 5-11
concatenation, 121-124, 295
conditional operators, 145-146,
    295
controls
    command buttons, 27
    CommandButton tool, 27
    creating, 26-29
    creating Line controls,
      256-257

    creating shape controls, 258
    described, 26-29, 295
    Enabled property, 128
coordinate factors, 282
coordinates
    understanding, 263
Counter variable and For Next
    loops, 212
cur prefix, 105
Currency data type, 101, 125, 295

D

data types, 100-101
date data type, 101
dbl prefix, 105
Debug button, 89
debug programs, use of
    comments, 88
decimal data types
    described, 101
    using, 125-126
decision making, 144-145
declaring, 104, 296
default printer, 243-244
Default property, 48, 296
diamond, use in flowcharts, 148
Dim statement, 104
Division form, 75
division operator (/), 72
Do Until loop, 190, 296
Do While loop, 190-192, 296
DoEvents statement, 198, 201-
    202, 296
Double data type, 125, 296
Draw button, 262

drawing
AutoRedraw, 274-275
boxes from code, 266-267
lines from code, 263-264
Point method, 274
PSet method, 273
Snake games, 272-282
with pixels, 273
dte prefix, 105

E

ellipsis, 42, 296
Enabled property, 128-130, 296
End buttton, 13, 25
End If statement, 147
End Select statement, 175
End statement, 41
EndDoc method, 243
endless loops, 199-200, 296
suspending program
execution, 201
error dialog box, 88
Error GoTo statement, 89-90
error handler (error-handling
routine), 89, 296
error trapping, 89, 296
event, 38, 296
event-driven, 38, 296
event procedure, 39, 296
exception, 88, 296
Existing tab, 4
Exit Sub statement, 93, 296
Exponentiation, 82, 296
exponentiation symbol (^), 82

F

factorial, 296
File menu, 6
FillColor property, 258
FillStyle property, 258

Fix function, 72-73, 84, 296
fixed-length strings, 118
flowcharts, 148-149, 296
focus, 30-32, 296
Font dialog box, 217
Font property of a label, 217-218
For Next loops
Counter variable, 212
described, 212, 296
For statement, 212
nesting, 215-216
Next statement, 212
Step keyword, 213-214
Form Layout window, 5, 13, 296
Form Load event procedure,
173-174
Format function, 126-128, 296
formats, samples, 127
formatting symbols, 127
form-level variable, 108, 278, 296
forms
About box, 219, 226-227
adding an image to, 42-43
adding controls to, 11
creating controls, 167-168,
26-29
creating label controls, 63-64
default background, 32
described, 20, 297
General Declarations section,
109
positioning, 13
printing, 242-243
resizing, 23-24
setting BackColor property, 32
splash screen, 219-225
types of, 221
using multiple forms, 219
viewing and modifying
properties, 23-25
forward slash, use of, 72
frame control, 167, 297
frm prefix, 25

G

General Declarations section of
Code Window, 109
global variable, 108, 297
graphics
adding image to a form, 42-43

H

handles, 24
hard-coded, 64, 297

I

If statement
checkboxes, 152-154
creating and reading
flowcharts, 148-149
decision making, 144-145
described, 297
If . . . Else statement, 150-
151
logical operators, 157-158
using, 146-147
using conditional operators,
145-146
image control, 42, 297
Image controls
img prefix, 44
naming, 44
setting, 44
Stretch property, 44
Visible property, 45
Image tool, 42
img prefix, 25, 44
ing prefix, 105
InputBox function, 195-198, 297
int prefix, 105
integer data types, 101
integer division operator (\), 74,
297

integers
    described, 74, 297
    performing division, 74
IntelliSense®, 40, 297
internal documentation, 87, 297
iteration structure, 190, 297

J

K

L

label control
    changing font settings, 217-218
    described, 63, 297
    mathematical operators, 63-64
labels
    using the AutoSize feature, 102
    using the Visible property feature, 86
landscape orientation, 167
lbl prefix, 25
Left property, 33
Line method
    color values, 264
    default measurement, 264
    described, 263, 297
    understanding coordinates, 263
    using, 264-265
line-continuation character, 66, 297
Line controls
    BorderColor property, 258
    BorderWidth property, 258
    changing properties of, 258-259
    described, 256
Line tool, 256

lines and shapes
    changing properties of line and shape controls, 258-260
    coordinates, 263
    creating line controls, 256-257
    creating shape controls, 258
    drawing boxes from code, 266-267
    drawing lines from code, 263
    endpoints, 264
    line method, 264-265
    manipulating control properties from code, 260-262
    ScaleMode property, 265
literals, 64, 297
Load event, 173, 297
Load Picture dialog box, 43
local variable, 108, 297
logical operators, 157-159, 297
long event procedures, 198-199
loops
    described, 190, 297
    endless loops, 199-200
    long event procedures, 198-199
    nested loops, 203
    using Do loops, 190-191
    using Do Until, 192-194
    using Do While, 191-192
    using the DoEvents statement, 198, 201-202
    with the InputBox function, 195-197

M

Make command, 49
    mathematical operators
    addition and assignment operators, 64-65
    calculating with numeric variables, 106
    creating Label controls, 63-64
    exponentiation, 82
    Fix function, 72-73

    integer division and using modulus, 74-76
    multiplication and division operators, 72
    order of operations, 82-85
    performing calculations, 62-63
    splitting code statements, 66-69
    subtraction operator, 69-71
    text boxes and the Val function, 65-66
    unary minus, 71-72
MaxButton property, 24
Maximize button, 21
MinButton, 24
memory locations (*See* variables)
menu bar, 5
Menu Editor
    Caption field, 234
    changing the indentation, 234
    Checked property, 237
    described, 232, 297
    name field, 234
    Not operator, 238
    Visible property, 238
menu event procedure
    writing code for, 235-236
menus
    check marks in, 237-239
    creating submenus, 239-240
    creating using the Menu Editor, 232-235
    described, 6
    inserting separator lines, 241
    naming menu items, 234
    writing code for Menu command, 235-236
message, 47, 297
message box, 92
method, 46, 297
Microsoft Visual Basic (*See* Visual Basic)
Microsoft Visual Studio (*See* Visual Basic)
modulus, 74, 297

modulus operator (Mod), 76

MouseDown event, 38

MouseUp event, 38

MsgBox function, 91-92, 297

multiple forms, 219-225

multiplication operator (*), 72

N

Name property, 25

nested For Next loops, 215-216

nested If statement
    described, 164, 298
    indenting code, 165
    using, 164-166

nested loops, 203

New Project dialog box, 3, 19

Not operator, 157, 238

numeric data versus text, 66

O

Object list box, 121

object naming prefixes, 25

object-oriented programming, 46-47

objects
    adding code to, 39
    changing properties of, 10
    described, 10, 298
    modifying properties, 23-26
    moving, resizing, and deleting, 28-29
    tab order, 30
    to disable, 128
    understanding focus, 30

On Error GoTo statement, 89

one-way selection structure, 150, 298

operations within parentheses, 83

operators
    described, 62-63, 298
    integer and modulus, 74
    logical, 157
    multiplication and division, 72

order of logical operators, 158
    using addition and assignment operators, 64-65
    using conditional operators, 145-146

option buttons
    adding code to, 170-173
    creating a frame control, 167-168
    described, 298
    in the frame, 169-170
    steps to use, 167
    using, 167-173

Option Explicit statement, 110-111, 298

option group, 168, 298

Or operator, 157

order of operations, 82, 158, 298

output
    use of the Format function, 126

output labels, 86

P

parallelogram, use in flowcharts, 148

parentheses, use of, 69

persistent graphic, 274, 298

Picture Box tool, 42

Picture property field, 43

pixels, 265
    changing colors of using the PSet method, 273
    Point method, 274

Point method, 274, 298

points, 265

portrait orientation, 167

prefixes (see object-naming prefixes)

Print statement
    described, 210
    in the active window, 211
    use of the semicolon, 215

Printer object, 243, 298

PrintForm command, 242, 298

printing
    a form, 242-243
    to default printer, 243-244

program flow around the error handler, 93-94

programs
    ending, 13
    handling run-time errors, 88
    MsgBox function, 91
    running, 12
    positioning a form in, 13
    setting additional properties, 32-33
    using color in, 32

project
    creating a new, 18-22
    described, 4, 298
    forms, 20
    saving, 22-23
    setting properties, 220-221

Project Explorer, 5, 7-9, 298

Project Explorer window
    docking, 8
    position of, 8

Project Properties dialog box, 220

Properties window
    described, 5, 10, 298
    setting BackColor property from, 32

properties
    Cancel and Default Command button, 48-49
    changed from Properties window, 10
    described, 10, 23, 298
    grouped by function, 10
    setting additional properties, 32-33
    setting from code, 46-48
    setting image properties, 44-45
    setting project properties, 220-221
    viewing and modifying, 23-26

PSet method, 273, 298

OBJECT	PREFIX	EXAMPLE
Check box	chk	chkComplete
Combo box	cbo	cboLanguage
Command button	cmd	cmdExit
Common dialog	dlg	dlgFileOpen
Directory list box	dir	dirSource
Drive list box	drv	drvTarget
File list box	fil	filSource
Form	frm	frmSnakeGame
Horizontal scroll bar	hsb	hsbSize
Image	img	imgHouse
Label	lbl	lblTotal
Line	lin	linDiagonal
List box	lst	lstStates
Menu	mnu	mnuFileExit
Option button	opt	optYesNo
Picture box	pic	picCow
Shape	shp	shpRectangle
Text box	txt	txtCompanyName
Timer	tmr	tmrAlarm
Toolbar	Tlb	tlbStandard
Vertical scroll bar	Vsb	vsbSpeed

DATA TYPE	PREFIX	EXAMPLE
Integer Data Types		
Byte	byt	bytAge
Integer	int	intNumber
Long	lng	lngHeight
Decimal Types		
Single	sng	sngAverage
Double	dbl	dblWeight
Currency	cur	curProfit
Other Types		
Boolean	bln	blnYesNo
Date (Time)	dtm	dtmDueDate
String	str	strName
Variant	vnt	vntValue

Microsoft® Visual Basic 5.0/6.0 Basics by Todd Knowlton and Stephen Collings
Quick Reference ©1999 by South-Western Educational Publishing

FEATURE	KEYBOARD SHORTCUT
Activate toolbox	ALT + V + X
Beginning of line	HOME
Bottom of current procedure	CTRL + PAGEDOWN
Copy selection to Clipboard	CTRL + C
Cut selection to Clipboard	CTRL + X
Delete current line	CTRL + Y
End of line	END
Exit Visual Basic	ALT + Q
Find	CTRL + F
Find Previous	SHIFT + F3
Find Next	F3
Help	F1
Menu Editor	CTRL + E
Move item one line down in Menu Editor	ALT + B
Move item one line up in Menu Editor	ALT + U
Move item to higher level in Menu Editor	ALT + L
Move item to lower level in Menu Editor	ALT + R
New Project	CTRL + N
Object list box in Code window	CTRL + F2
Open Project	CTRL + O
Paste Clipboard contents	CTRL + V
Print	CTRL + P
Project Explorer	CTRL + R
Properties window	CTRL + F2 or F4
Property beginning with letter	CTRL + SHIFT + LETTER
Replace	CTRL + H
Save Form	CTRL + S
Select All	CTRL + A
Shortcut menu	SHIFT + F10
Start (run) program	F5
Top of current procedure	CTRL + PAGEUP
Undo	CTRL + Z
View code for selected object	F7

Microsoft® Visual Basic 5.0/6.0 Basics by Todd Knowlton and Stephen Collings
Quick Reference ©1999 by South-Western Educational Publishing

Visible property, 45, 86
Visual Basic
    adding images, 42-43
    accessing the Code window,
      39
    components of compiler, 5-11
    creating a new project, 18-22
    creating menus, 232-236
    End statement, 41
    events, 38
    exiting, 14
    introduction to, 2

    opening an existing project, 4
    positioning a form, 13
    printing, 242-244
    running a program, 12
    saving a project, 22-23
    screen, 5
    starting, 3
    understanding focus, 30-32
    use of flowcharts in, 149
    viewing and modifying
      properties, 23-26
vnt prefix, 105

X

X coordinate, 263

Y

Y coordinate, 263

Q

Quit button, 282

quotation marks, use of in string variables, 119

R

radio buttons (*See* also option buttons), 167, 298

rectangle, use in flowcharts, 148

Restore button, 22

run-time errors
described, 298
handling, 88-91
trapping, 89

S

Save Project button, 23

ScaleMode property, 265-266, 298
using PSet method, 273

scope
described, 107, 298
levels of, 108

Select Case statement, 174-175, 298

SelLength property, 130, 298

SelStart property, 130, 298

separator lines
creating, 241
described, 299

Shape controls
default shape, 259
FillColor property, 258
FillStyle property, 258
changing properties of, 258-259
described, 258
manipulating properties from code, 260-262

Shape tool, 258

Single data type, 125, 299

Size command, creating, 239

Snake games
analyzing the code, 277-282
drawing with pixels, 273-275
how the snake is drawn, 275-277
running the game, 272-273
using AutoRedraw, 273

sng prefix, 105

software development tool, 2, 299

splash screen, 219-225, 299
adding labels to, 222

Start button, 12

standalone program, 49, 299

Standard EXE, 19

standard toolbar, 5-7, 299

Step keyword, 213-214

Stop Game button, 282

str prefix, 105

Stretch property, 44, 299

string data type, 101

string literal, 121, 299

strings
assigning text to, 119
concatenation, 121-124
described, 118, 299
use of quotation marks, 119
using the InputBox function, 195

submenus (cascading menus), 239-240, 299

subroutine, 40, 299

subtraction operator (-), 63, 69-71

T

tab order, 30, 299

task bar, 5

temporary graphic, 274, 299

term method, 46

text boxes, 65, 299
using the SelStart and SelLength properties, 130-132

text versus numeric data, 66

Tile Horizontally, 8

Tile Vertically, 8

title bar, 5, 22

Toggle Folders button, 8

tool tip, 6, 299

toolbox
CommandButton tool, 27
described, 5, 11, 299
Line tool, 256
positioning mouse pointer to show tool tips, 11
Shape tool, 258
Start button, 12

Top property, 33

truncation, 72, 299

twips, 33, 264-265, 299

two-way selection structure, 150, 299

txt prefix, 25

U

unary minus(-), 63, 71, 299

unary plus, 71

underscore character (*See* line-continuation character)

V

Val function, 66, 84, 100, 299

Value property, 154

variables
declaring, 104, 110
described, 101, 299
hard-code values, 106
outputting the value in a, 106
rules for naming, 104
scope, 107
string, 118-121
using, 105-106
using with mathematical operators, 106

variant, 110, 299

variant data type, 101, 110

VBP extension, 4

Visible method, 46-47